SIGN HERE FOR SACRIFICE

DEDICATION

Dedicated to every "grunt" regardless of rank or social standing who ever sweated and suffered for a distant cause.

IAN GARDNER

SIGN HERE FOR SACRIFICE

THE UNTOLD STORY OF THE THIRD BATTALION, 506TH AIRBORNE
VIETNAM 1968

OSPREY PUBLISHING
Bloomsbury Publishing Plc
Kemp House, Chawley Park, Cumnor Hill, Oxford OX2 9PH, UK
29 Earlsfort Terrace, Dublin 2, Ireland
1385 Broadway, 5th Floor, New York, NY 10018, USA
E-mail: info@ospreypublishing.com
www.ospreypublishing.com

OSPREY is a trademark of Osprey Publishing Ltd

First published in Great Britain in 2023

A catalog record for this book is available from the British Library.

ISBN: HB 978 1 4728 4942 7; PB 978 1 4728 4943 4; eBook 978 1 4728 4945 8;
ePDF 978 1 4728 4944 1; XML 978 1 4728 4941 0

23 24 25 26 27   10 9 8 7 6 5 4 3 2 1

Maps by Ian Gardner
Index by Zoe Ross

Typeset by Deanta Global Publishing Services, Chennai, India
Printed and bound in Great Britain by CPI (Group) UK Ltd, Croydon CR0 4YY

Osprey Publishing supports the Woodland Trust, the UK's leading woodland conservation charity.

To find out more about our authors and books visit www.ospreypublishing.com. Here you
will find extracts, author interviews, details of forthcoming events and the option to sign up
for our newsletter.

Contents

Acknowledgments

Without the incredible and tireless help of the John P. Geraci Chapter's Mike Krawczyk, Joe Alexander, Ron Ford, and David Rattee, none of this would have been achievable. Like me, David is English and connected by more than just blood to this incredible group. My learning curve has been immense, as has the realization of how complex the American journey to war in Vietnam actually was. I would also like to give special thanks to "Dee" Dallas for the battalion's After Action Reports and Mike Stuart for the original interview statements from January 2, 1968. Another debt of gratitude is also owed to "Jay" Eckhart for his fabulously colorful insights into daily life. The Da Lat Motorcycle Investigation Team: Steve Broering, Bjorn Christensson, Grant Angus, and Hoa, for going the extra mile. Also Darrin and Callum Courtney for their archive photographs, and last but not least, "Jerry" Berry for his back catalog of wonderful self-published books.

As usual, this section has been one of the hardest parts of the book to compile, as I am anxious not to forget any of my main contributors. If anyone's name has been overlooked, I hope you will accept my sincere apologies. My individual thanks are extended to the following: Chris Adams, Ed Bassista, Ed Blanco, Ralph Burdett, Steve Cook, "Bucky" Cox, Carl Decker, Jane Fulkerson, John Geraci Jr., Christine Geraci Free, Jerry Gomes, Gary Gressett, Carol Harrison, John Harrison, Joe Jerviss, Mark Jones, Andy Lovy, Tom Lundgren, Bob Mairs (RIP), Ray Mayfield, Nick Nahas, Ron Newton, Dave Rivers, Bill Robie, Jim Schlax, Al Thompson, Mike Trant (RIP), Frank Vinales, and Wayne Warren.

List of Illustrations

C Company commander Nick Nahas and his new bride Rosalie on their wedding day in 1964. (Nick Nahas)

Southern California boy Lieutenant Ron Newton from Second Platoon C Co was raised in the San Gabriel Valley and loved most water sports, including scuba diving. (Ron Newton)

Charlie Company platoon leaders, 1967, L–R: Lieutenant Wylie "Bucky" Cox (Maverick), Jim Kessinger (Hondo), and Ron Newton (Madman). (Ron Newton)

Platoon Sergeant Henry "Hardcore" Schiavone from Second Platoon C Company at the Dragon's Graveyard in November '67 with Private John Beatty holding mirror. (Ron Newton)

Lieutenant "Bucky" Cox (right) from Third Platoon C Co pictured with Platoon Sergeant Henry "RJ" Johnson and "Kit Carson Scout" – Vietnam, early 1968. ("Bucky" Cox Archive – Author's Collection)

Lieutenant Joe Alexander from A Company at Fort Campbell the day before 3/506 began their three-week journey to Vietnam. (Joe Alexander)

John Gfeller pictured a few years before he joined 3/506. The Alpha Weapons platoon sergeant was killed in action on February 19, 1968. (Patricia Gfeller Owen)

Ca Na Peninsula, Operation *Rose*, December '67, L–R: Battalion Sergeant Major "Snake" McCorkle, Medic Timothy Spatt, Lieutenant Herb Hohl III, and Corporal James Ellsworth from B Co. Ellsworth was killed in action on June 5, 1968 after being infused north with 2/327. (Joe Jerviss)

Members of Third Platoon, A Co seen here at the Enlisted Men's Club in Phan Rang, January 1968. L–R: James Chandler (1st Platoon), Martin "Pete" Knight, Raymond Bennett (standing), Lynn Berner (standing), Ed Bassista, Paul Clement (standing), Joe Klempin, Garry Gregory, Edgar "Jay" Eckhart, and Robert Hill. ("Jay" Eckhart)

Sergeants Ron Ford and Biven Patterson from Yazoo, Mississippi, seen here after the Inter Company Games Competition, end of September 1967. (Ron Ford)

Sergeant Mike Stuart from Second Platoon C Co wearing his jungle sweater during Operation *Klamath Falls*, December 1967. (Mike Stuart)

Mike Trant pictured at Firebase Bartlett north of Phan Thiet in March 1968. (Ron Ford)

Charlie Company radio operator Sergeant Mike Krawczyk pictured
in June '68 at Bao Loc being awarded a Purple Heart by new
Battalion Commander Walter Price. (Mike Krawcyk)

Lieutenant David "Mike" Pearson, leader of Third Battalion's
Quick Reaction element known as the Currahee Shock Force.
Coincidentally, Bob Mairs played college football with Mike's
older brother Roger while at university in Rhode Island. (US
Army)

SFC Philip Chassion was platoon sergeant for the Currahee Shock
Force before joining A Co in late January '68 as first sergeant.
"Chass" is seen here at LZ Betty giving a lesson on measuring
detonation chord. He was killed on February 2, during the Battle
of the Van Ta House. (Joe Jerviss)

Gear packed and ready, members of Second Platoon C Co wait
patiently for airfield transport at Fort Campbell. (Mike Stuart)

Troops from A Co at Fort Campbell's Army Airfield boarding their
flight to Alameda Naval Air Station near San Francisco, early
October '67. (Jim Schlax)

Men from C Company waiting to board troopship *General William
Weigel* at Oakland Naval Base in San Francisco. The *Weigel* had
already made several round trips to Vietnam and provided 3/506
with a new nickname – "boat troopers." (Mike Stuart)

Jerry Gomes (bottom left) with colleagues from the S&T Platoon on
their racks, under which many added signatures and messages
alongside similar graffiti etched by troops from World War II and
Korea. (Jerry Gomes)

Jerry Gomes seen here with some of S&T's heavily secured weapons.
(Jerry Gomes)

The *Weigel* passing underneath the Golden Gate Bridge en route to
Vietnam. (Mike Stuart)

Troops on deck saying goodbye to America. (Jim Schlax)

Lieutenant Jim Schlax from First Platoon A Co on board the *Weigel* en
route to Vietnam. (Jim Schlax)

Senior staff, possibly from the 503rd, preparing to receive another rush
of drunken troopers dockside at Subic Bay. (Jerry Gomes)

C Co sergeants partying at Subic Bay, L–R: Delbert Ellis, Billy Simmons
(WIA), Mike Stuart (standing), David Goddard, Nikolai Melkonian

Trooper from C Co standing watch over a potential exit point from the VC tunnel system at Son Hai. ("Bucky" Cox Archive – Author's Collection)

C Co clearing Son Hai on November 19, 1967. ("Bucky" Cox Archive – Author's Collection)

One of several combat assaults carried out by the 117th Army Helicopter Company "Slicks" into the Dragon's Graveyard during Operation *Rose* in November '67. (US Army)

C Co Weapons Platoon Leader Lieutenant Jim Moore dries out his clothing during Operation *Rose*, November '67. (Richard Pittman Archive © Mike Krawczyk)

81mm mortarmen Richard Pittman (left) and Willie Moss from C Co Weapons Platoon during a fire mission on Operation *Rose*, November '67. Moss was later wounded during the Battle of Phu Bon on February 6, 1968. (Richard Pittman Archive © Mike Krawczyk)

Richard Pittman from Weapons Platoon C Co giving his best 1,000yd stare during Operation *Rose*, 1967. (Richard Pittman Archive © Mike Krawczyk)

Typically, six canteens of water per day were just about adequate for each trooper. Space-saving water bladders (seen here) were also introduced and offered a more balanced load when carried in an average ruck. (US Army)

Members of C Co at Song Mao in early December 1967. ("Bucky" Cox Archive – Author's Collection)

View from helicopter during one of C Company's numerous combat assaults in Lam Dong Province during Operation *Klamath Falls*, December 1967. (Mike Stuart)

One of the first C-141s to arrive at Bien Hoa Air Force Base spearheading Operation *Eagle Thrust*, which began on December 13, 1967. In total, 369 sorties brought in over 9,500 troops from Second and Third brigades from Fort Campbell in five echelons. (NARA)

PLATE SECTION 2

Over Christmas '67, "Bucky" Cox was given a special security mission near Dai Ninh. Members of Third Platoon are seen here bathing in the nearby Da Nhim River, making the most of

assault on Song Be. L–R (foreground): Mike Pearson and Phil Chassion. (US Army)

Aerial view looking west across Phan Thiet toward LZ Betty (obscured by cloud), LZ Judy, Muong Man, and Ta Cu (694m). Distant feature top right is Nui Ong (1,302m), gateway to Bao Loc and Central Highlands. The water tower can be seen in the foreground and meandering Ca Ty River. (Bill Robie)

Downtown Phan Thiet looking northwest across Ca Ty River, bridge, and Highway 1. North of the water tower is Quang-Trung Camp, while due south below the tennis courts are Sector Headquarters and Government House, where fierce fighting took place during late February '68. Provincial Prison is situated out of shot further right. (Bill Robie)

Trucks carrying B Co leaving Phan Rang for Phan Thiet on January 17, 1968. (Joe Jerviss)

Sergeant Jeff Cunningham from C Co making final checks at Phan Rang before the motor march to Phan Thiet on January 17, 1968. (Richard Pittman Archive © Mike Krawczyk)

Driver Jerry Gomes from the S&T Platoon (seen here bottom left) en route to Phan Thiet after departing Phan Rang on January 17, 1968. (Jerry Gomes)

Captain Doug Alitz from Long Valley, New Jersey, assumed command of Charlie Company in January 1968. (US Army)

Mike Stuart from C Company posing outside one of the French-built concrete bunkers at LZ Betty near Phan Thiet, early 1968. After being sent home at the beginning of Tet, Mike was offered one-year preparation for West Point by the Army. Instead, after much deliberation, he decided to become a teacher. (Mike Stuart)

Third Battalion's HQ building at LZ Betty was situated next to the medivac pad. These original French interconnected terraces faced the eastern end of the runway and formed the operational offices for TF 3/506. (US Army)

View west from one of the 34ft watch towers at LZ Betty toward Ta Cu Mountain and LZ Judy. (US Army)

Commander of First Field Force Lieutenant General William Rosson, seen here at Phan Thiet on board the C&C Chopper with Lieutenant Colonel John Geraci. (US Army)

A UH-1H Huey from the 192nd Assault Helicopter Company delivering a squad from 3/506 during one of many combat assaults around Phan Thiet. Each helicopter cost $250K and a staggering 5,000 were lost during the Vietnam War. (US Army)

Troops from B Co at the Pick-Up Zone before flying to reinforce Alpha on February 2, 1968. Nicknamed the "Can Do" pad, all troop-carrying lifts at LZ Betty would start and finish here. (US Army)

Lieutenant Jim Schlax from A Co seen here in January '68 with his "Kit Carson Scout" Bong. It was hard to conceive that these ex-enemy soldiers were now sharing their rice and sleeping next to American platoon leaders and sergeants. (Jim Schlax)

One of many typical hamlets encountered in the area known as Disneyland. (Richard Pittman Archive © Mike Krawczyk)

End of January 1968: Richard Pittman and Clyde Braughton from C Co seen here during a break from security duty along Highway 1. Clyde died a few days later after being accidentally shot. At 20 years of age, "Brad" was one of those all-American boys who loved family, friends, school, and country. As per his instructions, "Brad's" G.I. Insurance payout went to his old high school, where it was used to fund a new football program. (Richard Pittman Archive © Mike Krawczyk)

During the first week of Tet, the enemy attacked the airfield with mortars. One of the rounds overshot and landed close to A Company but failed to detonate. Mike Trant (standing front right) and his colleagues are pictured where the dud came down. (US Army)

By way of commemorating C Company's first serious contact in December, the guys engraved Mike Daly's 9mm Chi-Com before presenting it to Captain Nahas as a leaving present. In rear areas, weapons such as this fetched high premiums, so it was generously agreed that Mike should receive the full black-market rate for his trophy. (Nick Nahas)

Members of C Co waiting their turn to be airlifted back to Phan Thiet before the Tet Offensive in January '68. (Mike Stuart)

View from the eastern side of the Van Ta House toward the shack that became Lieutenant John Harrison's command post during the battle on February 2, 1968. (Ed Blanco)

Damage inflicted by Second Platoon Alpha to the eastern side of Van Ta House during the battle on February 2, 1968. Roof of front porch can be seen top left. (Ed Blanco)

Pictured in April 2021, Mr. Van Ta's daughter Ngo Thi Don, now aged 79, sitting on porch opposite where Andy Daniel died on February 2, 1968. Over 50 years later, the scars of battle can still be seen on the rear of house. (Steve Broering)

February 1968, Phan Thiet, L–R: 2nd Lieutenant John Harrison, SSG Ray Mayfield, and medic Private First Class John Melgaard receiving their Silver Stars from Commander of the 101st Airborne Division Major General Olinto Barsanti while Lieutenant Colonel John Geraci proudly looks on. (US Army)

Radio operator David Stiles (left) and Emmett Clark from Second Platoon Alpha clearly showing helmet damage received during battle at Van Ta House on February 2, 1968. (US Army)

Lieutenant Colonel Geraci seen here on February 3 with Captain Gaffney and Alpha HQ following the battle at Van Ta House. (US Army)

One of many dead insurgents left behind on the soccer field during the first attack on Phan Thiet. (US Army)

Jerry Gomes outside what was left of the Civilian Provincial Hospital in Phan Thiet. (Jerry Gomes)

C Company moving past a huge bomb crater in Disneyland during early February 1968. (Richard Pittman Archive © Mike Krawczyk)

Doc Lovy (holding paperwork) overseeing wounded troopers being unloaded from a medivac chopper on the helipad at Phan Thiet. (US Army)

Liston Green from C Co taking a break while on patrol in Disneyland while an air strike is carried out in the middle distance, early February 1968. (Richard Pittman Archive © Mike Krawczyk)

Third Platoon C Co Radio operator Richard A. Williams. From the beginning, "RA" and Lieutenant "Bucky" Cox made a great communicative team and served together until March '68. ("Bucky" Cox Archive – Author's Collection)

In mid-February '68, Lieutenant Colonel Geraci said farewell to 3/506 and is seen here shaking hands with First Field Force Commander

Memorial service led by Bob Elton and Mike Pearson close to the
medivac pad and Battalion HQ at LZ Betty on June 1, 1968.
("Bucky" Cox Archive – Author's Collection)

Photo of C Company platoon leaders taken in late July 1968. L–R:
Bob Roos (2nd Ptn), Gordon "Gordy" Gant (3rd Ptn), and Dave
Rivers (1st Ptn). Roos took over Second Platoon when David
Bentley moved to E Co. Gant from Washington DC was leading
First Platoon when wounded on May 11. (David Rivers)

L–R: Commander of First Brigade Colonel John Collins (call sign
"Cotton Mouth"), Robert Elton, and "Snake" McCorkle seen here
during the change of command ceremony at Bao Loc on June
18, 1968. During the event, Elton was awarded the Silver Star.
(US Army)

List of Maps

Acronyms

AHC	Assault Helicopter Company
AIT	Advanced Infantry Training
AOT	Advanced Officer Training
AP	Air Force Police
APC	Armored Personnel Carrier
ARVN	Army of the Republic of Vietnam
C&C	Command and Control
CO	Commanding Officer
CP	Command Post
CSF	Currahee Shock Force
DEROS	Date Eligible for Return from Overseas
DMZ	Demilitarized Zone
ERV	Emergency Rendezvous
ETS	Expiry of Terms of Service
FAC	Forward Air Control
FDC	Fire Detection Center
FFV	First Field Force
FISCORD	Fire Support and Coordination System
FNGs	"Fucking New Guys"
HHC	Headquarters and Headquarters Company
HQ	Headquarters
IED	Improvised Explosive Device
KIA	Killed in Action
LASV	Liberation Army of South Vietnam

LAW	Light Armor Weapon
LBJ	Long Binh Jail
LNO	Liaison Officer
LRRP	Long-Range Reconnaissance Patrol
LZ	Landing Zone
MAAG	Military Advisory and Assistance Group
MACV	Military Assistance Command Vietnam
MACV-SOG	Military Assistance Command, Vietnam – Studies and Observations Group
MARS	Military Affiliate Radio System
MEDCAP	Medical Civic Action Program
MOS	Military Occupational Specialty
MP	Military Police
MPC	Military Payment Certificate
MSC	Medical Services Corps Officer
NCO	Non-Commissioned Officer
NLF	National Liberation Front
NVA	North Vietnamese Army
OAC	Officers' Advanced Course
OCS	Officer Candidate School
OJT	On-the-Job Training
OSS	Office of Strategic Services
PRU	Provincial Recon Unit
QRF	Quick Reaction Force
RA	Regular Army
RECONDO	Reconnaissance, Commando & Doughboy School
RnR	Rest and Recuperation
ROTC	Reserve Officer Training Corps
RTO	Radio Telephone Operator
S1	Personnel
S2	Intelligence
S3	Planning & Training
S4	Logistics
S5	Civil & Military Operations

S&D	Search and Destroy
SOP	Standard Operating Procedure
SP	Shore Patrol
S&T	Supply and Transportation
TQ	Tactical Questioning
VC	Viet Cong

Introduction

I never imagined for one minute that my previous works on Third Battalion, 506th Parachute Infantry Regiment during World War II would lead to something quite like *Sign Here for Sacrifice*. However, the synergy between the battalion's wartime commander Bob Wolverton and the Vietnam-era John Geraci is uncanny, as is the strength of character regarding both the officers and men. The men of '67 accepted that they were being groomed to actively participate in a faraway war. To be a paratrooper is to be part of a special brotherhood. These young troopers stood every inch as tall as their forebears in World War II. Twenty-two years later, it was their turn to carry the "Currahee" flag into battle and they did not intend to disappoint their leadership or country. Whether or not the Vietnam War was worth fighting is a discussion that we do not enter into in this book. Although politics is occasionally touched upon, it is first and foremost a story of service and duty.

For those of you who may be unaware of America's journey to war, this is just a brief overview of what ultimately led these young men to board a slow boat to South East Asia for this first tour in 1967.

The clock began ticking during the last weeks of World War II, when the battle-hardened troopers from Third Battalion, 506th Parachute Infantry Regiment, 101st Airborne Division were moving into Adolf Hitler's mountain home. Virtually at the same time, on the other side of the world in Southern China, a meeting was taking place between Nguyen Ai Quoc and the American Office of

Strategic Services (OSS). The 54-year-old exile had been and still was a major player in the communist revolutionary program dating back to the 1920s. Now reborn as Ho Chi Minh, which meant "Bringer of Light," Ai Quoc appeared disheveled and fragile as he sought US support for the independence of his country.

The three regions that made up Ho's country – Cochin China, Annam, and Tonkin – had been under French colonial control for the last 100 years, and at that time were still occupied by the Japanese. Although transparent about his political ambition, the future President of North Vietnam was determined to rid his country of both powers. As a scholar and teacher, Ho was well educated, and between the wars traveled to America, Great Britain, France, the Soviet Union, and China – where he married. In the early 1930s, at the request of the French, who had previously sentenced Ho to death, he was arrested in Hong Kong and put on trial by the British, who soon came under pressure from France for extradition. But on appeal, the matter was settled "out of court" and Ho escaped incognito to Moscow, where he continued to study and teach.

Six years later, Ho relocated to China and served as advisor to the Chinese communist armed forces. In 1941, he returned to Annam to lead the newly formed Viet Minh Independence Movement. The term "Viet Minh" was short for "Viet Nam Doc Lap Dong Minh Hoi." Created as a guerrilla force, the Viet Minh fought to overthrow their Japanese and French Vichy occupiers. Ho engineered many successful insurgent actions, all under the watchful and clandestine support of the United States.

At the end of World War II, the Viet Minh were powerless to stop either the Chinese, who accepted Japan's surrender in the North; or the British, who took surrender in the South. When General De Gaulle, leader of the Free French forces, demanded that China and the UK hand back control of "French" Indochina, his allies could do nothing but comply.

In September 1945, Ho Chi Minh declared independence from France and announced the creation of his Democratic Republic. The term "Viet" and "Nam" came from a conjunction of two old ethnic words, meaning "beyond" or "outsider" and "southern territory." In 1949, in an attempt to undermine Ho, France encouraged exiled Emperor Bao Dai to return, and he became a figurehead for their revitalized colonial plan.

The new regime was quickly recognized by the US, Britain, and other Western countries primarily to thwart Ho's growing communist expansion. But then Ho cleverly persuaded Bao Dai to abdicate and take on the honorary title of "Supreme Advisor." Feeling out of his depth, the self-indulgent playboy fled, and over the next three years divided his time between Hong Kong and the French Riviera. Bao Dai's sudden departure encouraged the Soviet Union and China to recognize and support Ho's fledgling Democratic Republic. This action set Vietnam on course for the First Indochina War that culminated in the unexpected northern defeat of French armed forces at Dien Bien Phu in 1954.

Out of 11,000 French paratroopers taken prisoner at Dien Bien Phu, 60 percent never came back from the camps. However, Western powers paid no heed to the incredible human effort shown by Ho's ill-equipped revolutionary force. Later, this turned out to be an inexcusable oversight for America, who after the Korean War (1950–53) dared to believe that it was possible to broker a successful balance between two regions. Today, few will understand that from the 1940s through to the Cuban Missile Crisis, America's greatest concern was the spread of communism.

When the French withdrew after Dien Bien Phu, Bao Dai returned and attempted to form a working government for Vietnam. On July 21, 1954, the Geneva Accords ended the First Indochina War along with French rule, effectively dividing the nascent country into two zones – north and south. However, Washington thwarted the emperor's plans by urging him to appoint the exiled politician Ngo Dinh Diem as prime minister for the South. As a devout Catholic, Diem had gathered much popularity within the Vatican, along with many US political and religious leaders. As the Geneva Settlement was never officially ratified, conflict quickly resumed, albeit without French intervention.

Diem was now political and military leader with Bao Dai as his figurehead and ceremonial chief. The following year, by way of a rigged referendum, Diem removed Bao Dai and his Nguyen Dynasty from power, declared the South a republic and himself president. Bao Dai wanted no part in Diem's Southern plan and fled back to France, never to return. The "last emperor" spent the remainder of his life in Paris and even found time to write a book called *Le Dragon d'Annam*. Ho's OSS meeting in 1945 could never have foreseen these shattering events that two decades later would spawn a war that cost another two million Vietnamese and over 58,000 American lives.

For the men in this book, the story really begins in December 1967, when the professional volunteers of the Third Battalion of the 506th Airborne (3/506) were sent west from their Southern coastal base at Song Mao into the Central Highlands and province of Lam Dong. The new mission coincided with a build-up from the Chinese-supported North Vietnamese Army (NVA) and proved a gritty introduction to the reality of a dirty, sweaty, insect-ridden war. Moreover, the Viet Cong, who would fight alongside the NVA, were not just a military force; they were a society equipped with total faith and the resolve to win. They would prove to be a determined, resourceful, and experienced enemy to the men of 3/506.

After New Year 1968, the battalion moved south by road back to the coast and Phan Thiet. The NVA had spent six months preparing and were now ready to unleash their forces across Southern Vietnam. The Tet Offensive began on January 31 with a coordinated series of deadly attacks. Now a specialized and self-sufficient task force, 3/506 along with South Vietnamese government and local forces were at the very heart of this month-long battle. Fighting in and around Phan Thiet was brutal, but the Currahee tenacity eventually prevailed. There was no other period like it and these young paratroopers made their mark in the dusty rice paddies and corpse-strewn streets.

Chronology of Significant Events

1945
September 2 Ho Chi Minh proclaims his Independent Democratic Republic of Vietnam in Hanoi.

1954
May 7 Ho's army defeats French forces in the North at Dien Bien Phu, causing France to relinquish colonial control.

July 1 Chief of the US Military Advisory and Assistance Group (MAAG) Colonel Edward Lansdale arrives in Saigon with 300 American advisors to begin working with senior civil servant Ngo Dinh Diem.

July 7 Bao Dai, the Emperor of South Vietnam, appoints Ngo Dinh Diem as his prime minister.

July 21 The Geneva Peace Conference divides Vietnam into North and South at the 17th Parallel, where a Demilitarized Zone is established.

1955
October 26 South Vietnam officially becomes a separate sovereign state known as the Republic of Vietnam and Ngo Dinh Diem becomes its president. Emperor Bao Dai flees in exile to France.

October Supported by North Vietnam, the Viet Cong begin a campaign of attacks against the South.

1960
America doubles its military training team to 685 advisors.

1961
January 20 John F. Kennedy takes over as president from Dwight D. Eisenhower and US confidence begins to decrease in Diem's dictatorship.

December 11 Direct US military aid to South Vietnam begins as two US Army helicopter companies arrive in Saigon.

1963
May–August Buddhist demonstrations occur against Diem's government.

November 2 President Ngo Dinh Diem is deposed and executed in a US-backed military coup.

November 22 President John F. Kennedy is assassinated and Vice President Lyndon B. Johnson steps into the White House.

1964
June General William Westmoreland takes over as head of Military Assistance Command Vietnam.

August 2 North Vietnamese torpedo boats attack two American warships in international waters off the Gulf of Tonkin.

August 7 Congress passes a resolution (the Tonkin Gulf Resolution) granting President Lyndon B. Johnson extensive military powers and permission to retaliate.

December 31 US armed forces in South Vietnam total 23,000 men.

1965
February 7 After the Viet Cong attack American bases, the US Air Force begins a strategic bombing campaign in the North.

March 8 US Marine Battalion dispatched to Vietnam, followed by a further steady build-up of troops.

June 19 Air Vice Marshal Nguyen Cao Ky becomes premier of South Vietnam.

1966

April 12 B-52s bomb targets in North Vietnam.

June 2 Operation *Hawthorne*, elements of First Brigade, 101st Airborne Division, participate in the relief of a Special Forces camp near Tak To in the Central Highlands.

September 14 Operation *Attleboro*, large-scale air-mobile search and destroy (S&D) mission by the 196th Light Infantry Brigade northeast of Saigon.

1967

January 8 Operation *Cedar Falls* launched north of Saigon as the 101st Airborne Division receives a warning order to activate Third Battalion, 506th Airborne Infantry (3/506).

February 22 Operation *Junction City* begins with mass parachute insertion by 173rd Airborne Brigade north of Saigon.

April 1 3/506 officially activated at Fort Campbell, Kentucky.

September 3 General Nguyen Van Thieu comes to power in South Vietnam.

October 3 3/506 leave Oakland Naval Base aboard the USNS *General William Weigel* en route to Vietnam.

November 11 Operation *Rose* (3/506).

December 1 Operation *Klamath Falls* (3/506).

December 13 Operation *Eagle Thrust*, Second and Third brigades, 101st Airborne Division arrive in Vietnam.

1968

January 2 The Battle of the Knoll (C Company).

January 17 Operation *San Angelo* launched by First and Third brigades, 101st Airborne Division, northeast of Saigon.

January 19 Operation *McLain*, LZ Betty (3/506).

January 21 The Siege of Khe Sanh.

January 23 North Korean torpedo boats seize the American surveillance vessel USS *Pueblo*.

January 30 Beginning of the Tet Offensive across South Vietnam.

January 31 Start of the month-long Siege of Phan Thiet (3/506).

February 2 The Battle of the Van Ta House (A Company).

February 6 The Battle of Phu Bon (A and C companies).

February 14 Lieutenant Colonel John Geraci hands over command of 3/506 to Lieutenant Colonel Robert Elton.

February 18 Second Battle of Phan Thiet (B and C companies).

February 19 Battle at Ca Ty River (A Company).

April 4 Martin Luther King Jr. murdered in Memphis, Tennessee.

April 25 Operation *MR-6*.

May 3 Peace overtures made by North Vietnam in Paris cause President Johnson to suspend aerial bombing campaign and announce that he will not be standing for a second term.

May 4/5 New communist offensive begins against towns and bases across the South.

May 11 The Battle of Song Mao.

May 19 Operation *Rockne Gold*.

June 6 Senator Robert F. Kennedy assassinated in Los Angeles, California.

June 8 Operation *Banjo Royce*.

June 18 Operation *Harmon Green* begins in Da Lat and Lieutenant Colonel Elton transfers command of Task Force 3/506 to Lieutenant Colonel Walter Price.

July 17 The Battle of Whiskey Mountain.

November 5 Republican Senator Richard Nixon wins election to become US President.

1969
January 31 US forces in Vietnam reach peak strength of 542,000 men.

July 8 Planned withdrawal of US troops begins.

November Massive anti-war demonstration in the United States.

1970
March 18 General Lon Nol deposes Prince Sihanouk as ruler of Cambodia and later declares a republic and receives direct military support from the US and South Vietnam.

May Violent anti-war demonstrations in America at US involvement in Cambodia.

June/July US forces withdrawn from Cambodia.

December 31 Congress repeals Tonkin Resolution.

1971
February 8–March 25 Operation *Lam Son 719*, 3/506 relieve Army of the Republic of Vietnam (ARVN) units near the DMZ as they prepare to move into Laos.

1972
March 30 North Vietnam launches conventional invasion of the South.

May North Vietnamese ports mined by US planes as bombing offensive is stepped up.

May 15 3/506 disbanded and stood down.

June ARVN troops hold back the North Vietnamese invasion.

August 12 Last US ground troops depart from Vietnam, leaving 43,000 Air Force and support personnel.

1973

January 15 US military operations against North Vietnam cease.

January 27 Peace agreement between US and North Vietnam signed.

March 29 Last US troops leave Vietnam.

1974

April Cambodian Lon Nol regime under increasing pressure from communist forces.

August 9 Richard Nixon resigns over the Watergate scandal and Vice President Gerald Ford is sworn into the White House.

1975

March 5 North Vietnamese Army launch final offensive against South Vietnam.

April 17 Phnom Penh falls to communist insurgents.

April 30 North Vietnamese troops enter Saigon: South Vietnam surrenders unconditionally as the last American helicopter takes off from the US Embassy.

Chapter 1

"Salute the New Dawn"

Reactivation – Fort Campbell, Kentucky

Over muffled engines and breaking waves, a troopship sailed into the late glow of sunset. Cooled by a gentle breeze, Lieutenant Joe Alexander and his platoon sergeant, John Gfeller, stood on deck silently contemplating. John turned to Joe and proffered, "Sir, you do know this is my first combat tour – don't you?" John was always stoic but his soft tone took the young platoon leader by surprise. This was the beginning of a disclaimer that had been long weighing on the sergeant's mind. Of course, Joe had always known, but it was never an issue.

Over the last few months, John had become Joe's trusted and dependable mentor, whose guidance and opinion were second to none. Being airborne was Gfeller's life and this war would either complete or end the circle for him. For the first time, Alexander realized they would be facing an uncertain future. Since the outset of this adventure, Joe had felt fearless, ten feet tall, bulletproof, infallible, and even invincible. The young lieutenant shivered as a sense of foreboding began flowing through his body. As they leaned against the railing, discussing options, family, and home, both accepted their jobs knowing that together they were strong. Through commitment and five months of solid preparation, perhaps somewhat naively both believed they were ready for whatever Vietnam could throw at them. Silence followed as the two stared into the Pacific's growing twilight. At that moment, Joe fully accepted the burden of leadership and belief in his commander, Lieutenant Colonel John Geraci, to make the right decisions, the decisions that would ultimately shape this story.

Originally from Brooklyn, John Philip Geraci (pronounced Jer-A'See) was born in 1925 into a tight, close-knit Italian family. Now at 42 years of age, Geraci was destined for legend and a new command reincarnated with the same ethos and *esprit de corps* shown during World War II by his then much younger counterpart – Lieutenant Colonel Robert Lee Wolverton. A fluent French speaker, Geraci had previously worked in Saigon as an advisor to the High Command of the Army of the Republic of Vietnam, known as ARVN. The US government's initial role was merely to advise and train the ARVN with absolutely no intention of ever becoming involved in combat.

In January '67, the Army had issued a warning order advising that two new independent battalions were about to be created. Third Battalion (Airborne), 506th Infantry was to be attached to the 101st Airborne Division at Fort Campbell, Kentucky; while Third Battalion, 503rd Infantry was scheduled to join the 82nd Airborne at Fort Bragg in North Carolina.

Although the iconic Screaming Eagle patch was still being worn, the division itself was a different and more complex animal compared to its World War II ancestor. By now, it had been structured into three brigades designated First, Second, and Third. Three battalions made up each brigade and each battalion numbered around 750 men. The volunteers for 3/506 were mostly well-motivated Regular Army and drawn predominantly from Second and Third brigades at Campbell.

This additional maneuver battalion was to have a full and current parachute capability. The plan was to take over business in Vietnam's South-Central region inside the Tactical Zone operated by II Corps around Phan Rang. Three other battalions, who collectively made up First Brigade, had been in the country since the end of July '65. Owing to their own nomadic nature, many areas surrounding base camp at Phan Rang had been neglected for some time. It was vitally important to fill this gap and allow First Brigade to concentrate further north, where enemy activity appeared to be increasing.

Luckily for Lieutenant Colonel Geraci, the man in charge of First Brigade was none other than Salve H. Matheson. Now a brigadier general, Matheson had been a highly valued member of Colonel Robert F. Sink's staff during World War II. Salve had jumped into Normandy and Holland with many of the men who now served in his current airborne army. Matheson was over the moon about this new directive and took it upon himself to remotely mentor from his northern headquarters at Chu Lai. Unlike most other 101st units who were now wearing a subdued olive drab eagle field patch, as a statement of intent, 3/506 was going to war wearing the traditional full-colour embroidered version.

WRAPPED INSIDE A DIFFERENT FLAG

Reactivated on May 1, 1967, the Third Battalion (Airborne), 506th Infantry was now on course for its own rendezvous with destiny. Officially written as 3-506, 1st Brigade (Separate), 101st Airborne Infantry Division, perhaps as a nod to lineage, many seniors still preferred 3/506. Whatever the preference, John Geraci set out to inspire his new brotherhood, aptly nicknamed "the Currahee Battalion," with a spirit and belief not seen since those trailblazing days of 1942. In itself, the word "Currahee" was significant and referenced Bob Sink's original "Native American" regimental motto, meaning "stands alone." Mount Currahee was also the Appalachian mountain in Georgia that dominated Camp Toccoa – birthplace of the 506.

John Geraci joined the Marine Corps on his 18th birthday in early '43 and shipped out to the Pacific as a wireman. After the war, he went back to college and studied English and Philosophy, earning extra money as a door-to-door salesman. On New Year's Day 1949, then an Army reservist, John was called up to attend

Officer Candidate School (OCS). Three months later, he was posted to 35th Infantry Regiment and sent to Korea. The next 12 months earned the young officer two Silver Stars and a solid reputation as an inspirational and natural rifle platoon leader. However, Vietnam would become John's third and perhaps most significant experience of conflict. During his first tour in 1960, with the Military Assistance Advisory Group known as MAAG, Geraci's ability to speak several languages, especially French, proved invaluable. Promotion to lieutenant colonel soon followed, along with a staff appointment to the Joint Unconventional Warfare Task Force led by Major General William Yarborough – who opened John's eyes to the extreme world of airborne soldiering.

A second tour in '63 brought John into contact with Major General Duong Van Minh, who was open to the possibilities of regime change. At that point, President of the Republic of South Vietnam, Ngo Dinh Diem, and his sectarian government were attracting negative attention due to their regular breaches of human rights. Diem had grasped power in '56 after a rigged referendum deposed playboy puppet Emperor Bao Dai from his opulent mountain palace in Da Lat.

Assisted by American military and economic aid, the new president was able to counter a growing communist insurgency from Ho Chi Minh's Democratic Republic in the North. Diem was from a prominent Catholic family and the nepotism he displayed toward Catholics in the military and civil service proved to be his undoing. This preference was blatantly obvious to many downtrodden religious groups, especially Buddhists – who then made up around 80 percent of the population.

Diem was an autocratic and vicious dictator who crushed all freethinking opposition members in his path. As a direct consequence, communist interest and influence began to flourish across Southern Vietnam. One week prior to Buddha's annual birthday celebration, Diem's government decided to ban displays of all religious paraphernalia. However, on May 8, 1963, flags were flown close to the northern border in Hue. Pronounced "Wey," the ancient city was a symbolic cultural and religious center, and many went out onto the streets to demonstrate. Nine people were killed and the protest rallies that inevitably followed resulted in hundreds more deaths.

Buddhist leader and long-time anti-war activist Trich Tri Quang sent a manifesto to Saigon demanding equality – which Diem arrogantly ignored. With rising instability, the somewhat ideological American government became ever more concerned. Further persecution followed and as a direct result, a nun and three monks burned themselves to death in protest. One self-immolation in particular made TV news all over the globe and pushed President John F. Kennedy to actively pursue the regime change that John Geraci had previously been sent to negotiate. Somewhat reluctantly, Kennedy gave approval for the ARVN to go ahead and depose President Diem. Subsequently, Diem and his brother were arrested and unexpectedly executed. In the three months following this coup d'état, the man America chose to lead South Vietnam, General Duong Van Minh, was unable to establish a secure government. As a consequence, the northern insurgency began to gain more traction. With around 16,000 US training advisors now in country, on November 22, 1963 – three weeks after the ARVN took control – JFK was assassinated along with the American dream.

NEW HORIZONS

During the summer of '66, Geraci returned to Fort Campbell and moved into 1030 Drennan Park with his wife Rita and their five kids – Vicki, Christine, John Jr., Jeff, and toddler Jane.

Back in Vietnam, General Duong Van Minh had long since been deposed, leaving the country in turmoil and at war with the North. In early '67, after his stint as commander of 2-502, John gladly accepted the task of forming and leading Third Battalion. Truly blessed to have Matheson as his guiding star, together they would go on to create an accelerated five-month program for deployment. From his headquarters close to the border with North Vietnam, Brigadier Matheson accepted co-responsibility for training and was already pushing for a series of vitally important exercises over the swamps of Georgia and hills of Eastern Tennessee.

Although First Brigade was still drawing parachute pay, they had not jumped since '65. Back then, Matheson put on a demonstration drop for General William Westmoreland and outgoing US Ambassador Maxwell D. Taylor. In Korea, Westmoreland had commanded 187th Airborne Regimental Combat Team and was well versed in the advantages of military parachuting. The general was no fool and during his long career had worked alongside some of America's greatest military leaders, including Max Taylor, who had led the 101st into France on D-Day.

In '67, as head of Military Assistance Command Vietnam or MACV, Westmoreland was subordinate only to current US Ambassador Ellsworth F. Bunker, the State Department, and Commander in Chief of the Pacific Fleet, Admiral Ulysses S. Grant Sharp Jr., based over 6,000 miles away in Honolulu. Officially, it was Westmoreland's job to control and coordinate operations in Southern Vietnam. However, the Navy, Marine Corps, and Air Force ultimately answered to Admiral Sharp, who along with new President Lyndon B. Johnson also determined America's aerial bombing policy against the North.

Pre-war, "Westpoint" man Westmoreland had been working on a tactical timetable for victory and hoped to be out of Vietnam by 1970. This could only be successful on assumption that he would have unrestricted access to American troops and logistical bases large enough to support them. In the zone specifically operated by II Corps, it had taken far longer than expected to roll out the main supply hubs at Qui Nhon and Cam Ranh Bay. Ironically, these crucial delays only served to provide North Vietnam with more time to plan and execute its next big move.

Ultimately, the MACV commander wanted American forces to search out the enemy while government troops took on counter-insurgency duties in the villages. This combination of US military might and ARVN pacification had been designed to force the North Vietnamese Army out into the open or perhaps even a withdrawal, but so far neither seemed to be working. As per his request, Westmoreland was given more troops and 1967 would see the largest commitment so far – 449,000 men. However, out of this number only around 15 percent were destined to physically engage with the enemy, with 3/506 among their number. The year 1968 would be a bloody one, with Third Battalion crucially involved in some of the fiercest fighting down south inside II Corps Zone.

SECOND GENERATION HEROES

Captain Freeman "Dee" Dallas and Sergeant First Class John Boes were the first to learn about the new outfit. At the time, Dallas was working at Third Brigade as assistant logistics officer and had just returned from compassionate leave after the death of his eldest son. "Dee's" brigade commander, Colonel John Hayes, called him to his office, where one of the outfit's most senior supply sergeants, John Boes, was also waiting. Boes had already served one tour in Vietnam and of course knew just about every trick in the logistical supply book.

Hayes leaned across his desk and explained they were being temporarily assigned to a special project under stewardship of Brigadier Matheson. Their job, which was not negotiable, meant finding a suitable area on base capable of accommodating up to 800 people. "Dee" and John were slightly dumbfounded but before they could regroup, Hayes fired off another bombshell and explained that Dallas was also responsible for procuring every single item of equipment and only had a few weeks to complete the job.

When a new unit is "stood up," usually orders are issued authorizing a small cadre of a dozen or so people to make all necessary preparations before the troops arrive. But this was just "Dee" and John, and still trying to figure out what had just happened, they drove over to an empty barracks on the western side of base. Although it had not been in use for a long time, the site was close to Third Brigade Headquarters and ideally situated next to the base railway between Kentucky, Missouri, and Colorado avenues.

Thankfully, when hundreds of new beds, furniture, and lockers arrived, a detail was sent by Colonel Hayes to assist with humping and shifting. The next few weeks turned into a blur as the guys worked long and hard to get everything up and running. It was only when completion drew near that "Dee" heard they were not going to be kept on. This was a punch in the guts for the duo, now so heavily invested that any prospect of walking away seemed unthinkable. Hayes was sympathetic and introduced "Dee" directly to Colonel Geraci, who after realizing what a fantastic job they had done, hired them on the spot. Thus, Dallas and Boes became the first to be officially assigned to Third Battalion, and formed the nucleus of a fledgling Logistics Department. Even though Hayes knew he had lost two of his top guys, it did not stop him from throwing a fabulous leaving party at the Officers' Club!

With everything now "official," Dallas and Boes set out to create a bespoke first-class equipment list designed to cover every eventuality. From previous experience, Boes knew that all official allowances would be nowhere near enough to support their needs in Vietnam. Dallas purposely over-ordered on everything, including military shipping containers known as "CONEX boxes." Subsequently, any "excess" that could be pilfered was hidden away from the inflexible and petty Divisional Inspection Teams.

Table of organization was the same for Geraci, as it was for any other home-based battalion commander starting from the top with Headquarters and Headquarters Company. Abbreviated to HHC, the company also encompassed a specialist heavy mortar and reconnaissance platoon. For his command sergeant major or "top kick," Geraci chose William McCorkle, who had fought alongside him in Korea. Known to all as "Snake," McCorkle was from Denver and although a little wild and crazy, "Snake" was to be a perfect fit for the role. With things now neatly falling into place, recruiting for HHC could begin, starting with Captain Jay Cope and First Sergeant John McDonald.

Although capable of taking temporary command of a rifle company, most of the senior rear echelon housekeepers were selected on their specific administrative skills, such as the new Civil and Military Operations Officer Captain Douglas Alitz, and George Fisher, who arrived a month or so later to take over as battalion executive officer. Major Fisher was a calm, neat, proper Princeton type and not the gung-ho death-from-above paratrooper one might expect. During the early "seniors" meetings, Geraci made it crystal clear that his company commanders answered directly to him and not the lawyer-like departmental heads.

The new planning and operations officer or S-3, Major Robert Mairs III, call sign "Fat Cat," was in the words of his brother officers "one cool dude" and quite different from his colleagues now filling the upper echelons of HHC. Although born in NYC, Bob was really a surrogate New Englander, having moved to Rhode Island at the tender age of two. Despite being 6'2" and weighing 190lb, Bob had always been airborne, except for one or two "malfunctions" earlier in his career. At the end of March 1967, Mairs, who was then executive officer for 2-506, took on a new role as S-3 to Third Brigade. During an earlier field exercise, Bob had staged a mock World War II-style parachute drop using dummy troopers. Bob's subterfuge influenced the opposing force, led by Geraci, to fail quite spectacularly. Geraci never forgot what Mairs had done and when it came to picking his new S-3, he knew exactly who he wanted beside him in the chopper. Bob was divorced at the time and living a single man's existence between brigade officers' quarters and an apartment in Hopkinsville. Geraci gave off an air of approachability and Mairs, unlike many other senior team members, was never afraid to speak his mind. It was a special bond, and happy to let Bob get on with the job, John rarely questioned his ideas or decisions.

Vietnam was a platoon leader's war and all Geraci had to ensure was that his troops were fed and given access to plenty of ammunition and positive guidance. Surprisingly, Geraci was never one for heaping praise on anybody, especially the young lieutenants. However, if anyone ever screwed up, including "Fat Cat," then they would feel the full weight of John's fiery Italian temper.

Not long after Mairs signed on, Captain Teddy J. Booth was appointed as his aerial planning officer or S-3 Air. It was Teddy's job among others to coordinate all future airlifts, and he was damned good at it. With Teddy on board, the Air Force then assigned majors Pratz and Sexton, call signs "Jacksprat" and "Razorback," along with their Cessna "Bird Dog" spotter aircraft. Pratz was to be Third Battalion's dedicated forward air control pilot and Sexton his air intelligence officer. The two men were close friends and even shared a place in Clarksville with their respective families.

THIS IS YOUR CAPTAIN SPEAKING

The battalion's rifle companies were designated Alpha, Bravo, and Charlie, and subdivided into four platoons. Each company usually consisted of around 160 soldiers under overall command of a captain, executive officer, and first sergeant. Individually, the platoons were numbered and led by a second lieutenant and a cadre platoon sergeant. Broken into four squads, each platoon usually operated six fire teams, all supported by two M60 machine-gun crews. Often referred to as "Weapons," the Fourth Platoon was by nature much smaller in size and designed specifically to provide heavy firepower for the company via its 81mm mortar, and 90mm and jeep-mounted 106mm recoilless rifles.

Things were not working out at Alpha for Captain Fred McCoy, and after a couple of months plans were made to replace him with 37-year-old Thomas Gaffney. Tom had always been John's first choice but back in January, when first approached, he had been unavailable. Originally born in Hawaii and brought up in California, Gaffney was probably one of the best line commanders at that time. Tom could think on his feet and was always an inspiration to everyone around him. This time, Geraci was not about to let bureaucracy get in the way, especially as Gaffney was about to ship out to MACV in Saigon!

John pulled a few last-minute strings and had Tom's movement orders changed. In disbelief, Gaffney phoned Washington, who confirmed it was all above board! As Tom lived on base at Werner Park with his wife Corine and their three children, he headed home to discuss options. A couple of hours later, Gaffney walked into the orderly room where McCoy was clearing his desk. On June 21, 1967, ownership of A Company officially transferred to Gaffney, who next to the colonel was now the most combat-experienced officer in the battalion. Tom would go on to imbue his men with a sense of belonging to something that was special and quite unique. The new Alpha boss was committed to the oath, a warrior, who wanted to lead his "kids" every step of the way.

Tom Gaffney had trained as a radio operator shortly after the end of World War II, before signing up for airborne and being posted to Japan. Returning to the States, he volunteered to serve in Korea and worked as a high-speed radio-cryptologist until 1950. When the North decided to invade, Gaffney saw action and finished his tour as a senior NCO. Back in the US, he was assigned to a new signal company preparing for the reinvasion of Korea. During this period, Tom transferred to the 82nd at Bragg and was sent back to Japan and the newly reorganized 187th Airborne Regimental Combat Team then under the command of Westmoreland. Within a few days, Gaffney was made an assistant platoon sergeant and sent back to Korea to take his place on the Main Line of Resistance. During one action, Tom found himself in charge and rallied against stiff resistance. It was for this reason that Westmoreland personally recommended him for a battlefield commission.

After his father died in early '54, Tom took a new posting at Campbell. Three years later, re-formed into the 1st Airborne Battle Group, 187th Infantry, the outfit was sent to Germany. Several tours followed, including in the Lebanon and a stint with Special Forces in Laos. Over two further tours, Gaffney provided training against communist Pathet-Lao insurgents for the Laotian Airborne and an indigenous Mountain Guerrilla Force. Coming up through the ranks, Tom did not have much time for the young West Pointers who were being brought in to run Bravo and Charlie companies … but eventually his attitude toward them changed and he became more of a father figure, always on hand with advice and criticism. By the time Gaffney took over Alpha, Jim Schlax had First Platoon followed by John Harrison (who was also acting XO), Len Liebler, and Joe Alexander.

Dashing, energetic, intelligent, and athletic, 25-year-old William Landgraf was given command of B Company. From Sarasota in

Florida, at 6'3" Landgraf had been an "all-American" captain of the swimming team at West Point. Landgraf liked things done his way and this turned out to be a definite advantage overseas when the companies began to operate more independently. One of the tallest officers in Battalion, and a stickler for regulation, the captain always insisted that web gear and uniform be worn in correct textbook fashion. Final alignment for Bravo was First Sergeant Arthur Roberts, XO Milton Menjivar, and platoon leaders Herbert Hohl III, Stephen Cook, Donald Love, and James Muschett. Landgraf was a great guy and militarily speaking, at least in the beginning, appeared to be a more decisive character than his younger friend and colleague Nick Nahas.

Lebanese by descent, Captain Nicholas Nahas hailed from Beaumont in Texas and was appointed to head up Charlie. Nick came in from Germany, where his boss Lieutenant Colonel Ted Crozier had previously served with Geraci. When Nick received orders to return to Campbell in March, Crozier was kind enough to put in a good word. Much to Nick's surprise, West Point classmates Bill Landgraf and Doug Alitz (who hailed from New Jersey) also came in from Germany at the same time.

Nahas had spent a year at Texas A&M before entering West Point aged 17 in the summer of 1960, when William Westmoreland was superintendent. After Nick's junior year, the cadets were sent on advanced officer training (AOT) to various military posts in Europe and elsewhere. Typically on AOT, a cadet would be a platoon leader, but since the students were not yet commissioned, the "post" carried the tongue-in-cheek title of "third lieutenant." Nick was sent to Worms in Germany with the 48th Mechanized Infantry, where he briefly crossed paths with "Dee" Dallas.

When the "Class of '64" graduated, it was decided that they would not attend Officers' Basic. Instead, the rookies were fast-tracked straight to Ranger and then Airborne School. During training, Nick picked up a painful leg injury and was forced to go on sick call by one of the instructors. However, the following week, because he was set to marry his sweetheart Rosalie and did not want to jeopardize the wedding or his pending parachute course, he convinced a doctor to sign his return to duty slip. A few weeks later, Nick and Rosalie were on a ship to Germany, where he spent the next two and a half years back at Worms working first as a platoon, then recon leader, before finishing up as a company commander under Colonel Crozier.

Doctor Andy Lovy had been assigned to the 501st and was determined to see out his tour quietly at Campbell. After graduating Optometry School, Lovy was preparing for a new career as an osteopath when his draft papers arrived. Having just left a country practice in West Virginia for a partnership in Milwaukee, Andy was not thrilled to be joining the military, especially when being an Army optometrist required three years' service as a second lieutenant. However, luckily for Andy, the rules changed at that time to allow osteopathic doctors like him to be directly commissioned into the Medical Corps. Specializing in "medicine" also meant a shorter enlistment and came with the rank of captain. So, it seemed like a win-win situation for this young doctor, who quickly realized an opportunity to improve his skills.

However, during a party on base, "Dee" Dallas introduced him to Geraci and everything changed. John enthusiastically explained about the unit and asked if Andy would be interested in taking on the role of his battalion surgeon? Andy's wife Madeline convinced him to accept and two weeks later, doubts crept in when Geraci invited him over to play bridge and then golf the following Sunday. Lovy hated both with equal passion and when he plucked up the courage to confess, John's answer was priceless: "Christ Almighty! Every doctor that I've ever known plays bridge and golf – just what the hell is wrong with you, captain?"

SONS OF THE NEW BEGINNING

By now, word of the new unit had spread to such an extent that Geraci was fielding an avalanche of requests; he had a free hand, especially when it came to cadre NCOs who – for the most part – had already served at least one tour in Vietnam. Virgil Craft was a typically tough type in his early thirties who became Nick

Nahas's first sergeant. Virgil had not been particularly popular in his previous role with the 187th Airborne, who were part of Third Brigade. However, Captain Nahas tagged him as a good listener who seemed to understand and care about what his junior officers had to say. A select few cadre members had been to Ranger School and it was a major plus for Nick to have two as platoon sergeants in his company – Henry "Hardcore" Schiavone (pronounced Sha-vone-eh) and Henry "RJ" Johnson.

Most of the recently commissioned young lieutenants, known as "butter bars," came from the same two OCS classes, graduating one week apart. During those early days, due to incompatibility between some cadre and their platoon leaders, Charlie Company eventually settled into Roy Somers as executive officer – followed by platoon leaders James Kessinger, Ronald Newton, Wylie "Bucky" Cox, and James Moore.

These young officers from C Co were historically close-knit. Born in Arkansas and raised in New Mexico, "Bucky" Cox had known Jim Kessinger well before they were roommates at OCS. Not yet 20 years old, Cox was already married and living off base in Clarksville. Philosopher Jim was four years "Bucky's" senior and felt strongly about the growing loss of life and US policy in Vietnam. Believing Cuba to be the biggest threat, Jim felt that America should leave Asia to the communists and let China become a buffer zone similar to Russia with Europe. Over the coming months, Kessinger would have many heated barroom "discussions" with colleagues, including Doc Lovy, who believed that America had a responsibility to contain the spread and turn back all threats to Western existence and way of life.

As a freshman, Joe Alexander was not particularly fond of class, taking exams, or for that matter the Reserve Officer Training Corps (ROTC). However, when he attended a local land grant college, it was compulsory for all male students to be in the cadet program. In September 1965, with war escalating, President Johnson increased the draft. Ironically, as a college student Joe was exempt, but by early '66, the appeal of a college education no longer seemed attractive and he began to look around for a new challenge. A few days later, at the post office in Johnson City, Tennessee, Alexander struck up a conversation with an Army recruiter. His options were simple: volunteer as "RA" and serve three years, or be drafted and serve two. For the enlisted man, "RA" or Regular Army was a prefix in front of his service number that meant he had signed up voluntarily. Typically, regular enlistment was followed by a further three years in the reserves, whereas a draftee only served two years active but four years as a reservist. As Joe was from the volunteer state, his first question to the recruiting sergeant was how could he volunteer to be drafted? The recruiter was still laughing as he handed Alexander his pen.

Joe was assigned to the 39th Infantry Regiment at Fort Riley, Kansas. Being part of 9th Infantry Division, the regiment was on alert for future deployment, although like so many other units, nobody really knew when. Due to Joe's experience with ROTC, he was quickly earmarked for promotion, and as a big, fit guy, assigned to the 90mm recoilless rifle team. The 39th was a good introduction and taught Joe respect for his senior NCOs and the value of teamwork. Midway through basic training, his name appeared on a bulletin board as being eligible for OCS. Graduating in March of '67 and commissioned into the infantry, Joe was still looking to widen his horizons. Several classmates had long-term prior service and because of their enthusiasm for all things airborne, Joe decided to apply for the paratroops.

On April 17, 1967, Lieutenant Alexander reported into 3/506. Initially placed with Master Sergeant Bill Wright and Sergeant First Class Billie Kirk, Joe helped to get the Planning & Training department up and running. The best teachers were always guys like Kirk and Wright and Jim Goree from Intelligence, all of whom played their part in Alexander's professional education. Eventually, Joe was given Third Platoon, A Co after his predecessor moved across to HHC. Toward the end of summer, just prior to a major field exercise in Eastern Tennessee, Joe, because of his previous work with recoilless rifles, swapped with Lenny Liebler and took over Weapons. Initially, Liebler did not make a good first impression with Third Platoon. Unlike Joe, Len came across as somewhat aloof and superior, but in fact this was merely a front to hide his concerns and fears for what lay ahead.

Up until the reshuffle, Alexander had little to do with Weapons Platoon Sergeant John Gfeller, who originated from Kansas but lived locally in Clarksville. John already had a reputation for being professional and exceptionally knowledgeable of all things mortar and anti-tank. Sharp and smartly dressed, even at 35 years of age, John was fitter than most of his younger colleagues. Proud and unflappable, Gfeller had been to Korea in '53. Believing in firm, strong leadership, John set the bar particularly high and despite his own close relationship with the men, actively discouraged Joe from doing the same.

CAN ANY OF YOU TYPE?

As Second and Third brigades were still not on alert status, it made 3/506 a far more attractive proposition for the young paratroopers. The opportunity to serve with a bespoke unit like this really appealed to those now seemingly stuck in limbo. Many had been inspired by the 173rd Airborne Brigade, who had recently jumped into battle north of Saigon at the beginning of Operation *Junction City*. Almost every soldier now serving in the division had previously been through eight weeks of basic training at places like Fort Gordon, Dix, and Hood, followed by a further two months of advanced infantry training (AIT) before signing up for jump school at Fort Benning in Georgia.

Twenty-eight-year-old Platoon Sergeant Joe Jerviss from Hawaii came from the 509th Airborne/Mechanized Infantry in Germany and was posted back to Fort Campbell in February '66, where he ended up in a dead-end training job. Married to his childhood sweetheart Josephine, Joe – nicknamed "Pineapple" – was a family man with five kids. Bill Wright was aware of Joe's dissatisfaction and at the 789 Club for senior NCOs introduced his friend to "Snake" McCorkle. "Snake" was happy to talk and before Joe knew what had happened, he was sent over to fledgling B Company. Joe was one of the first to join Bravo's ranks on April 26 and one week later, as he walked into the battalion office, he had a feeling of déjà vu. The misshapen officer's cap sitting on the table looked almost identical to that of his last platoon leader – Bill Landgraf! Back then in Germany, Joe had been responsible for giving Landgraf his first cigarette. Conversely, Joe's first-ever Article 15* came from Bill as punishment for being intoxicated and urinating on his wife Nancy's car while she was still in it!

When Landgraf walked in, Joe's first thought was *No way*, but he needn't have worried, as the captain seemed genuinely glad to see him. Shortly afterward, Jerviss was introduced to Jim Muschett and Herbert Hohl III. Struck by Herb's statuesque presence, he signed on for First Platoon. Joe promised to enable and mold his new charge into the best platoon leader he had ever worked with, and all Herb had to do in return was listen and be receptive to "Pineapple's" ideas and experience. It turned out to be a brilliant pairing, with Herb leading from the front and Joe sweeping up the rear.

Bravo's First Sergeant Arthur Roberts was a Korean War veteran and arrived in August after original top kick, John Garcia, was transferred to the 502 owing to his uncontrollable heavy drinking. Roberts was a solid "beans and bullets" garrison leader who never raised his voice when enforcing discipline or distributing orders.

Growing up dirt poor in Illinois did not stop "Jay" Eckhart and his seven brothers and sisters from finishing high school or going on to further education. But the moment "Jay" turned 18 in October '66, he signed on for airborne training. Basic was at Fort Campbell and afterward there were eight weeks of AIT at Fort Gordon in Georgia. The supervisors back in garrison were all staff NCOs but the instructors at Gordon were combat veterans quick to impress on the candidates the serious nature of war. Finally, at jump school, the intake was divided down into several groups each holding around 60 students. Every morning at 0330hrs, the candidates were up for PT and a

---

*Designed for internal use by a commanding officer as punishment for all minor acts of misconduct.

seven-mile perimeter run. Anyone unable to keep pace with their instructors, who were traditionally known by the term "black hat," was thrown in the jack wagon and posted out as regular infantry, who were always derogatively referred to as "legs."

Just like the parachutes, training at Benning had not really changed since 1942. The physical aspects of a two-week ground school were tough enough but made harder during the summer by exceptionally hot and humid weather. Mounted 40ft in the air, stairs loaded with "jumpers," the outdoor exit trainer was a big apparatus to conquer. "Jay" looked across at his black hat, shouted his name and course number, before being dispatched down a 300ft-long zip wire. From one bottle test to another, he progressed to the 250ft-high jump towers. Everyone was excited but when it was time to release the safety line and descend under canopy, the pucker factor suddenly became very real.

Packed full of adrenaline and exhilaration, but equally scary, week three was all about parachuting. The syndicates were marched out to draw and fit 'chutes before forming up on the airfield flight line. Jumps one and two were clean fatigue and usually carried out from a C-119 Flying Boxcar. Being stick leader on three of the five lobs* meant Eckhart would be first man out. The reality of being number one finally hit when both port and starboard C-130 doors were opened and the order came to stand, hook up, and fit equipment! After the jumpmaster was satisfied, he called for equipment check then action stations ... and everyone shuffled toward their respective exits. With one foot on the starboard step, hands braced, "Jay" stared down at the undulating ground and waited. Half a second later, the green light flicked on and he was out into a warm embryonic slipstream and under the tail. Twenty seconds later, through a PA system at about 300ft, battling against ground rush, "Jay" could hear the instructor below giving corrections on drift and landing position. Feet together – knees bent – elbows in – chin on chest, and he was down. Then it was

---

* The term most paratroopers use for a descent under canopy.

harness release drills and a long walk back to the truck. After his final qualifying equipment jump, along with the other successful candidates, Eckhart was presented with his wings "blood" style.* From the parade ground, a small fleet of buses took everyone back to Campbell and as he was about to disperse on two weeks' leave, "Jay" and a dozen other enlisted men learned that they were destined for 3/506.

Originally, Ronnie Ford was born in Chicago, but by the age of five his parents had divorced and he ended up living in California with his mother and younger sister. Ron was only 17 when graduating jump school on December 23, 1965. It had been a huge class and like Ron most were straight out of AIT. A vast majority of his intake went to fill slots with the 173rd Airborne in Vietnam. But as Ford's 18th birthday was not until January 9, he was held back and sent to Fort Campbell. Arriving on Christmas Eve, Ron went into a holding company before being assigned to Second Brigade. Back then, 30-year-old Tom Gentry, who also lived locally, was his platoon sergeant. Being in the 101st meant a huge amount, but Ronnie was always in trouble. Ford was a tough kid in need of discipline and Gentry certainly gave it to him. After staying with 2-501 for about a year and afraid he was going to miss the big show, Ron volunteered along with Gentry for the new battalion with a "ready to rock 'n' roll" attitude.

Mike Stuart had been serving as a technical corporal with Third Battalion, 187th Airborne Infantry Regiment that along with 1/506 and 2/506 made up Third Brigade. Mike thought it was both his patriotic and family duty to go to war, save South Vietnam, and halt communist expansion across Asia. Like so many others, he had grown up during the Cold War, where "containing communism" was a byword for romantic notions of military sacrifice.

---

* "Blood style" refers to the fact that the metal wings are punched into the recipient with pin extended.

Edward Bassista lived in Perth Amboy, New Jersey and wanted to join the 173rd, specifically to go to Vietnam, but instead ended up serving with Mike Stuart under Virgil Craft. After eight weeks' basic, Mike and Ed were allowed to wear the eagle patch minus its "airborne" rocker tab. Stuart and Bassista were part of a pre-AIT jump school scheme that had not been used since the Korean War. Three weeks later, despite the unusual winter temperatures and three inches of snow, Ed and Mike limped away as qualified paratroopers for a well-earned two weeks' leave. The boys returned to Campbell for their AIT before being shipped out to Norway on Operation *Bar Cross*. It was around this time that Ed heard that Colonel Hayes was looking to train three five-man Long Range Recon Patrol teams at Fort Campbell and by mid-January '67, Bassista was in RECONDO School.

The Reconnaissance, Commando, and Doughboy School was a countrywide combat leadership course modeled on the pre-existing eight-week Ranger program. Condensed down into three weeks, the in-house course at Campbell was run by New Englander First Lieutenant David "Mike" Pearson, and covered advanced navigation, demolition, hand-to-hand combat, patrolling, and medical training. The climax of "week one" was a grueling confidence course culminating in a 60ft rope drop followed by a zip wire known as the "slide for life." Suspended 110ft above a lake, every student had to launch himself down the cable until instructed to let go and plummet into the chilly water below. Both exercises were a test of guts and drive, and not for the faint-hearted. The remaining two weeks were split down into five different patrol missions that included dialing in a live real-time air strike. Firstly, a request was made for a strafing run with 20mm cannon. This was followed by a seven-second delay bomb that would penetrate through trees and explode on the ground. With the canopy gone, the next thing on the menu was a concoction of 200lb ordnance followed by napalm. Out of 60 who started, Bassista was among those that made the final cut and qualified to wear the coveted tab before being assigned to LRRP Team 3.

At the age of 21, Bassista was even more desperate to get into the war. But like everyone else at Campbell, despite his latest assignment, he was going nowhere fast. However, when the government lowered the eyesight restrictions for helicopter crew, Ed decided to "re-up," slang for re-enlisting, and take a shot at becoming a Huey pilot. At that time, first sergeant of Third Brigade's HQ Company was Theron Gergen, who also happened to be a good friend of Tom Gaffney's. Larger than life, "Bull" as he was known had been at the legendary Battle of la Drang Valley with Colonel Hal Moore back in '65. "Bull" had also previously worked with John Geraci at the Ranger School and like Bassista was immensely proud of the RECONDO rocker on his right shoulder. Gergen was as tough as he was terrifying. Short in stature and broad of chest, many walked softly around him and depending on mood, he either liked or loathed you. Luckily, on this particular morning he was feeling nothing but love for Bassista, and when Ed happened to mention about his impending re-up to Army Aviation, naturally Gergen asked why.

"Bull's" solution to Ed's problem came as a revelation. The first sergeant had recently been headhunted by Geraci as cadre and when he told Ed that 3/506 would be going to Vietnam – well, that was it. After promising to make all the necessary arrangements, "Bull" had Ed go back to the "re-up" sergeant and tell him where to stick the paperwork! Consequently, when the time came, Ed, now joined by Mike Stuart, gathered on base with the other NCOs at the Joe Mann Theater for a welcoming speech. After completing initial documentation, everyone received a promotion by one grade in rank. However, rather disappointingly, the two friends learned they were being posted to different companies – Ed to Alpha with Gergen and Mike to Charlie Company and Virgil Craft.

In February '67, two months after he had qualified for RECONDO, Ray Mayfield applied to 3/506 and was posted into A Company. Ray grew up in Texas, joined the Regular Army to avoid being drafted, and then volunteered for airborne. Until Geraci could figure out what to do with him, Ray was initially sent to Weapons due to his previous experience with the 106mm recoilless rifle.

"Jay" Eckhart reported in along with his buddy Daryl Anderson to Building 6923, where the main offices of Alpha were also situated. Housed in separate buildings, each company block-bordered onto Mainville field and parade ground. Running from each landing, long corridors connected into numerous squad bays. Passing by the four-man NCO accommodation on the top floor, "Jay" and Daryl stopped outside "Bull" Gergen's office and knocked politely. After several minutes, the first sergeant looked up from his desk and growled for them to enter. Shoulder to shoulder, they presented their joining instructions. "Bull's" first question was, "Can any of you broke-dick privates type?" Unanimously, the answer came back, "No, sir" – in that moment, "Jay" and Daryl were not about to admit to being good at anything, let alone typing. "Bull" shook his head with disappointment and sent them to Staff Sergeant Manfred Fellmann and Third Platoon. Obnoxious and in his mid-thirties, Fellmann had been a German boy soldier during the last days of World War II.

Walking into the bay, "Jay" and Daryl were allocated to different squads. After finding his bunk, Eckhart was directed to an office across the street to sign out his individual set of furniture from Supply Sergeant Bill Norris. Norris shoved a form in "Jay's" direction and told him to indicate on "metal wall locker" and "wooden footlocker with tray." That done, he gestured toward a stack of heavy boxes. Ten minutes later, as "Jay" came back sweating and red-faced, the corporal lying on the opposite bunk enquired sarcastically, "You idiot, why on earth didn't you ask for some help?" Easygoing and with an appreciation for irony, Thomas Vaughan from Oklahoma would go on to become a great friend. Vaughan also knew Ed Bassista and they had been close since their time together in 3/187 LRRPs.

Although drafted from Chicago in January '66, Mike Trant's transition was slightly different. Firstly, Mike's joining date had to be postponed until April due to a minor brush with the law, and after induction he was sent to Fort Polk, Louisiana. Here the troops were billeted together in single-storey buildings that had once housed German prisoners of war. Due to the exceptionally humid climate, basic was hard-going, especially with only running allowed between tasks.

Airborne Recruiters were never far away and mentioned to Mike about the extra $55 a month for enlisted and $110 a month for officers. Attracted by this additional pay, Trant decided to put his name down for jump school before qualifying for OCS with another recruit – John Harrison. Everything seemed to be going to plan until by complete accident he sent a letter intended for a friend to his mother. While on the phone to her cousin, Mike's mom playfully talked about his bad language and future plans for becoming a lieutenant. Completely misunderstanding what she had said, the cousin called Mike's commander, whom by chance he had known from his own time in the military. Things quickly escalated when the base chaplain then accused Mike of being depraved! After an argument, Mike's company commander withdrew his recommendation to attend OCS, dashing Mike's future hopes for a decent career in the Army.

Later, while at Fort Ord, Trant's name was called for jump school. In truth, his original enthusiasm had dipped, but by going to Benning, he believed it would purchase more training time and keep him out of Vietnam. With less than 12 months remaining until his expiration date, known to all as ETS, Mike took what he naively thought was another opportunity to delay and successfully applied for 3/506.

As Mike stood in the chow line on his first day in battalion, a lieutenant walked up and wished him good morning. Trant's jaw dropped – it was John Harrison, who had Alpha's Second Platoon and was also doubling as executive officer to Tom Gaffney. After a quick catch-up, John explained that Alpha was looking for an assistant in the supply room and encouraged Mike to apply. Ever the opportunist, Mike figured that by conning his way into the Logistical Department, it would be a nice little rear echelon gig, where he could quietly serve out the remainder of his time. Half jokingly during the interview with Bill Norris, Michael heaped it on thick and boasted he could type at least 100 words a minute!

Knowing "Bull" was still searching for competent clerks, Norris was more than happy to oblige.

Mike Krawczyk's father Leonard was a career soldier who had served in Korea and stoked his son's lifelong interest in World War II history. The moment Krawczyk turned 18 in early '66, he volunteered for the Army and airborne forces. Out of 800 students on his jumps course, only around 50 percent made it through the miserably hot weather. One of the clerks at Campbell's replacement depot convinced Mike and several others to try for Second Brigade's 501st Signal Company, which turned out to be a total disappointment. Eventually, through word of mouth, Mike got hold of a recruiting number for 3/506. When his orders finally came through, Mike and his chum Cleo Delong were posted to Charlie and subsequently assigned to Captain Nahas as his top-tier signallers.

One of C Company's most popular squad leaders turned out to be a 20-year-old kid from West Palm Beach in Florida called Paul Cline. Sergeant Cline had been specially selected out of basic to be fast-tracked up the ranks via a program known colloquially as "shake 'n' bake." Paul had played football at Florida State and had been inspired to volunteer for airborne by his father, who fought as a paratrooper in World War II. Staff Sergeant Max Cadena was the polar opposite to Cline. Max had prior service in Vietnam with First Cavalry Division and was as good a field sergeant as any platoon leader could wish for. However, in garrison, Max was a disheveled raging alcoholic with a hangdog expression who often drank himself into oblivion. From the moment he was aware, Captain Nahas struggled to tolerate Max's behavior and over the coming months was forced to have him confined on numerous occasions to dry out.

By now, a few single seniors were sharing rented accommodation off post, such as Alpha's Stacy Raynor and Biven Patterson. Biven Bextal Patterson had gone to the University of Mississippi on a baseball scholarship and was an incredible pitcher.

It was customary for company commanders and their first sergeants to oversee monthly pay parades. A private E-1 in '67 made $90.50 a month plus jump pay, and after tax and other incidentals there was nothing really left for luxuries. Ever the maverick, during one particular gathering, because two of his soldiers were "temporarily unavailable," Gaffney made a point of personally taking their wages across to the stockade. When Nick and Bill enquired why he would be doing such a thing, he explained that from experience it was only right and proper. After asking what he meant by "experience," the two captains were taken aback to learn that Tom had served time in Japan at the infamous "Big Eight" military prison.

After payday, everyone would gather on Friday night at the Bastogne Bar. The only beer available was a weak canned variety, but nobody really cared. The functional bar had its own jukebox, easy-wash linoleum floor, unbreakable windows, and an outside seating area for those warm Kentucky nights. It was here that the guys got to know their bunk buddies and began to develop bonds that would become so important in Vietnam. Everyone thought Ralph Burdett from Jim Schlax's platoon was merely drunk when he said he was actually English and had joined the Army on a green card! But it was in fact true; Sergeant Burdett had originated from Luton in Bedfordshire and came to Montreal as a child with his parents. Two years later, the family qualified as permanent residents and were able to move across the border, where Ralph's dad had an older brother living in New Jersey.

"Jay" Eckhart was sharing his cubicle with a short, rotund Texan named Thomas Dees. Tom had worked on a huge farm in East Texas called "King Ranch." The drunken tales he spouted about life before the Army seemed totally impossible, but in absence of any war stories there was nothing else to BS about. "Jay" was one of only two below the rank of corporal in his platoon to finish high school … and many like Dees actually resented him for it.

The arrival every evening of a mobile pizza wagon could be frustrating for those with empty wallets. Occasionally, someone would announce, "I'll buy if someone flies." With that, the entire room would scramble and whoever reached the cash first and made it downstairs to the "roach coach" won entitlement to an equal share in whatever was on offer.

An informal officers' club at the base hospital, known as "the annex," was frequented by most of the young lieutenants, especially during Friday night's happy hour. On the odd occasion when Geraci dropped by, he would announce, "OK, guys, who is the J.O.P.?" At that point, the most "junior officer present" had to come forward and begrudgingly pay for the evening's drinks! Despite this random threat to finances, the "annex" proved a great place for John's juniors to kick back, relax, and chat up the women – who to be fair were mostly married to senior officers and as such way beyond their pay grade.

FROM ANOTHER PLACE

Within any medical detachment there was usually an administrative assistant known as a medical services corps officer or MSC, and that man was Lieutenant Curtis Washington. Graduating university with a degree in Psychology, Curt, an African American, completed his officer training as a member of the Armored Branch. However, because of his degree, when Curt originally came to Fort Campbell, he was reassigned to the Medical Service Corps and sent to study in Texas. Andy Lovy quickly set about cross-training Washington as his medical assistant and soon the two became inseparable both on and off base.

Andy was totally committed to the actions and competency of his team. To that end, he placed a senior medic with each rifle company to oversee the line guys who were embedded within each platoon. These five seniors had all served previously in Vietnam. However, it was clear from the outset that the line medics did not have anywhere near the level of knowledge Andy was expecting. Out of the 40 lessons that he had planned and projected, only five were ever fully delivered. Because of this, permission was given for a series of three-week hospital attachments specifically designed to give selected individuals hands-on experience in Emergency, Surgical, Orthopedic, and Internal Medicine.

Lovy took guys like Mark Jones under his wing. Mark had already done his medical training at Fort Sam Houston in Texas, although his first military occupational speciality or MOS was artillery. While at Fort Benning, Jones achieved a high-enough rating for medical school and with the guarantee of a 30-day leave, he signed up. However, despite the perks, he found Sam Houston inadequate. Half of the module was related to a hospital setting while the other covered basic first aid. It was only when Mark found himself with Doc Lovy that he really began to learn what battlefield medicine was all about. Unfortunately, there was not enough time available for Andy to put everyone through this bespoke course.

However, those who showed exceptional ability were sent across to Lieutenant David "Mike" Pearson and the Currahee Shock Force (CSF). Pearson's colorful nature and his .357 Smith & Wesson manifested the call sign "Paladin," reflecting Richard Boone's character from the popular TV Show *Have Gun – Will Travel*. Former Ranger Pearson was brought in to train and lead the CSF in jungle warfare. This Quick Reaction Force (QRF) was made up of just two small sections – anti-tank and recon.

Pearson's second in command was 34-year-old Sergeant First Class Philip "Chass" Chassion. A highly respected career soldier, "Chass" lived locally in Clarksville with his wife Joyce and their three children James, Phyllis, and Patricia. Originally from New England, Phil joined the military when he was 18 and had previously served in Korea, Europe, and Vietnam. Coming from a huge family of 13 kids, "Chass" could never keep up with his mail but always tried to make time for his twin brother David.

Just like his best buddy "Chass," 32-year-old Sergeant First Class James Bunn had already spent some time in C Company by the time he joined Alpha at the end of September. Originally from Alabama, Jim had enlisted when he was 17 and already had one tour under his belt with 2/502. Jim lived on base with his wife Rachel and three daughters Desiree, Cindy, and Carol, and could have remained in the States, but that was not the way he was wired. Bunn was eventually assigned as a platoon sergeant to John Harrison, where his mission as he saw it was to pass everything he had ever learned onto his new charges.

Chapter 2

"To the Limit and Beyond"
Training for Vietnam

Even though most of the platoons were still not fully up to strength, squad-level snap shooting sessions using BB pellet guns began to enhance instinctive skills until new rifles could be delivered. The M16 was prone to jamming, partly owing to poor-quality ammunition. However, several refinements had now been introduced, such as replacing its magnesium bolts and using heavier buffer springs to slow down rate of fire. In Vietnam, all rifles needed to be cleaned and oiled at least twice a day with alternative lubricants other than the ineffective standard-issue "LSA."

Newly armed, the battalion threw itself into a series of scenarios, beginning with Exercise *Goblin Hunt 1*. The first field problem began on May 22, when Geraci and his men became a guerrilla-style aggressor against Division at the Land Between the Lakes. Situated about 30 miles west of Campbell, this vast wild forest spanned 170,000 acres between the big lakes of Kentucky and Barkley.

By simulating an insurgent force, it was hoped that the battalion would gain some practical understanding of the VC. As bandit leader, Geraci adopted the guise of "Juan Mal Hombre" – meaning "John the Bad Guy" – a name he had taken from recent "WANTED" posters pinned up by his previous outfit. The sudden proliferation of flyers offered three cases of beer or a three-day leave pass as potential "reward" for Juan's capture. The name stuck and from then on the colonel's call sign became "Mal Hombre," and was even used by his family in preference to Papa or Dad!

The battalion was able to familiarize itself and comfortably implement "Mal Hombre's" plans for rebellion. John's experience and that of his cadre made for a formidable opponent. Hundreds of yards of communications cable were cut by 3/506, rendering inter-brigade dialogue virtually nonexistent. The colonel also had a small number of Special Forces teams parachuted in to work alongside him. As per standard operational procedures, the SF guys were there to tutor hit-and-run attacks alongside escape and evasion techniques. *Goblin Hunt* gave Geraci the opportunity to determine what he had and where he needed to improve. Using helicopters, trucks, and all other available vehicles, Second and Third brigades mobilized everything they had to put John and his men out of bussiness.

Joe Alexander was attached to a Special Forces sergeant and directed specifically against Second Brigade. During the first week, he cached supplies and planned options before Division deployed its hunter force. Joe was captured and spent three days in a makeshift prisoner-of-war compound. He never forgot the experience of tactical questioning, especially its interrogation phase. At the end of TQ, Joe was dumped in the middle of nowhere and ordered to find his way back to friendly forces.

While living off the land with Ronnie Ford, Mike Trant got permission from a local farmer for them to sleep in his barn. That night, as they tried to get comfortable, Ron noticed Michael had a few little titbits squirreled away. Mike only agreed to share his expensive chocolate on condition that Ron rolled on top of him like a human comforter! Nose to nose, they quietly passed the time discussing their dysfunctional families, including mothers who never wrote and their connections to Chicago. Mike's family lived in Oak Park, then a "crime-free" suburb of the city. Oak Park was free of crime for good reason – most of the successful mobsters lived there, including his friends the Battaglias. Patriarch Sam Battaglia had links back to the legendary Al Capone and the early days of organized crime. It transpired that Mike's mother had remarried after his father was killed in a hit-and-run accident. By the time a new sister and two brothers came along, Trant was in his early teens and hanging out regularly at the Battaglias. Mom Angela was a lifesaver and despite her husband Sam being incarcerated always found time to send her surrogate son luxurious weekly welfare packages. When Ron eagerly agreed to join Mike for a big party at the Battaglias, he could never have known that it would be the birth of a lifelong do-or-die friendship between him and Mike.

Bob Baldwin and his buddy Wayne Warren from C Company were paired up and inserted by helicopter for the escape and evasion phase. Bob was 23 and came from Cleburne in Texas. Strangely enough, it was his girlfriend who had actually talked him into volunteering for Nam. Wayne was captured and waiting to be interrogated when a jeep pulled up. As he was being driven to a nearby country store, the driver told him that his grandmother had just died and he needed to phone home. A few days later, Virgil Craft callously denied Wayne's request for compassionate leave and in doing so turned most of the company against him.

Undercover in one of the local hospitals, Andy Lovy and three of his medics were working as orderlies. The doc decided to make a covert trip back to Campbell and "steal" a drug known as Methaline, which crucially turned blue when introduced to water. Commonly used to treat urinary tract infections, the dark-green powder was vital to Andy's upcoming audacious plan. Lovy successfully posed at Campbell's dispensary as an inspector from the surgeon general's office. Once inside, he gathered up a dozen or so vials before heading back to the Land Between the Lakes. The small bottles were then distributed among the team that then included Ron Ford, whose collective job was to try to infiltrate both brigades and to introduce the powder into their mobile potable water systems.

Armed with some of the vials and a can of bright-yellow spray paint, Ronnie set off alone in a jeep. It was not long before he was stopped, but he managed to convince security that he was from 2/501, C Company and lost. Clearing the checkpoint, Ron headed toward his target before parking up and walking the last few hundred yards. Suddenly, a challenge uttered out from the darkness and Ford immediately went on a verbal offensive. The sentry apologized and Ron continued until he arrived in a tented encampment where quite unbelievably everyone seemed to be asleep. Looking around, Ford could just make out a few vehicles and then BINGO – a water trailer. Carefully opening the hatch, he poured in the agent. Before leaving, there was one more job that needed doing. Taking the can of yellow paint, he mischievously sprayed THRUSH, as in the evil bad guys from TV's *The Man from U.N.C.L.E.* on a parked vehicle! Further temptation led him into a tent, where he again stenciled THRUSH in big letters across the canvas. It was time to bug out and lay up nearby. People were running around everywhere when Ron's eyes opened. Calmly, the sergeant stood up and in half-light casually began walking toward his emergency rendezvous or ERV. It was not long before the abandoned jeep was located and search parties dispatched.

Similar to what the VC did with local farmers in Vietnam, "Mal Hombre" had designated local civilians to secretly work alongside his force. Traveling through the forest, Ronnie finally reached his ERV, where a clandestine "fifth columnist" was waiting with an old truck.

When Lovy declared the "games" over and Third Battalion had won, Division immediately disagreed. That was until Andy asked a senior commander at Second Brigade to visit the latrine. But with his urine and everyone else at brigade now turning blue, Divisional HQ realized they had fallen victim to Lovy's underhand "germ" warfare and half-heartedly acquiesced, although the 101st commander Ben Sternberg refused to admit any form of a defeat. On Saturday, June 3, as jets swooped low overhead, the Divisional band marched triumphantly into Lando de Lagos aka Dover, Tennessee.

Hamming it up with a bandit-style false mustache, "Mal Hombre" – along with machine-gun-toting "Snake" McCorkle – begrudgingly capitulated on the courthouse steps to Sternberg and Mayor Herman Tippit. In front of a large, enthusiastic crowd, General Sternberg joked to Tippit that it had been a privilege to rescue his "country" from the evil clutches of "Juan Mal Hombre."

Before a closing display from the 101st free fall team, Geraci joined four local women, who had acted as fifth column, to dedicate and sing a couple of old Civil War folk songs to the general ... of course Vietnam would never and could never be this simple, but nevertheless some positive lessons were learned.

Back at base, regular timed physical tests were introduced, including a hefty assault course followed by a one-mile full-on sprint. Those who passed were issued new 1942-style purple shorts, emblazoned with the traditional World War II-era 506 Para-Dice patch. Each company would also do calisthenics in its own area before forming up for regular long-distance runs. Wearing their heritage pants and freshly printed Currahee T-shirts, the super-fit troopers jogged in formation around base, chanting cadence ditties such as, "The captain's face was turning green – somebody pissed in his canteen," followed by a more serious, "Blood, guts, kill, kill, blood, guts, kill, kill."

By August, many NCOs were being sent on courses, and for the first time were able to mix with colleagues far away from the confines of Campbell. Ed Bassista connected with Ronnie Ford while on a two-week jungle expert survival course at The Army School of the Americas in Panama. For some reason, the two had never seemed to get on, but that all changed at Fort Gulick. On a rare day off, they indulged in local "nightlife" and still had enough change left over for a slap-up four-course meal. During the course, students learned how to kill, pluck, and cook poultry. Rather than wring each bird's neck, several people bit off the heads. Impressed when Ed followed suit, Ron's admiration rapidly changed as his buddy poured warm blood directly into his mouth!

After a long, hot, sweaty jungle march, Ed, Ron, and two other troopers finally reached their designated spot and began negotiating for a raft. The Panamanian soldier manning their stand seemed unusually difficult and quickly lowered his attention toward a dagger strapped to Ed's leg. Bassista was not about to give up the expensive Mark I Gerber combat knife for "a shitty boat." Things quickly escalated and Bassista without warning dragged his argumentative opponent to the ground. Placing the razor-sharp edge firmly against the man's throat, Ed screamed, "OK, you fucker, if you want it – here it is!" Ron was speechless as Ed – unable to contain his rage – spat and drooled over the terrified Panamanian ... needless to say, they got what they wanted.

SPIRITS OF THE STORM

Major General Olinto Mark Barsanti replaced Ben Sternberg on July 1. Although a veteran of World War II and Korea, and well-liked in Washington, the new "leg" commander drew early criticism from his troops, including Geraci, who referred to him as "Top Wop." However, the previous director of US Materiel Command had been hand-picked to specifically oversee the newly agreed Divisional movement order to Vietnam. When Westmoreland requested that the date be brought forward, 3/506 became his first choice for spearhead. To gauge Geraci's readiness, Barsanti levied a two-day command maintenance inspection. Luckily, like with so many other things, Tom Gaffney was well versed and understood exactly what needed to be done. Impressed by Alpha's efforts, "Mal Hombre" asked Tom to take his supply crew and assist Bill and Nick with their own preparations. This cross-leadership spirit resulted in a Preparation for Overseas Movement score unequaled by any other unit on base for two years.

Most of the execs dreaded weekends when the boys were off base on pass. Those who could afford it took the Greyhound from Campbell's main PX and headed for Nashville along Route 41A. Everyone else stayed on camp and gathered at air-conditioned nightspots such as the bowling alley or cinema. As planned, Ron Ford went home to Chicago with Mike Trant, who despite being unhappy about going to Vietnam, still dragged them into a boozy fight on Rush Street with a group of disrespectful hippies. That night, before going to the Battaglias, Mike's mother got a little drunk and said something to Ron that he never forgot ... "We love Michael – we just don't like him." And it was true ...

Along with further platoon training came helicopter drills, authentic village clearance, and Landing Zone or LZ techniques.

Integrated within the program was a short RECONDO-style course teaching lower ranks how to deal with fast-flowing rivers and mountainous terrain. Rappeling, aerial re-supply, patrolling, and familiarization with explosives were also included in the package.

Things began to get serious when 3/506 arrived at Fort Stewart in Georgia for Operation *Crocigator*. The two-week program was to begin with a full operational parachute insertion. Early on the morning of July 10, one of "Bucky" Cox's squad leaders approached him as he made final preparations. Even though his friend Max Cadena was now on Ron Newton's team, "Bucky" was gutted to learn that Max was drunk and behaving badly. Cox could not understand what had gone wrong, especially since Cadena was still under "booze watch" back at base. Cox knew if Nick Nahas got so much as a whiff, then Max's butt would be toast. Newton and Cox closed ranks to help Cadena service his heavy equipment container and get ready for the bus. Once at the airfield, they helped him 'chute up and "poured" him onto the plane. The low-level jump into the Okefenokee Swamps turned out to be horrendous for everybody as the drop zone was inundated with trees and knee-deep, foul-smelling water.

The marshland was also home to alligators, bears, and several varieties of deadly snake. The only thing missing to complete the scenario were wild elephants and tigers. Due to re-supply problems, people were forced to live off the land and drink brackish water just to stay hydrated. Switching roles, 3/506 was now part of the main aggressor force, with simulated access to artillery and air power. However, due to the advanced timetable, extra time needed to fully practice these disciplines was no longer available. This small oversight would turn out to be a big problem during the battalion's first two months in Vietnam.

BURNING SKY

The Divisional Planning & Training Section ran regular five-day jumpmaster courses for officers and senior NCOs at Campbell. Two days of intensive ground training at the Advanced Airborne

School were followed by three days' dispatching. Shortly before the end of Joe Alexander's course, he was called back to base. Although Geraci was still cleaning up after *Crocigator*, he had been tasked to support a State of Emergency declared to quench growing civil unrest in Detroit. On July 23, the city had erupted into mass rioting that during a five-day period claimed the lives of over 40 people. Joe and several others were sent across to help "Mal Hombre" organize loading schedules at the airfield. While Joe had been away, the battalion underwent instruction on various methods of riot control. Sitting on bleachers, the troopers listened to outdoor lectures concerning the worsening situation in Detroit … but what they were not being told was why the riots had started. The Detroit Police Department had previously raided an event and arrested around 90 people. The event had in fact been a welcome home party for two African American soldiers. The media did all it could to portray the situation as a confrontation between black residents and a system that suppressed and exploited them. The adverse effect this had on the black guys within the battalion proved worrying. Guys like Sergeant Charles "Pete" Dozier personally intervened and calmed things down. "Pete" was Joe Alexander's section chief from Charles Town, West Virginia. The battalion was fully multi-racial and those of color depended on African American seniors like "Pete" to give them fair representation. Everyone was relieved when the top brass decided not to send 3/506 into Detroit.

Transported by truck to the Tennessee/Georgia border in August, "Mal Hombre" and "Fat Cat" prepared for their final exercise, Operation *Night Eagle*. Alongside Second and Third brigades, a seven-day jungle-style program was set up in the Cherokee National Forest. Here a narrow strip of the Appalachian Mountain chain resembled Vietnam's Central Highlands. Divisional elements were once again playing hunter force but no matter how tough conditions seemed to be, this was nothing compared to the real thing. Early deployment had put "Mal Hombre" on a collision course with the rainy season, where warmer temperatures bred 100-percent humidity and squalid conditions. Unlike the North, which had four discernable seasons, the provinces of Ninh and Binh Thuan were heavily inundated with humid rain from May to November.

During *Night Eagle*, the medics removed thousands of ticks called "chiggers." Mutual discomfort built cohesion, but at times it was hard to stay focused in the subtropical Appalachian humidity. But it was imperative as vital ambush and counter-ambush drills gave way to long-distance patrolling. Third Battalion struck at every opportunity and covered over 80 miles on foot. Squad leaders were tasked to plan their own ambushes and prepare patrol routes, as well as to work with their "eye in the sky" Jim Pratz, who was constantly circling overhead in the "Bird Dog." To make things even harder, the only maps made available were ultra basic and nearly 30 years old. Consequently, with no grids or coordinates, ground navigation was pushed to its very limits. One of the sergeants from Charlie, Jeff Cunningham, sprang a perfectly prepared ambush on Captain Nahas. Unable to detect any sign or presence, Nick was greatly impressed by just how far his men had come during the last couple of months.

"Dee" Dallas and John Boes began to drill down into actions on WIA, KIA, medivac, ammo, unworkable radios, chopper loading and unloading, etc. "Dee's" other concern was to ensure everyone on radio watch wrote down their re-supply, known as "arrows," and medivac requests correctly. Although there were not that many helicopters available for *Night Eagle*, it was still important for all radio operators to understand correct procedure when dealing with aviation assets. While the battalion was away in Tennessee, Weapons Platoon remained at Fort Campbell to conduct live-fire training. John Gfeller put Joe Alexander through his own advanced support weapons course, including the complexities of erecting an RC-292 antenna system!

TIME TO SAY YOUR GOODBYES

With deployment looming, those married and living on base had the added pressure of having to relocate their families. September was divided by two periods of leave. Andy Lovy and

Curt Washington opted to take the second cycle, giving them time to double-check their medical equipment before it was sent to USNS *General William Weigel* at Oakland Naval Base in San Francisco. As designated loading officer, Curt was in charge of the troopship manifest and went out of his way to make sure all medical containers were given priority "last on/first off" listing ... well, that was the theory.

Rosalie Nahas handed back the keys to 1206B Werner Avenue and moved 700 miles with her one-year-old son to be close to Nick's folks in Texas. Luckily, his father, a retired colonel with over 30 years' service, fully understood the support Rosalie now needed.

Those who had to fly home used the airport at Nashville, while everyone else took the Greyhound. Michael Shepherd from First Platoon B Company was Canadian and Joe Jerviss made a bet with a doubting Herb Hohl that Mike would come back! It was ironic that many young men went to Canada to avoid the draft and here was Shepherd, a full-blooded Canadian citizen, enthusiastically filling his boots in the US paratroops!

A long road trip lay ahead of Jerviss, who was about to drive Josephine and the kids across to California so they could catch the military flight home to Honolulu. Jim Bunn was planning to drive Rachel and their kids home to his mom's in Oklahoma. As it was en route, he suggested they should drive together at least as far as Mangum, where Joe said his goodbyes and continued north to Travis Air Force Base.

After spending their first week in Chicago, it was Mike Trant's turn to meet Ron Ford's family in California. The two chums arrived in St Louis a day early to catch the military hop and ended up looking for seats in a busy bar just outside base. Everyone was pretty loose, especially one of the Air Force guys, who came over and asked if they wanted to join him. How could they refuse; the table was full of lovely ladies who seemed interested in the two sharp-looking paratroopers. One girl, after learning he would soon be in Vietnam, immediately snuggled up close to Ron and began stroking his thigh. Her friend quickly followed suit with Mike. The boys could not believe what was happening and later thanked the Air Force man profusely when he got up and left. The next morning, after saying goodbye to the two girls, Ron and Mike were on a flight to the West Coast. Five hours later, Michael was standing in front of Ron's mom. At the time, she was living in a small hotel room with his 16-year-old sister, her boyfriend, and their newborn baby.

The following Saturday, after a brilliant week letting off steam, it was time to return to Fort Campbell. But before leaving, they stopped by the hotel for a last farewell to Ron's family. It was clear that money was tight and against Mike's wishes, Ron gave his sister every collective dollar they had remaining in their float. After a hard and difficult goodbye, she dropped them off at Travis.

But with just 24 hours to get back, there were no flights available! As the guys pleaded at "check-in," one suddenly came up for Delaware. When they arrived at Dover Air Force Base, they discovered their next flight did not leave until the early hours of Sunday morning. To pass the time, they begged, borrowed, and stole enough money to cover beer and snacks. Mike was still drunk when Ron dragged him into the departure lounge. The news was not good and the flight they were hoping for had been canceled. Being more sober, Ron turned and announced he was going off to find breakfast. It was still dark outside as Mike sank onto a couch, curled up, and went to sleep.

Fifteen minutes later, Trant was awoken and told there was a plane leaving shortly for Oklahoma! After stumbling in and out of several buildings, he eventually found his pal patiently waiting in a chow line. Back at the terminal, they ran into the pilot, who handed them two packed lunches and pointed to a twin-propped C-47. However, "check-in" then refused permission to board. The Sky Train was full of field-grade types and it was clear that they did not wish to share their flight with what they perceived were a pair of disheveled drunken bums.

Mike found a telephone and rang Alpha's orderly room, whereupon John Friday picked up. Mike was desperately trying to explain when Captain Gaffney came on: "There's no being late, private! Go to the Air Force Police and turn yourselves in as AWOL.

Trust me, son, the APs will take you to the nearest civilian airport and purchase any necessary tickets – go get it done!"

Naturally, they followed Gaffney's instructions, but as the APs checked through their travel warrants, they realized the two friends were not officially AWOL until the next morning. Eyes to the sky in frustration, they headed back to the departure lounge, where thankfully their pilot had been looking for them. "Where have you two been? I told you to get on my aircraft." After telling the pilot what had happened, he blurted, "Fuck that, it's my plane and I decide who flies." A few minutes later, Mike and Ronnie were on board and sitting well out of everyone's way. Once airborne, Mike munched through his packed lunch and just moments later threw it all back up.

After acquiring two more flights, they finally made it to Nashville and ran into a couple of buddies from Alpha working a shuttle run. Totally shattered, the duo hitched a ride back to Campbell and made morning parade with just minutes to spare. Gaffney did a double take when he saw them swaying to attention and with a smile whispered, "I will talk to the pair of you later – welcome home!"

New clothing, boots, and rucksacks were issued along with a bunch of other useless stuff that would later end up buried in foxholes around Phan Rang. With new nametags and patches, everyone gathered for final platoon and company photographs. After processing at Johnson Field, several hundred cases of beer were dumped into ice-filled portable rubber reservoirs. Fluttering in the breeze, flags from every state hung neatly from a line of trees. After an inter-company games competition, everyone decanted to nearby woods for a last supper of celebration.

Chapter 3

"The Things We Cannot Change"

Shipping Out

Colonel Geraci and his Advance Party were flying to Vietnam and had planned to leave on October 4 but their medivac *Hercules* became delayed due to engine problems. Accompanying Geraci were Bob Mairs, "Dee" Dallas, and Mike Pearson, along with company executives Karl Perry, Milton Menjivar, and Roy Somers, plus around 20 personnel from various S departments. The officers had a collection to purchase beer and gathered in "Dee's" office to watch a big football game. Later that evening, still in party mood, Dallas and Pearson headed to the Officers' Club with John Boes for another session with majors Mairs, Pratz, and Sexton, and Master Sergeant Jim Goree.

Two days later, "Mal Hombre" and his intrepid team finally got off the tarmac and made it to Travis, where their aircraft suffered further mechanical issues. This second breakdown caused another ten-hour delay and opportunity to visit the nearest watering hole. Over 72 hours, the C-130 hopped between islands, stopping briefly in Hawaii to refuel and change crew before flying on to Wake Island, Guam, and the Philippines. Finally, on October 8, deprived of sleep, the Advance Party touched down at Phan Rang.

Prior to Geraci's departure, a fleet of trucks brought the battalion to Campbell's Army Airfield, where several charter planes belonging to Modern Airlines were waiting. Piled into baggage trailers, the brand-new duffels and equipment were loaded into each respective hold. Before boarding, medic Larry Briggs questioned Max Cadena's uncontrollable shaking and was immediately silenced by Virgil Craft.

The main cabin of Alpha's aircraft quickly filled with cigarette smoke as the 707 taxied out and took off. Arriving safely at Alameda Naval Air Station, the troops were bussed a short distance to San Francisco Harbor, where they spent that night at the aptly titled Camp Hell. From "Hell," their twin-funneled, gray-painted vintage troopship was clearly visible in the distance. Top speed 20kts, 622ft long, and 75ft wide, USNS *Weigel* would be home for the next three weeks.

Boarding began after dockside assembly and roll call. Joining 3/506 on *Weigel*'s penultimate voyage were 3/503, 324th Signal, and 201st Aviation companies, plus a small contingent destined for Third Marine Amphibious Force. Ray Mayfield was now working at Alpha HQ and had already been on board for several days with a small team led by Major Fisher. Guides were on hand to direct each company to its pre-designated berths. Each compartment was stacked with rows of foldable bunks. Men billeted centrally were luckier than those who found themselves in the vomit-inducing stern or bow sections. If that was not bad enough, S&T were bunked in the bowels directly above a noisy propeller shaft.

Due to an absence of bedding, everyone was told to use poncho liners, but with conditions below deck being so warm, it was not necessary. The enlisted guys had access to communal saltwater showers and un-partitioned toilets. Rank most definitely had its privilege, as the officers, warrant officers, and top-three-tier NCOs settled into shared private cabins.

Curt Washington and Andy Lovy were assigned a room with Bill Landgraf and Junior Communications Officer Jack Jordan. After introducing himself to onboard doctors Rosenberg and Takahashi, Andy began to set out his tentative plan for joint medical coverage. At approximately 1430hrs on October 3, *Weigel* left port and the clock began ticking. There were no heartbroken girlfriends or wives to wave goodbye, just a military band on a dank, cargo-littered dock blasting out their own version of a musical epitaph.

Many were already feeling unwell before *Weigel* even reached the magnificent Golden Gate Bridge. Jerry Gomes headed topside just as they passed underneath. For Gomes, this was a profound moment because he had driven across "the city of fog" countless times on his old commute to work.

During first sick call, Larry Briggs diagnosed Max Cadena with severe anemia. Captain Nahas was fuming when he had to explain to Major Fisher that his sergeant was now in need of an urgent blood transfusion. Being O negative, Max's blood type was rare and compatible with only a handful of people on board, one of whom was Fisher! The four pints of blood subsequently donated were just about enough to raise Cadena's red cell count back to normal. Not just a top-flight medic, Larry was also a gifted piano player with a great voice, who made it his mission to entertain while on board.

Now based with his men in the air-conditioned infirmary, it was Lovy's job to check inoculation records and bring everyone up to date with their shots. Minor surgeries were also carried out, such as the removal of John Harrison's ingrowing toenails. John had been suffering for a while and took the opportunity to get both big toes treated while he had the chance. Dozens of lectures were provided by all departments during the voyage, but Philip Chassion's "How to Survive and Fight" was always popular and often concluded by him saying, "If you have faith then keep hold, for you will be sure to need it over the coming months."

An impromptu stop was made at Midway Island to offload members of the 503rd who had tested positive for hepatitis E. It transpired that they had all ingested contaminated water during their final exercise. As a precautionary measure, Lovy and his counterpart in 3/503, Doctor Golden, inoculated everyone who had been in close contact and imposed stricter hygiene rules and mess schedules. Consequently, most galley staff and mess stewards were quarantined. After a negative test result, Chris Adams was ordered to take over from one of the stewards. Despite his initial objections, it turned out to be a blessing in disguise, as Adams now had a cabin with its own shower and bathroom. He was sharing with a guy called Harold from the 503rd, and it did not take long for them to discover a lucrative opportunity. Once Sam the baker joined their team, Chris and Harold's "bakery business" soon grew exponentially. In order to keep up with demand, Sam produced dozens of extra pastries and pies for "customers" who waited patiently every evening behind the Officers' Mess.

As *Weigel* crossed the International Date Line on October 10, all crew and guests officially entered into a traditional ceremony known as "Royal Domain of the Golden Dragon." Shortly afterward, a severe typhoon battered *Weigel* for several hours. Below decks, it was utterly miserable, as raw sewage combined with vomit to swamp every compartment. Enough damage was caused to force the ship's captain to change course and put in for emergency repairs at Luzon.

SUBIC BAY, THE PHILIPPINES, OCTOBER 19, 1967

"WELCOME TO SUBIC BAY" read a sign, as the guys gawped in awe at a gigantic aircraft carrier moored nearby. With the unexpected bonus of shore leave, Joe Alexander was appointed duty officer responsible for timely and orderly return to ship. Nick Nahas's first reaction was to laugh when told that his company had to be back on board by 0100hrs! Off limits to anyone below staff sergeant, Sam the baker and his buddies were getting ready to party in nearby Olongapo.

Harold and Chris were desperate to go along with Sam and spend their ill-gotten gains. Luckily, he came up with some spare civilian clothing and relevant passes. Decked out in Hawaiian shirts, Bermuda shorts, and flip-flops, Chris and Harold fell in with the crew and disappeared off base. Back then, Olongapo town was one long shithole of a street full of pickpockets, a thriving sex industry, and shack-style bars. Naively, Andy Lovy, Bill Landgraf, and Jim Kessinger had the same idea. Hailing a garishly painted vintage taxi jeep, they headed for one club in particular that had been well recommended. But Olongapo's trash-filled streets seemed oppressive and ugly. The club was just too bawdy for Andy and Jim, who soon made their excuses and left.

As designated provost marshal, John Harrison sensed things were not about to go well, when a white Shore Patrol pick-up truck drove onto the dock. Until that moment, there had been no hint of trouble, but as its inebriated cargo spewed onto the ground, John's upbeat holiday mood slumped. Called down from the ship by an angry lieutenant commander, Harrison was ordered to quell a riot at the Enlisted Men's club. It seemed that some troopers had taken over and now had several bartenders and a couple of men from the Naval Shore Patrol all held captive! John immediately triggered his Rapid Response Group, led by "Bull" Gergen. When they arrived, Harrison found the Navy Police outside slapping black-painted truncheons into their palms. The main entrance was littered with unopened beer cans thrown by those now holed up inside.

John saluted as a Shore Patrol officer impatiently announced he was about to break skulls. Stepping back, Harrison urged him to think again. The officer smiled, smugly looked around at his men, and replied, "You go right ahead, lieutenant, be my guest." With that, "Bull" bellowed, "Port arms," and the response team advanced with their pickax handles into a protective line. As they reached the entrance, Gergen glanced down at John's feet and burst into laughter. Wearing flip-flops with both toes still heavily bandaged, Harrison looked ridiculous as he pushed open the front door.

Luckily, most of those inside came from A Co and upon seeing "Bull" quickly backed down. In reality, after being locked into a large, semi-refrigerated storeroom, the SPs had sheepishly accepted an invite to join Alpha's little party. Things were not as bad as they first seemed, and all official charges were quickly dropped. After agreeing damages, Harrison made his way back to ship with the sullen culprits. Back on board, just when John thought things could not get any worse, another white pick-up came weaving into view and crashed into a concrete bollard.

A dozen men jumped out and made for the stern. From his position at the bow, hindered by flip-flops, John was outrun as the last soldier disappeared inside *Weigel*. It was only then he noticed four semi-naked SPs inside the abandoned vehicle's rear cage and trudged back to help. Among personal items scattered across the front passenger seat were equipment belts, a Master-at-Arms badge, and two walkie-talkies. Apprehensively, John released the captives, who were absolutely livid.

An approaching siren indicated the "truck jacking" had not gone unnoticed. Followed by a gray sedan, a jeep came tearing along the pier and screeched to a halt. Inside was the same officer John had squared away earlier. But this time he had come looking for Major Fisher. As *Weigel* was sealed off, Fisher came down and got into the sedan. Thirty minutes later, he returned ashen-faced and without a word went straight to his cabin. Lieutenant Harrison never found out what Fisher had said but the SPs were immediately stood down and sent back to their respective duties.

Meanwhile, a live band at the Officers' Club had been fabulous and as Doc Lovy merrily made his way back to ship, he bumped into Bill Landgraf. The captain had been completely cleaned out by a thief in Olangapo. Drunken troopers from B Company were arguing on the dock. Roger Shannon did not want to board and it took Andy and Bill over half an hour to convince him otherwise. The doc should have quit while he was ahead, but went to calm another guy shouting his mouth off further along the quay. After ten abusive minutes, Andy escorted the man, who was a helicopter pilot, to where Phil Chassion and a few Naval heavies were quietly waiting to put him to "bed."

On Sunday morning, about 30 guys headed out to a nearby golf course, where its clubhouse served a great cooked breakfast. When the bar opened at 1100hrs, copious amounts of San Miguel flowed until around mid-afternoon, when Subic's Shore Patrol arrived! The revelers soon found themselves facing a line of ubiquitous white Navy pick-ups. Ray Mayfield, Phil Vernon, and several friends compliantly clambered into the rear cage of one flatbed. While Rich McDaniel rode up front, Ray and the others sat down opposite a group of 503rd troopers. Within seconds, a fight erupted and then suddenly stopped to let Phil Vernon locate a missing tooth. Once Phil's crown had been returned, the brawl recommenced with renewed vigor, before "Mac" was ordered to step in and regain control.

Chapter 4

"Only the Strong Survive"

Orientation and Deployment – October 28
–November 30, 1967

Covering a distance of almost 7,000 nautical miles, the *Weigel* continued on across the South China Sea before docking at Qui Nhon to offload the 503rd. After the other units disembarked at various locations along the coast, 3/506 finally reached Cam Ranh Bay on October 26. "Mal Hombre" and the Advance Party were waiting dockside with Brigadier General Matheson and Deputy Commander of First Field Force (1 FFV) Brigadier George Blanchard. From its headquarters at Nha Trang, the mission of 1 FFV was to provide combat assistance to II Corps in the Central Highlands. Over the last two years, several aggressive formations had been attached and rotated through Blanchard's organization, including the 173rd Airborne, First Brigade, and now 3/506. As the troops formed up for a big welcome parade, Bob Mairs stood proudly next to Geraci, cradling his Thompson submachine gun recently "acquired" from the VC. Post-ceremony, the American Red Cross ladies served up donuts before the boys were trucked 60 miles south to Phan Rang.

The Proficiency School at Phan Rang was said to be one of the finest in Vietnam, being home to First Brigade's rear detachment. Salve Matheson was closely tied to Third Battalion's inaugural

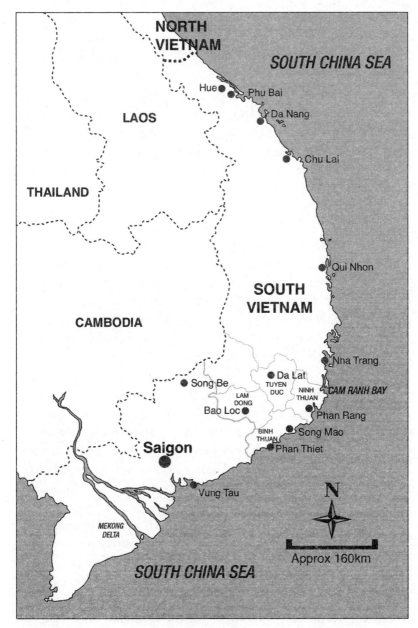

MAP 1: 3/506 South Vietnam Overview, 1967: Operational Areas
and Points of Interest

schedule, along with his legendary Command Sergeant Major Paul Huff. Situated against a backdrop of rugged hill country and outgoing South Korean artillery, the sprawling bomber base had its own air-conditioned luxury barracks, flushing toilets, showers, and swimming pool.

However, home for the troopers was a collection of ramshackle huts and dusty tents, oil drum trashcans, and basic open latrines. The battalion was set to acclimatize for the next few weeks but even here on the coast it was still wet, warm, and unbearably humid. For inexperienced soldiers with an eagerness to perform, keeping everyone hydrated proved to be a real concern for the directing staff.

Completely self-contained, the purpose of "P" training was to realistically refresh everything learned previously in the States, with emphasis on enemy tactics, booby traps, culture, and tropical diseases. Malaria-infected mosquitoes were a constant threat and combined weekly doses of Chloroquine and Primaquine – known as "Monday/Monday" pills – were essential, as was a mosquito net. Other hazards could be found in food and water, where dysentery, cholera, hepatitis, and typhoid were rife.

Five days of range work followed, during which time Alpha Platoon Sergeant Tom Gentry was hospitalized by a random ricochet. From here, the men moved on to orientation by the US and Royal Australian air forces, covering aircraft familiarization and ordnance. "Mal Hombre's" troopers came to love the Australians, especially their Enlisted Men's Club, and although a fair walk from camp, it always had an endless supply of scrumptious ice-cold rum and coke.

At the time, William Westmoreland was touring divisional bases with ARVN General Cao Van Vien. The two visited 3/506 at Phan Rang on the 8th to welcome and emphasize their five-nation Free World Military Allied Force that also included New Zealand and Taiwan. Over lunch with Colonel Geraci, Westmoreland went on to explain his plans and thoughts for the future. With almost half of the interior being uninhabitable jungle, swamp, and scrub, he fervently maintained that the enemy had to be found and engaged in these more remote areas. Rapid helicopter deployment was now key and had been well tested up north by First Cavalry. The original idea of helicopter combat assault had been Westmoreland's and aptly demonstrated his mantra – mobility plus firepower equaled attrition. After praising Geraci's troopers for epitomizing the American fighting spirit, Westmoreland spoke about their recent parachute exercise and how crucial it had been to fulfilling his vision. Westmoreland's visit left everybody with a renewed sense of purpose, knowing that they were now the only solid divisional choice for its future airborne combat operations.

Yet, many departments had still not received their vehicles or containers. Consequently, people were forced to bum rides to visit nearby towns such as Thap Cham, with its popular steam baths and ancient dynastic ruins. Finally, when the CONEX boxes did arrive, dedicated shower blocks and accommodation tents were erected. Frustratingly, Andy Lovy and his men had to move their main aid tent at least six times before they finally got it into a position that "Snake" McCorkle approved. Before long, Lovy was receiving his first patients who had predominately fallen victim to snakebite. When Andy came back from a meeting, he was surprised to see a large Confederate flag pinned to the aid tent and politely asked for it to be removed. The two medics responsible argued it represented Alabama and therefore was not connected in any way to prejudice. The medical detachment was a multiracial team serving multiracial patients and Andy felt that it did not seem right to be driving a wedge between the two. He could not order the flag to be taken down but instead asked everyone to be considerate. A few minutes later, the "stars and bars" disappeared never to return.

"Bull" told Ray Mayfield to get some tent lighting installed so the boys could write home to their mothers. Ray had only just finished when Gergen ordered him to burn away the excrement. Mayfield explained that being raised in the country, he was more adept at putting lime on the poop rather than fuel. "Bull" showed no interest in Ray's reticence and instead went into great detail, explaining correct use of gasoline. Mayfield was right to be nervous, because only a few days earlier, medic Mark Jones had been rushed to hospital after having both arms scorched by a fireball. Despite Ray's overly careful efforts to torch the waste, most still remained unburned. Afterward, "Bull," completely stone-faced and much to everyone's stifled amusement, scolded, "Goddamn it, Mayfield, what did I friggin' well tell ya – you gotta stir that friggin' shit before you Goddamn burn it!" The saying went on to become a euphemism for the ongoing mission and saw much comical use over the coming months.

ON-THE-JOB TRAINING – CHU LAI

From Phan Rang, the coastal flats of Southern Vietnam curved 350 miles north toward Quang Tin Province and the US Marine enclave of Chu Lai. On October 29, most of the officers and first sergeants were flown here for seven days' operational experience with 2/327. Known as on-the-job training (OJT), 2/327 were part of First Brigade and aptly nicknamed the "No Slack Battalion."

Recently promoted to captain, Mike Pearson spent his first few days in the 1 Corps Zone with "no slacks" Logistical team and evenings frequenting their "May 13 Club," where he met Lieutenant John McKnight Jr. John was in charge of the Hawk Recon Platoon and of course shared much in common with Pearson. McKnight's father had been a company commander in 3/506 during World War II and was captured shortly after dawn on D-Day.

While Geraci and Mairs renewed old friendships, the juniors were partnered up with their opposite numbers to get a feel for how northern operations were being conducted. Andy Lovy hooked up with the exec from the 101st Medical Company Don Johnson and Greg Kole, battalion surgeon for 320th Artillery. That night, everyone joined Salve Matheson and his staff for dinner and drinks at the club. Matheson's mess was a large, rustic, no-frills tent, and when he and his Deputy Brigade Commander Colonel Oscar Davis were holding court, they could be a formidable pain in the ass. Always in the name of fun, "Matt" and Davis took great pleasure in teasing their guests before toasting with flaming shots of cognac, known to all as "afterburners."

First Brigade had been based at Chu Lai since the beginning of September as part of Operation *Wheeler*. The NVA were building up in the nearby Song Thu Bon and Song Tranh valleys, confiscating local food and other supplies while staging for big city targets along the coast. *Wheeler* had seen the largest single sweep to date conducted by the Screaming Eagles. In early October, Typhoon Carla triggered an epic monsoon that raked Chu Lai with torrential rain and winds of up to 90mph. Despite this unusually extreme weather, 2/327 still managed to maintain pressure on the enemy's fragmented Second Division. But after seven weeks of vicious combat and over 800 North Vietnamese soldiers killed, the fight still remained largely unresolved.

Among those sent into the mountains was John Harrison, who while patrolling came under direct enemy fire for the very first time. It was a totally different experience than he imagined. When the bullet cracked overhead, despite everything he had been told or thought he knew, John just sat down in the open. Afterward, the platoon leader to whom Harrison was attached explained that new officers often moved with a different rhythm and were always singled out by snipers. When they found the body, John's shooter was old-school Viet Cong using a poorly maintained vintage Russian bolt-action rifle. Even after what had just happened, John still found it hard to conceive that a dirty, 65-year-old weapon such as this man's Mosin–Nagant could be something lethal ... but make no mistake – it was.

Useful tips on how to improve and re-rig equipment were also taken on board. For instance, all rucksacks were metal-framed, with bag section at base and straps for bedroll uppermost. It was better to turn the sack around to spread any load, leaving the lower frame free to secure a poncho roll and sandbags. Another good piece of advice was when cut in half, a C-Ration box, placed between the frame and sack, could provide effective cushioning for your lower back. The guys were also encouraged to remove a useless narrow waist strap from their "rucks" and run it through the M16 carry handle. This way, when hanging from the shoulder, a rifle was always ready and available for use.

MACV devised a countrywide system of remote hilltop artillery fortifications known as firebases and Chu Lai was no exception. From here, long-range patrols would seek out contacts before calling in search and destroy battalions such as 3/506. These firebases were designed to channel insurgents into corridors where artillery and airpower could then be more accurately directed against them.

Andy Lovy and Curt Washington were out on a morning flight to the command post (CP) with "No Slack Quack," Dr. Richard Porter. The CP was situated within a heavily protected firebase overlooking the Song Tranh Valley. After an unusually quiet night up on the hill, leaving Mike Pearson behind at the Tactical Operations Center (TOC), Andy and Curt accepted a lift from Lieutenant Colonel Edmund Abood – call sign "Black Panther." The "no slack" CO was conducting a reconnaissance flight in his Command and Control chopper and thought it would be a good opportunity for Andy and Curt to see where some of his recent battles had taken place.

Later that same day, "Mal Hombre" and "Fat Cat" were making a low-level pass in "Black Panther's" helicopter when someone below stepped on a mine. Much to "Fat Cat's" surprise, "Mal Hombre" turned his head away and refused to look. Nobody enjoyed seeing anyone get hurt but the casualty had lost a leg and needed urgent extraction. As there was no place to land, Bob volunteered to rappel down and oversee the lift. When the major returned with the wounded trooper, John still refused to acknowledge the injured kid's presence. Afterward, when the guy was offloaded to a medivac, John admitted to Bob that despite having been a soldier for over 20 years, he still struggled to cope with any form of high-level suffering.

That afternoon, Dr. Porter took Lovy and Washington out on one of his medical civic action missions known as MEDCAP. The program was designed to assist civilians with their medical needs and show that America was actively supporting them. After obtaining the necessary access permissions from a local village chief, the doctors began to set up shop. The philosophy was to treat and train villagers in basic first aid and by doing so hopefully dilute future enemy influence. The Vietnamese National Police usually escorted all Civil Affairs teams to politely coerce any reluctant villagers from their homes. Mothers soon appeared with babies along with the elderly. Soon a line grew to more than 50 people, the majority of whom were treated for malaria and various simple skin infections caused by poor hygiene. Before departing, as a gesture of goodwill, Porter distributed soap, candy, and cigarettes … all of which seemed to be well appreciated.

Exhausted and disheveled, Andy returned to Phan Rang only to find that "Dee" Dallas had "borrowed" his camp bed for a VIP guest. Lovy was fuming and the fact that the visitor was Brigadier General Matheson made no difference. "Matt" had come for a special meeting with "Dee" and John Boes. Upon entering, "Dee" was surprised to see Major Robert Elton, the brigade's head of logistics, sitting in the corner. Matheson cut to the chase and asked "Dee" for urgent help with procuring a number of highly specific spare parts for his vehicles. With that, Elton nodded, leaned forward, and handed Dallas two sheets of paper full of stock numbers. John and "Dee" looked through the list for a couple of minutes before nonchalantly confirming that none of it would be a problem. All thanks to John's brilliant albeit unconventional forward planning, Matheson and Elton were rendered speechless and proffered no further questions on the whys and wherefores of their pending delivery.

Curt Washington went back to Chu Lai for a second time on the understanding that he was going to learn more about the "no slack" CP. A helicopter dropped him off at an isolated outpost and within minutes the platoon leader there had gathered his men and began to march. When Curt ventured to ask where they were going, the lieutenant pointed to a range of mountains a few miles away. Curt then enquired about the whereabouts of Lieutenant Colonel Abood's command post. "Hell no, that's way up over there," came back the reply. It was then that the penny dropped but it was too damn late. Curt had to endure a grueling eight-hour march, two ambushes, and one serious casualty.

On-the-job training lesson two – never get off a chopper without first confirming your exact location!

Back in Phan Rang, in an attempt to gain more perspective, the company commanders took turns to ride shotgun on bombing missions against enemy base camps north of Saigon. After spending a horrendous couple of hours strapped into the backseat of an F-100F Super Sabre, Nick Nahas was still naive enough to believe that being "Army" was a much better option than Air Force!

During his time at Alpha Headquarters, Mike Trant had formed a solid bond with Armorer Carl "Skip" Rattee. Both were draftees who loved to party and both had fallen victim to the bullying nature of Bill Norris. Norris may have been a brilliant supply sergeant but he treated them like they were his personal valets and even tried to have "Skip" busted for complaining. Company training NCO, Sergeant Bob Bell, knew they were unhappy and invited Mike and Carl to join him for a few days out in the field. But things did not quite work out as expected when Joe Alexander and John Gfeller selected them for their new outfit.

At that time, most of the battalion's 81mm mortars and recoilless rifles were being withdrawn into storage and the three Weapons platoons re-structured to provide an additional rifle arm for each company. Although these new configurations were designated as a Fourth Infantry Platoon, they temporarily lacked the manpower and equipment necessary to function as such. Consequently, lieutenants Alexander, Muschett, and Moore now found themselves acting as reserve or back-up for their respective companies. Over the following few weeks, additional fire team leaders, radiomen, and grunts filtered in to bring numbers up to a more acceptable level. Rattee and Trant joined Lieutenant Alexander's new platoon, along with several others, including radio operator Tom Vaughan and medic Jose "Joe" Ramos. Alexander's original core platoon was very close-knit and Mike found it almost impossible to fit in. However, this was not the case for New Englander "Skip," who was ecstatic about his new role as a fire team leader under Sergeant Marcel "Frenchy" Coulon.

It had been just over a month since leaving San Francisco, and with nights growing cooler, the final monsoon rains turned everything into a sea of thick red mud. For several days, the only way in or out of base was by air, especially after the main bridge outside Cam Ranh Bay was sabotaged. At the same time, Captain Doug Alitz was organizing the battalion's first MEDCAP with Doc Lovy and local district chief Captain Viet Tan. On that first trip, Andy was proud to have inoculated more than 300 people for cholera and distributed various medications along with over 80lb of soap.

Chapter 5

"The Dragon's Graveyard"

Operation *Rose* – November 1967

After eight months' fighting in the northern zone, Matheson and his men handed over responsibility to the 198th Infantry Brigade and departed Chu Lai to join Operation *Klamath Falls*. The entire brigade would now be based at Phan Rang but working out of Bao Loc – 60 miles due west in the Central Highlands. Primarily, the new mission was to locate and neutralize the enemy across Lam Dong and Binh Thuan provinces and bring security to a section of road between Phan Rang, Phan Thiet, and Xuan Loc known as QL1 or Highway 1.

Poorly surfaced and in places barely wide enough for the big transporters, Highway 1 was in a terrible state. The US government had recently increased road funding and sent huge amounts of equipment and heavy plant. But sadly, most of this cash found its way into the pockets of corrupt Vietnamese "entrepreneurs" who rather than roads, built ostentatious bars, restaurants, and nightclubs in Saigon.

While the brigade headed out to Bao Loc, 3/506 along with several local provincial recon units or PRUs was assigned to an area due south of Phan Rang. As the battalion's first airmobile combat helicopter assault, Operation *Rose* was brainchild to Geraci and Mairs. The Viet Cong at that time were made up of a mixture of Main Force battalions and Local Force companies and complex in organization.

Seven years earlier, anti-American forces had combined to become the National Liberation Front. Shortly afterward, with assistance from Ho Chi Minh, the NLF established its Liberation Army of South Vietnam (LASV) that went on to become the current Main Force Viet Cong.

Third Battalion's mission was designed to encompass a series of planned Search and Destroy patrols in the Padaran Hills to locate and eliminate a troublesome base operated by a Local Force company from the 270th VC Battalion. However, most of the information available regarding this unit was already one month out of date. The cape's western hills were and still are among the most amazing maritime massifs in Vietnam. Bordering Ca Na Bay, the beautiful Cape of Padaran gave way to a wall of rocky cliffs proliferated by dragon trees, venomous snakes, and insanely aggressive fire ants.

The operation gave "Mal Hombre" and "Fat Cat" a chance to test and confirm the procedures they had been developing back in America. It would also prove to be a superb "beat-up" for future missions such as Song Mao and Bao Loc. While the Southern and Eastern lowlands were home to a large fishing community, Padaran's western hills belonged to the elusive Cham and Raglai tribes. These ancient indigenous people worshipped a variety of red monolithic features that overlooked many steep valleys in the patrol area. Tallest of these were Da Bac and Deo Ca, whose sacred stony peaks rose to a height of nearly 650m. The terrain was unforgiving and tough. Thick brush and dense forest covered undulating high ground cut by fast-flowing streams that drained eastward into vast coastal salt fields.

Neatly bound by a single road known as Route 407, the Eastern lowlands reached out into the bustling fishing community of Son Hai, where Doc Lovy had recently carried out his first MEDCAP. The village and its surrounds were perfect cover for the nearby secret VC base and storage area. An important hub for coastal infiltration, "Base 35" was purportedly being used by the insurgents for rest and training. Despite numbering over 100 soldiers and

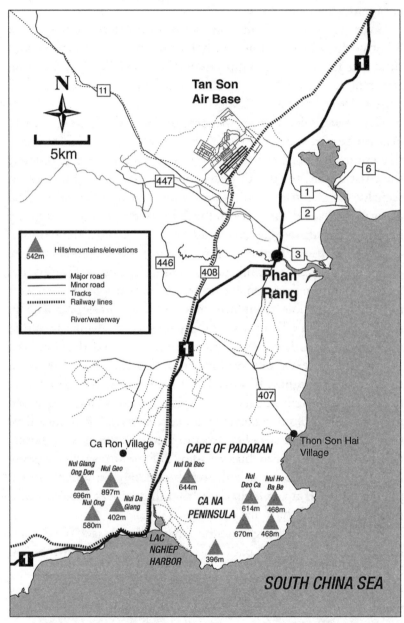

MAP 2: Operation *Rose*, December 1967: The Dragon's Graveyard

armed with World War II-era rifles, the female-led locally recruited company were not to be underestimated.

Normally semi-arid, the late monsoon climate would prove a hefty baptism for the young paratroopers as they entered into their first game of cat and mouse. Wet and humid, the search grids east and west of Highway 1 encompassed the two aforementioned rugged, elevated ranges. Gaffney and Landgraf were allocated to the eastern massif encompassing Da Bac while Nick Nahas and Mike Pearson headed west. This included both Highway 1 and a railway that coursed south down the valley before doglegging sharply along the coast toward the city of Phan Thiet. Geraci was also to provide security for the myriad of engineering works being carried out along Route 1 and assist the Vietnamese National Police with their ongoing checkpoints and roadblocks.

Across in the Alpha lines at Phan Rang, Jim Bunn and Corporal Wally Couch were making sure that all vital kit was packed and ready. Operational equipment loads right across the battalion were now almost double compared to that of training. The average troop was now carrying 400 rounds of 5.56mm while the M60 boys humped 600 rounds of 7.62 link. Each soldier would also be carrying an extra 100-round box of M60 ammo plus two or three claymore mines. It was even worse for the M79 grenadiers, known as "thumper men," whose load was always dictated by up to 80 rounds of 40mm explosive projectiles, each weighing a little over half a pound. Radio operators carried a full pack just like any rifleman but the added burden of a PRC-25 or "25" and spare batteries also made for a hefty combination. The weight of war plus rations and up to eight canteens of water left little space for personal essentials or home comforts.

The commander of the 117th Helicopter Assault Company, Major David Jayne, was patiently waiting for "Mal Hombre" and "Fat Cat" out on the helipad with his Command and Control chopper. David's face and hands had been badly burned back in '59 when the helicopter he was flying for the Inter-American Geodetic Survey crashed during takeoff in Guatemala. Extraordinarily, after three years in hospital and 28 operations, David had only just re-qualified and volunteered for Vietnam. John and Bob would soon come to adore Major Jayne for his maturity and cohesive understanding of their bespoke needs.

Even after one month in country, when the time came to board the choppers on Veterans Day, nobody was really ready for the unusual climate. Drenched in sweat, at 1200hrs, the troopers flew out under the watchful eyes of "Mal Hombre" and "Fat Cat," who were hovering on point overhead. A few hours earlier, D Company 2-320 Artillery, known as the "Red Legs," were airlifted by Chinook along with their guns and A Co from 2nd Squadron, 17th Cavalry to establish a firebase along the highway two miles north of Lac Nghiep Harbor. Aptly codenamed "Team Custer," the cavalry guys, whose motto was "Have Gun Will Travel," had been attached to First Brigade for some time. Not only tasked with night security for artillery, Custer was also to act as an important screening force for Highway 1.

The main assault was staggered into three consecutive lifts flown by a total of 13 Huey UH-1Ds. Bill Landgraf and B Company were first to touch down on LZ Tampa, situated in rice scrub flatland leading to the vast sand dunes of Mui Dinh. As the door gunners hosed their M60s, four accompanying gunships broke away to clear the site with rockets. Bravo seemed to have drawn the short straw and were forced to call in fast air within minutes of landing. The next couple of hours saw them busy clearing Punji pits while their attached engineers disarmed several IEDs. Not long afterward, the company engaged ten khaki-clad insurgents … and the game was on.

Being diverted by smoke and small pockets of bushfire, Tom Gaffney eventually set down onto a saddle three miles due south of Landgraf. Because of the deceptively long grass on LZ Atlanta, some of Gaffney's men dropped almost ten feet before their jungle boots reached terra firma. Chris Adams pitched forward and smashed his face into the hard ground. At the time, Chris thought he was luckier than Tom Vaughan, who was immediately flown back to base with two broken toes. Shortly before Alpha moved out, Lieutenant Alexander noticed his Gerber Mark 1 lying on the ground and blood dripping from one hand. Attached to Joe's pistol belt, the razor-sharp "throat slasher" – purchased from Bricks Military Surplus in Clarksville – had broken loose, puncturing his palm. Joe quietly doctored himself up, said nothing, and stored the blade out of harm's way in his rucksack, where it remained for the rest of his tour. By mid-afternoon, 150 Alpha troopers were slowly climbing toward their first target feature – marked on Gaffney's map as spot height "614."

Seven miles away, Nick Nahas and his men dropped into the valley close to Highway 1. Nick was already minus one platoon, which had been taken to guard "Mal Hombre's" CP over on the summit of Da Bac. A couple of miles south, Mike Pearson and the CSF dismounted below the western massif near an ancient settlement known as Ca Ron.

When the time came for Alpha to set up for the night, the hideously sloping loose stone and shale made it almost impossible to dig in. Under such heavy loads and steep terrain, the first day had taken a toll both physically and mentally. But despite feeling utterly exhausted, there was a job to be done and listening and night ambush patrols still had to be deployed.

Like everyone else, C Company had been humping all day when Nahas reached the summit of one particular hill. It was getting dark as Nick began to form his perimeter and dig in. Suddenly, the sound of rotor blades grew louder and "Mal Hombre's" voice came on the radio. Nick's signaller Mike Krawczyk handed over the receiver as Geraci pointed out that they were on the wrong fucking feature! No amount of pleading was going to make the boss change his mind and Nick was forced to pick up sticks and relocate. Halfway through his diatribe, "Mal Hombre" was totally unaware that "Fat Cat" had cut off his microphone to interject with his own more balanced and sensitive view.

The other hill was higher, steeper, and even tougher to climb, and once the company had dragged itself to the top, everyone was finished. Ever the nice guy, Nick told Mike and Cleo Delong to get some sleep while he stood radio watch. Nick was comatose when Mike woke around 0300hrs. Without disturbing the boss, the young sergeant quietly took back control and patiently continued to monitor both radios until first light.

Mike Pearson and Phil Chassion struck camp beside a stream teeming with fish of all sizes. Phil, a keen angler, was marvelling at the abundant, crystal-clear water when Staff Sergeant Roger Dall came back from patrol severely dehydrated and on the verge of collapse. Dall was one of "Paladin's" most experienced team members and seeing him like this was truly alarming. "Pete" Dozier from Joe Alexander's platoon cramped up so bad that, unable to walk, he had to be airlifted out. After a damp night on the hills, everyone saddled up, scraped off the ants, and commenced with their individual missions.

Nervous of ambush and booby traps, Alpha humped north across the hilltops toward Phuoc Hai. Not surprisingly, movement turned out to be much slower than water consumption. Again, B Company was first to make contact and went into action on the slopes northwest of Gaffney. Third Platoon from B Co had come under fire from a small complex of camouflaged bunkers. Bill Landgraf called in artillery and air support but when his men checked afterward, they found nothing. Thirty minutes later, in a nearby shallow draw, Bravo's point squad turned the flank of what they believed was an intended ambush. During the shoot-out, one enemy soldier was killed and Private Winston "Speedy" Hamilton and two other troopers wounded.

By mid-afternoon, John Harrison was upstream from Lieutenant Donald Love, screening another part of the valley where twice he had been fired on. Owing to thick brush, visibility was down to less than 25m, making it almost impossible to determine from which direction the shots had come. Walking "slack" for Corporal Andy Daniel, Chris Adams was finding the going difficult owing to copious dense undergrowth. Ideally after first contact, the job of any "slack" man was to provide covering fire while "point" reloaded. The squad would then move up under cover from the point while their platoon leader decided whether to fight through or send his two remaining squads in on the flanks. Suddenly, Harrison's security spotted five VC and frantically broke trail.

During the company sweep, Tom Gentry, who had only just returned to duty with Jim Schlax, tripped over thick undergrowth and broke his arm.

Before the medivac arrived to hoist Gentry out, Bravo moved downhill into the marshes toward Dong Hai. The moment everyone was clear, Gaffney brought down artillery before pushing forward to set up his perimeter for the evening. That night, Alpha set out an L-shaped ambush along tracks where they had earlier encountered the VC. With claymores and trip flares set, the men waited all night in pouring rain, but nobody came.

WATCH MY TRACER

Gaffney and Landgraf were now getting closer to the main foothill base below Ho Ba Be. As the CSF was already engaged, "Mal Hombre" decided to call in two long-range patrol teams from Brigade. However, due to a heavy offshore swell, their planned arrival by boat had to be postponed until sea and wind conditions were more favorable.

Since arriving in Vietnam, Ed Bassista had opted to walk point for Lenny Liebler, where he was best able to keep his lieutenant on course. Lenny's appalling navigational skills were beginning to concern everyone in the platoon, who out of loyalty said nothing to Tom Gaffney. Luckily for Len, "Mal Hombre" had recently asked Gaffney to back off and allow his platoon leaders more space to make their own decisions. Liebler was never popular with Gaffney, who ironically due to the colonel's intervention didn't found out about Len's map-reading issues until many years later.

After being given Tom Vaughan's old radio, "Jay" Eckhart was now begrudgingly working in Third Squad as Sergeant Garry Gregory's radio operator. Most of the communicating was done on tactical or logistical matters. If another radio operator called, it was usually for a conference at the platoon or company CP. Under those circumstances, "Jay" would relay the information; otherwise he was not authorized to participate beyond, "This is 3-3, wait."

Jokingly, "Jay" always said that his basic "G-2" for being a good radio operator was a strong back and the ability to walk.

Pausing on a bend, one of Liebler's guys, Reg Jackson, spotted a group of individuals emerging from behind a large rock formation wearing NVA uniforms! The NVA table of organization was much like the American equivalent, with squads, platoons, and companies. Nobody was expecting to see the North Vietnamese Army this far south and word of the sighting quickly rippled around. Immediately raising his rifle, Jackson got off a short burst before the soldiers vanished into the brush. Several similar contacts were made throughout the afternoon and Gaffney was concerned enough to call "Mal Hombre" in for an emergency meeting. Rather worryingly afterward, as David Jayne pulled back on the controls, the C&C was hit several times by enemy small-arms fire. Meanwhile, over to the west of Dong Hai, after several small skirmishes, B Co came across two recently occupied huts furnished with a sleeping area large enough to accommodate up to 20 people.

MONDAY MAYHEM

The weather seemed relentless and even with ponchos it was impossible to keep dry. By now, to alleviate inevitable sweat rash, everyone had gone commando and discarded their underwear. Despite recent high winds and rain, Andy Lovy decided to fly out on the first re-supply from Phan Rang to the CP and spend some time on the hills with his medics. He also brought in a new batch of "Monday-Monday" pills, plus a bulging mailbag containing extras from home such as Kool-Aid and various hot sauces. Usually after dropping in a water purification tablet, it was customary to follow up with a pre-sweetened additive such as fruit-flavoured Kool-Aid or Lipton Lemon Tea ... that made anything taste palatable.

While Andy was returning to Phan Rang with Captain Dallas, "Dee" happened to glance down from the helicopter and noticed three armed men running through the undergrowth. Alerting the door gunner, "Dee" gave direction with tracer fire from his

Thompson. At that moment, their pilot put in a steep right-hand bank to get a better view. Squatting by the open door, "Dee" pitched forward off the flight deck. Left hand gripping his seat, Doc Lovy instantly reached out with the other, and grabbing "Dee" by the belt, yanked him back on board. Dallas sat down in a cold sweat, looked at Andy, grinned sheepishly, and said, "Wow, Doc, these webbing belts sure are strong aren't they?" No other words were said during the flight back to base as both pondered on "Dee's" potential free fall into the afterlife.

The rifle companies were now operating in squad-size patrols, with Gaffney and Nahas moving eastward while Landgraf and Pearson covered north and southwest. Searching for mines, Team Custer discovered another enemy sleeping area alongside Highway 1. Recently vacated, the VC had been stopping trucks and buses to levy tax charges and identify ARVN personnel.

Despite violent squalls of localized rain, people were still falling like flies to heat exhaustion and malaria. "Bucky" Cox quickly got used to judging pace and inserting rest breaks by monitoring his radio operator "RA" Williams, thumper, and M60 guys. Over in Alpha, when a medivac flew in to evacuate one of their heat victims, Wally Couch from John Harrison's platoon shot himself in the foot. Ironically, Wally was previously a garrison trooper from Germany, where most of his time had been taken up by the pistol team. It was a chicken-shit thing to do and when Captain Gaffney and Jim Bunn found out it was self-inflicted, they went ballistic. Following Couch's unexpected departure, Ronnie Ford agreed to take over as fire team leader.

While Chris Adams was waiting for Couch and the heat casualties to be evacuated, he noticed a couple of weird-looking worms hanging from an adjacent bush. As Bunn walked by, he told Chris that these were in fact Indo-Pacific land leeches and if he ever found one on his body then he should smother it with insect repellent until the insidious creature fell off!

Days quickly blurred into one another … stand to – chow – patrol – dig – chow – sleep – ambush – stand to – chow, etc. Everything not sealed became drenched and impossible to dry. Eventually, people stopped bitching as they became more accustomed to the environment. Typically, if the metal parts of an M16 were not completely covered in lubricant, they would be red with rust by morning. LSA, known to the guys as "monkey cum," was great for inhibiting carbon but it had to be used liberally because the excessive conditions altered its overall viscosity.

Blackened faces followed every gun battle, owing to a mix of cordite and LSA. Combined with cigarettes and "C-Rat sweat," the "GI" smell was a dead giveaway to the VC, who in turn stank of Nuoc Mam fish oil used for cooking. During their first major contact, First Platoon put up an impressive burst of fully automatic. Just as Jim Schlax was about to order "ceasefire," he was horrified to see his guys reaching for their cleaning rods to un-jam their rifles. Switching to semi-automatic seemed to resolve Jim's immediate problem but it was clear that current-issue 5.56mm ammunition was still not entirely fit for purpose. As a direct consequence, many began to order in bottles of Hoppe's cleaning solvent from home to replace the LSA. Hoppe's, as a less viscous lubricant, allowed the M16 to function more efficiently on both full- and semi-automatic settings. Although the unique smell – similar to cologne – actually made everyone even more recognizable to the insurgency, it was a risk many were willing to accept.

Eventually, the weather improved enough for Brigade LRRPs to come ashore, whereupon Team "5" was immediately deployed into a valley below the eastern massif. During late afternoon, while moving to a better vantage point, "5" encountered a small group of NVA on the ridge above them. One NVA who died during the gun battle turned out to be a nurse. While searching bodies, the team became aware of a larger force approaching and decided to withdraw. Pursued downhill with rockets and automatic weapons, they were soon in deep trouble and called for extraction. With the only helicopter available being "Mal Hombre's," the boss was able to direct David Jayne, while Jim Pratz flew his "Bird Dog," aptly nicknamed "Mini-Phantom," in low to mark an emergency pick-up zone or PZ. Team "5" was extracted in the nick of time and mercifully survived to fight another day.

FRONT TOWARD THE ENEMY

Straddling the last week, Phase 2 was launched on November 18. A new directive saw Bravo continue with its S&D mission and Charlie airlifted into the eastern scrubs to establish a blocking force alongside Gaffney above Son Hai. Among the first to be given opportunity to shower and shave, Alpha also enjoyed a hot meal and invitation for those who wished to join Protestant clergyman Captain Otis Smith for a mobile Sunday service. Chappie Smith concluded with the battalion's prayer, which midway paid tribute to the last combat casualties suffered by 3/506 in World War II.

Over the next few days, Joe Alexander and his reconstituted platoon did great work recovering several caches of medical supplies, rice, clothing, important documentation, and equipment, plus what appeared to be a makeshift field kitchen. At one point, Joe took the plunge and called in his first successful air strike. Impressed by the confidence-boosting professionalism shown by the pilot and FAC, Joe radioed a message of thanks and let slip that they had just popped his cherry. Alexander was taken aback when the pilot from US Air National Guard announced he had only been in Vietnam for two weeks and this was also his first mission.

Ordered to link up with First Brigade's MP Co, MACV, and the 3-45 ARVN, Nick Nahas helped facilitate the evacuation of Son Hai's 250 inhabitants to Phan Rang. Afterward, as C Company searched through the supposedly empty village, several people were seen on the beach trying to escape via boat. When warnings were ignored, the Americans opened fire, killing four Vietnamese men and wounding a 12-year-old boy. The survivors pleaded innocence but provided no plausible explanation for why and what they had been doing. Tragically, one of those who died turned out to be the young boy's father – it was not a good day for Nick and the boys. After being interviewed in Phan Rang, some villagers revealed that the local VC force were already gone and heading north.

A Co remained in position, acting as Immediate Attack Force, while more caves and bunkers emerged. The dog tracker team working with Alpha picked up a trail that eventually led Gaffney to a semi-occupied base camp, where they killed one insurgent and recovered a selection of weapons.

CLOSE QUARTERS

Route 407 had only just been declared clear of mines, when on the 24th, shortly before 0800hrs, another tragedy struck. Doc Lovy was traveling in a MEDCAP convoy from Son Hai toward Highway 1 and Thon Vu Bon. Elements of Team Custer and ARVN were providing security when their lead vehicle exploded. Three of the occupants were thrown clear, except for a Vietnamese interpreter who became impaled between the windshield and steering wheel. Expecting to be ambushed, everyone dismounted and took cover, but nothing happened. Several minutes passed before Andy and his driver went forward to help. While waiting for the Air Force to strafe in preparation for dust-off, Lovy tried his best to keep the ARVN soldier stable. Andy was surprised by the amount of blast damage inflicted to the casualty's skin by a "protective" layer of sandbags that covered the jeep's footwell and floor. Eventually, a dust-off arrived from the 254th HAC, followed by a Chinook or "Hook" to airlift the wrecked vehicle.

Meanwhile, slightly further south on the eastern massif, Joe Alexander exhumed the three-week-old bullet-riddled remains of a very young-looking woman. The local VC commander was reputed to be a woman and apparently identifiable by a single breast. Captain Bob Robinson from Intelligence requested that the body be stripped and a breast check carried out. Known as "Magoo" and terrified of snakes, Roosevelt Howell was carefully examining the corpse when a large serpent slithered out and scared the life out of him. After the commotion had subsided, Joe was able to ascertain that two breasts were present and the individual had been a nurse. Sadly, exhumations like this would soon become part of everyday life for Joe and his colleagues in Vietnam.

On the saddle below spot height 614, Captain Landgraf's troops stumbled across a large abandoned base that had been previously missed by Gaffney. Cloverleaf patrolling continued while Team

Custer looked after the engineers. While Bravo and Charlie screened the northeastern flatlands, Alpha relocated west by helicopter to the highway. The following day, B and C companies combined for helicopter assaults onto salt flats east of the harbor. Captain Nahas was tasked to sweep around Lac Nghiep while a convoy of trucks took Bill Landgraf along the coast for a night surveillance mission near Vinh Hoa.

By the end of November, Operation *Rose* had moved into its final phase, with everyone being withdrawn across the Provincial Border into Binh Thuan near Highway 1. It had been a tedious but demanding introduction to war, but overall *Rose* served to deny and force the insurgents to withdraw north toward Lam Dong and First Brigade.

Digging in on the steep scree-covered slopes overlooking Ca Na Bay was not easy. But paradise comes in many forms and the beach sunset was truly breathtaking. Everyone's feet had taken a battering and regular powdering had now become an essential routine. Glad not to be humping, Chris Adams rummaged through his rucksack for a baby bottle containing Canadian Club Whisky. Chris's mother regularly sent over surreptitious bundles of the spirit-filled plastic feeders hidden inside coffee canisters. Lighting up a cigarette, Adams passed the prohibited teat-topped bottle to a friend, who gleefully sucked away like a desperate infant. The next day, after mail call, hot chow was brought in for a late Thanksgiving supper. It was also payday and the extra $65 Hazardous Duty Allowance no longer seemed anywhere near as generous as the guys had originally thought.

Chapter 6

"Battle Troopers"

Operation *Klamath Falls* – December 1967

Marking its return to the II Corps Area of Operations, First Brigade had launched Operation *Klamath Falls* out of Bao Loc on December 1. Third Battalion's role was to remain on the coast and screen Highway 1. On day two, 3/506 were in convoy heading southwest along the seafront toward Hai Ninh and the old French airfield at Song Mao.

Situated below foothills leading to Vietnam's majestic Central Highlands and Bao Loc, the tarmac strip at Song Mao was crucial to the new mission. Once again, Geraci and Mairs would be working alongside 117th AHC and Team Custer, who knew the area well. Also remaining were the Red Legs' artillery and sappers from A Company, 326th Airborne Engineer Battalion. Each Rifle company still had its own tracker dog section, although over the last few weeks the canine pups had proved slightly more of a hindrance than an asset. Phase 1 saw the men airlifted out across marshland and hills onto four separate LZs – Corine, Nancy, Rose, and Peggy – named after the spouses of all four company commanders.

The idea was to create a circular containment area with a firebase at its core. Corine was obviously designated to Alpha, whose mission was to block all possible exit routes along the Long Song River Valley. Gaffney and his men were landed 20km due east into an open patch of wooded lowland close to the villages of Tinh Cham and Tinh Viet.

As part of a much larger pan-provincial organization collectively known as Military Region 6, the 840th Viet Cong Main Force were also operating in the area. Bravo were inserted on a high plateau above Alpha specifically to block egress while Nick Nahas offloaded west onto undulating jungle-covered hills. Each insertion was intended to deny potential attack routes toward the coast and Highway 1. Meanwhile, "Paladin," "Chass," and the Shock Force deployed alongside artillery and heavy mortars to establish a Tactical Command Post within the central firebase at Peggy.

OUR BLOOD IS FOREVER

Immediately after landing, Captain Landgraf headed southeast looking for trouble and soon found it. Lieutenant Love had sent out a "cloverleaf" patrol from his platoon. A standard cloverleaf usually consisted of three or four squads deployed in a semi-circular pattern, hence the term. On this occasion, a force of around 15 insurgents all wearing American helmets and ponchos quietly shadowed one of Love's returning squads. Momentarily confused by the American clothing, "Speedy" Hamilton hesitated, and in that split second was mortally wounded by a grenade. Back at Song Mao, because Major Fisher had not actually got around to allocating the aid station with a phone or radio, Andy Lovy was completely unaware of any incoming casualties.

After the dust-off arrived, Andy flew out with "Speedy" and corporals Erskine Widemon and Calvin Harrison to the 326th Medical Clearing Station at Phan Thiet. Widemon was bleeding profusely from the deep shrapnel wound in his groin. Reluctant to apply a tourniquet, Andy enlarged the hole in Erskine's upper thigh, inserted two fingers, and discovered that the femoral artery had been cut. Squeezing both ends, the doc was able to temporarily arrest bleeding and then pack out with sterile gauze and a compression bandage. The two surgeons who greeted Lovy at Phan Thiet would not believe that Widemon's artery was severed nor agree to him needing urgent evacuation to Vung Tau. That was until they removed the dressings with inevitable consequences.

While Widemon was undergoing an emergency blood transfusion, a call came in from the helipad. A member of Lovy's dust-off crew had stepped from the helicopter to speak with a friend. At that exact moment, downdraft from a low-flying transport plane caused the Huey's rotating blades to flex downward with catastrophic results. Within seconds, Andy was giving CPR on the tarmac. A tracheotomy soon followed, skillfully executed by one of the clearing station doctors. Ultimately, the 18-year-old's life was restored by Vung Tau's brilliant team of neurological specialists. But "Speedy" Hamilton was not as lucky and died in surgery later that afternoon.

BALANCE OF POWER

Over the last few years, many Vietnamese country doctors had been murdered by the Viet Cong as they strove to destabilize and terrorize the civilian population. Consequently, Captain Doug Alitz was striving to deliver quality MEDCAP into the villages and towns along Highway 1. Everything seemed to be going well until Doc Lovy found out his pills were being appropriated by the local VC. A large number of children were suffering from an eye disease known as trachoma that if left unchecked often leads to blindness. With no medication available from Brigade, Lovy's practice partner in Milwaukee came to the rescue. But despite this successful outcome, it was clear to Andy that he was not going to win the battle for hearts and minds anytime soon.

Meanwhile, contacts began occurring over to the east, beginning with Sergeant Andy Rivera, who was Phil Vernon's dependable fire team leader in Alpha. Vernon was scaling a ridge when he noticed smoke coming from somewhere below. Summoning Rivera, Phil notified Jim Schlax, who ordered the two NCOs to take a closer look. Leading the way, Rivera silently descended through a corridor of rocks and noticed the distinctive smell of fish oil. One by one, Rivera's squad moved along a small gully and up onto a ledge from where they could see a campfire. As Rivera moved for a better look, three other fires came into view, along with a dozen or so VC sitting around eating lunch. One insurgent stood and walked a couple of steps before comically tripping over. Suddenly, the laughter stopped as the man raised his hand and pointed up toward Rivera.

Andy squeezed off a short burst and dropped in several grenades. Instantly, the enemy bolted, abandoning everything – including two dead colleagues. Another brief exchange forced Rivera to take cover as the VC returned for their comrades. Moving beyond the clearing, Rivera engaged and killed another insurgent emerging from a cave. Inside, Andy found medical supplies and journals while his squad collected seven carbines and two rifles from the campsite.

Nearby, John Harrison found another cave directly below a feature known as Bong Cam. The place was furnished and even had sleeping accommodation for up to 40 people. John also recovered 400lb of rice that had originally been sent as aid by the US government. Alpha was reinserted by helicopter into a remote rice paddy valley alongside the Song Tan River. Over the next two days, Gaffney and his men searched fruitlessly around the waterway. Typically, much of this lowland terrain was even more arduous due to the proliferation of foul-smelling, humid swamps. When Alpha returned to base on December 9, it was announced that a MACV compound 35km north of Song Mao had been attacked and overrun by members of the 186th Main Force Battalion. Tahine, a tiny Montagnard settlement, was situated in a logging valley alongside the Da Queyon River. Montagnard was an old French term meaning "People of the Mountain." Most common were the artisan M'nong, aristocratic Rotee, and warrior Jurai, who collectively refused to be intimidated by the VC. Easily recognizable by their darker skin, the features of a Montagnard were similar to those of an Aboriginal tribesman. After France's defeat at Dien Bien Phu, the communists had terrorized many indigenous villages, turning them into a perfect anti-guerrilla force. The "Yards" had created a resistance movement that was now crucial to America, crushing insurgent strategy within the

Highlands. Although discipline was poor, these mountain peoples showed incredible strength, loyalty, and energy. Although over 61,000 "Yards" served with the US Army, the war destroyed most of their villages and led to over 200,000 being killed.

Built on a small knoll at the northern end of Tahine, the SF compound was made up of six buildings and occupied by local Montagnard militia. A party was in full swing when the attack came. As a MACV-led ARVN relief force flew in to assist, the helicopters came under heavy fire. After one Huey crashed, the government troops aborted and callously left four American advisors to their fate.

THE IRON TRIANGLE

On December 9, 3/506 and all its supporting elements began to extract by Chinook back to Song Mao in preparation for the second phase. After drawing four days' rations, A and C companies created a joint perimeter and patiently waited. The next morning at 1100hrs, Bravo, followed by the CSF, flew out for a special last-minute mission to Tahine. Shortly after landing, Captain Landgraf soon discovered the murdered MACV men whose battered bodies lay barefoot by the fort entrance, hands restrained behind their backs. Wild pigs gorged on entrails protruding from a bloated torso surrounded by dozens of mutilated indigenous corpses. Joe Jerviss and Private Marshall Hill attached ropes to the ankles of each American body before pulling them clear of any potential booby traps. It appeared to be an inside job because the 186 VC had gained entry via a tunnel leading up from the village. Screening actions from Landgraf and Pearson enabled MACV to safely conduct a follow-up investigation and provide medical assistance to any injured locals. Later that evening, after being relieved by South Vietnamese troops, the CSF returned by chopper to Song Mao.

"Dee" Dallas carefully nudged his heavily loaded two-and-a-half-ton truck up onto the ramp of a C-130 Hercules. On arrival at Bao Loc, as Dallas and Boes were getting ready to drive across

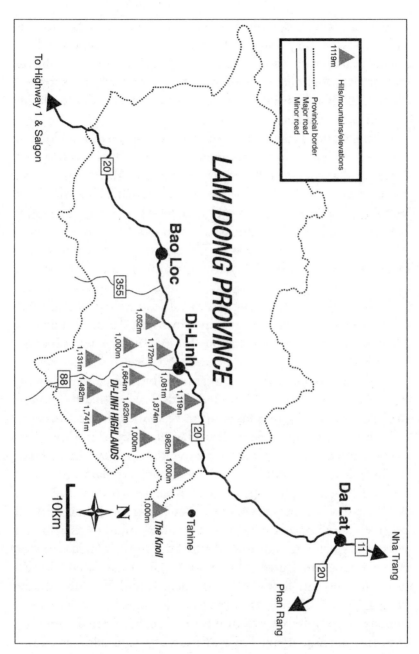

MAP 3: Operation *Klamath Falls*, Bao Loc and the Di-Linh Highlands, December 1967

to the new base area, Brigadier General Matheson pulled up and inquired what they had in the back. "Sir, our soldiers will be having steak tonight and a decent hot breakfast tomorrow before they insert." Mightily impressed by "Dee's" reply, "Matt" responded, "Well, captain, please inform the colonel that I'll be over for dinner tonight, so it had better be good!"

Gaffney and Nahas followed on in staggered lifts looking forward to cooler mountain temperatures. Tom flew out first with Schlax and Harrison followed by Liebler and Alexander. The aid station and much of HHC had already relocated, along with "Mal Hombre's" Tactical Operations Center. However, being close to the helicopter flightline brought in dust and dirt from constant rotor wash. New Battalion Executive Officer Major Houston Hauser began his tenure positively by arranging for all future air traffic to use a different flight path.

Beyond Bao Loc, a succession of substantial rolling hills dominated the horizon from north to south. Situated alongside Highway 20, the town was famous for its tea and silk production. The main road dissected Lam Dong Province from east to west, connecting Saigon to Phan Rang and Nha Trang. Twenty miles further east were the Di-Linh Highlands that boasted the region's highest peak at 1,874m, plus an ultra-modern hydroelectric dam.

Feeling marginalized by Major Hauser, Lovy and Washington decided to pay a visit to the clearing station at Phan Thiet. Here, the brigade surgeon, Major Richie, was able to explain where their medical supplies would be coming from and to which surgical hospitals their casualties would now be going. While there, Andy became unwell and had to be hospitalized by Major Richie for tests. The following morning, Andy discharged himself and flew back to Bao with Curt, whereupon Major Hauser accused them of leaving the battalion without his permission. The conversation became heated and quickly overflowed into argument when Hauser implied that Andy had acted unprofessionally. After the incident with Erskine Widemon, Lovy was not about to allow his ethics to be called into question again. Afterward, relations between Dr. Lovy and the management team spiraled rapidly downhill.

In 1967, the province covered an area approximately 60 miles wide by 35 miles deep. The Da Dang River defined the region's northern outreach close to covert North Vietnamese supply routes. The previous rainy season had hampered enemy movement along the border with neutral Laos and Cambodia. These beautiful mountains had been home to the first French hill stations where early colonizers came to seek relief from stifling heat. Now, however, although the nights were growing colder, warmer daytime temperatures turned out to be a double-edged sword for the Americans. After Tahine, it was clear that the 186th Main Force and elements from Headquarters MR-6 had a heavy presence in western Lam Dong. The 186th had already set up several base camps along Highway 20. Here, local hamlet guerrilla teams from 490th Local Force Company could operate tax points to obtain rice, medical, and other vital supplies from the defenseless villagers.

The NVA had been quietly bringing troops, weapons, and equipment across Lam Dong's northern border with Quang Duc via Cambodia and the Ho Chi Minh Trail. In daylight, the web of jungle roads and trails looked empty, but by night thousands of vehicles were using darkness to reinforce and supply the insurgency. The only successful solution to date had been from high-flying American B-52 bombers and ground attack aircraft from the Royal Lao Air Force, but it was a monumental task.

Originally begun in 1959, the road system now totaled a network of some 8,500 miles. Although officially neutral, and with a coalition government, Laos remained militarily divided between the Royal Lao Forces and Pathet Lao. The Pathet Lao guerrillas were supported by North Vietnam and held much of the countryside, including the important border supply routes. Back in '66, General Westmoreland wanted to invade far enough into Laos to cut the trail, but risks of escalation and potential American casualties seemed far too great for him to gamble.

Because US forces controlled the air space, evasion was now easier than escape. The skill of deception and camouflage was something to behold. The only way to combat this was for each

Rifle company to saturate its designated area of operations. The new AO, codenamed "Lela," was located 30km southeast in mountains below Highway 20. The next ten days would be spent "dancing" around the Tactical Headquarters, spending two or three days in one valley before being flown to another and beginning the search process all over again. One time, unable to see the onboard compass, Nick Nahas was confused as to where he had been placed and called down artillery onto coordinates he thought were nearby. After confirmation that the shells were on their way, Nick waited and waited before realizing that the company were not even on the same map!

Back at Song Mao, Mike Pearson initiated the first helicopter assault by flying in with the CSF to secure and make way for the "Hooks" bringing in "Mal Hombre's" Tactical Headquarters. Situated on a high open plateau near the tiny settlement of Sre Boh, at 1,071m the command post, Battalion's heavy mortars, and Red Legs' artillery firebase were collectively situated between Route 88 and Highway 20. Two hours later, Bravo flew in direct from Tahine, followed by Alpha and Charlie from Bao Loc onto adjacent LZs surrounding the firebase.

Meanwhile, as the first part of Operation *Eagle Thrust*, General Barsanti arrived in country on December 13, at Bien Hoa Air Force Base near Saigon. The general wasted no time in deploying Second and Third brigades to enhance the ongoing US troop build-up around the Southern capital.

Two days later, after moving a couple of miles' southeast, A Co destroyed a large base camp that had been built directly below a ridge close to fresh water. There were no roads and few villages here, just a series of ancient Asian elephant trails undulating across hills and mountains. Another similar-sized camp was found further west by Len Liebler. Working across the valley from Liebler, Bravo found two more camps that totaled 15 huts, six kitchens, and a vast tunnel system. "Mal Hombre" knew he was getting closer by the military paraphernalia left behind in these various locations, including a strange man-made wooden contraption built to bore sight a heavy mortar.

CARBINE KILLERS

Soon, each platoon, including Joe Alexander's, began to stage its own independent ambush operations. During this period, Joe hardly ever saw the other platoon leaders, but the experience he gained was invaluable. The only time he really heard from Gaffney was usually around 2200hrs, when he would radio across coded coordinates and instructions for the next set of ambushes. Contacts continued to increase over the next few days until during the early hours of Tuesday, December 19, Gaffney lost his first man, Private Edgar Campbell. By then, Alpha had moved further north toward the elevated settlement of Ap Klong Jum, overlooking the single-track Route 88 that led to Di-Linh. Elements from John Harrison's platoon were waiting in ambush when a patrol from 145th Main Force VC crept in shortly after 0430hrs.

In charge of the first ambush site was old-school, 27-year-old Texan Staff Sergeant Jearl Keefer. Keefer's squad were part of a larger tactic known as a "pinwheel" alongside nine other squads from Alpha. Remotely setting up one of these pinwheel ambushes required every ounce of map appreciation and creative ingenuity. On this occasion, Gaffney had found the perfect place where a shallow, partially forested valley could force any approaching troops to "bounce around" into his other sites. The company control group was placed centrally in readiness to assist. Each platoon had moved into its designated area, forming a hub around its respective lieutenant. The VC always moved at night and any one of their patrols could easily represent the tip of a much larger force. Therefore, it was essential for Gaffney's command position to be located somewhere that was easy to defend and rendezvous on. That night, Gaffney and Harrison, along with John's remaining two squads, were providing security and a Quick Reaction Force.

As the enemy quietly approached Keefer, Ed Campbell's un-silenced "25" suddenly registered a transmission. Alerted, the insurgents quickly withdrew under a hail of automatic fire. Ironically, Ed was only acting as a stand-in and his inexperience with the "25" no doubt served to compromise Keefer's security.

Harrison immediately took one squad plus medic John Melgaard and made for the nearby ridge. Keefer had been shot in the right buttock and for the most part seemed comfortable. However, Campbell had been wounded in the left arm and leg but more importantly had taken a third bullet to his neck. Melgaard immediately went to work underneath a poncho with his flashlight while Harrison called for medivac. The ambush site was on a steep slope with only a small gap in the canopy above for evacuation. Standing on a tree stump holding a strobe marker, John did his best to guide the pilot in. As the minutes ticked by, Campbell's condition got worse and it was clear he had to be evacuated immediately.

The pilot's flying skills were utterly incredible. With barely enough room for the chopper, he slowly descended under direction from his door gunners and held off in a low hover with rotors narrowly missing the slope. As Harrison loaded his two troopers, the pilot compensated for the extra weight and rose vertically back up through the canopy. It was an amazing piece of night flying and as the bird disappeared into the blackness, a burst of gunfire erupted from First Platoon.

The same enemy patrol that ran into Keefer had just triggered "Mac" McDaniel's ambush. In the gunfight, one insurgent threw down his rocket launcher and ran off as corporals Tommie Davis and Alfred Johnson opened up with their machine gun. Paperwork found afterward on the dead showed that they were part of a larger migration of forces. Along with the discarded launcher, First Platoon recovered two rockets, an AK-47, six rucksacks, and several grenades. When "Mac's" men were still searching the black-uniformed bodies, a third ambush was successfully unleashed.

The following morning, "Mal Hombre" flew in to inform Gaffney that Ed Campbell had died on the way to hospital. Campbell was Alpha's first KIA and as with "Speedy" Hamilton and B Company, his death was hard to accept. Losing Staff Sergeant Keefer at such an early stage was also a blow for Harrison, especially as he had him earmarked to replace John Friday as his next platoon sergeant.

THE GREAT DELUSION

December 20 was Lieutenant Liebler's 21st birthday and together with his intrepid, dysfunctional platoon, he was straddling a valley when he noticed movement in the forest up ahead. Looking through binoculars, Ed Bassista could clearly see that it was a colony of albino monkeys, but Len was already on Lynn Berner's radio dialing up a barrage of "Fuck You" (slang for 18 rounds of high explosive). Reaching across, Ed snatched the handset away and immediately canceled his call to Alpha 6 – Gaffney's call sign. Afterward, Len bribed the platoon to keep quiet by pledging them $100-worth of beer on the next stand-down. Later, when the time came to deliver his promise, Lenny did not have the money, so Bassista sold his beloved Gerber to cover the costs.

From his time with LRRPs, Bassista had taken the use of claymore mines to a whole new level. As squad leader, Ed always deployed 12 mines while in ambush – six in the kill zone, two on each flank, two in the rear, and two directly in front of the squad position. Bassista instilled into his guys not to talk or fire unless being overrun. Afterward, if any wounded were identified, Ed would go out by himself, pick up an abandoned AK or M1 carbine, and finish them off. Although ruthless, it was exceptionally efficient, especially in the more remote areas where fanatical prisoners were a liability. Bizarrely, a few days earlier, Ed came across an old hut containing skeletal remains of a small child surrounded by beautiful tribal offerings. The place looked spooky and fearful of potential "Yard" retribution, Bassista forbade his guys from taking souvenirs.

A small element of CSF accompanied Doug Alitz, Doc Lovy, and Curt Washington on a local MEDCAP mission just north of Bao Loc Airfield. The older people were first in line and when they thought everything was safe, the younger women and children followed suit. In total, around 100 people were checked and treated. Later that evening, Andy and Curt told Mike Pearson that a man (probably political cadre NVA) had been hanging around asking questions in Vietnamese. This was alarming because the "Yards" spoke a completely different dialect to any mainstream Vietnamese.

Pearson had already agreed to a meeting at the same village on another matter. The next day, when "Paladin" arrived, there was nobody around. However, the same man who had spoken to Lovy stepped out from a hut. Mike quickly headed back to base and returned with Lovy and a small security team, but the man was gone. When their indigenous police officer found the chief's wife, she told him that her husband had gone fishing and flatly refused to reveal the mystery man's identity. Subsequently, protection was doubled for all future MEDCAP missions. But the incident highlighted important language issues and a need for permanently attached tribal translators.

By contrast, in another "Yard" village, Andy and the team were invited to a banquet prepared by several elders. The meal looked amazing but contained certain items that Lovy was unable to eat due to his religion. Not wishing to offend anybody, Andy turned to Doug Alitz and asked for advice. Overhearing their conversation, one of the Montagnards enquired in perfect English, "Captain, are you by any chance Jewish?" After everything they had experienced over recent days, Andy could never have imagined such an educated response. With a wave of his hand, the chief had everything replaced with fresh bread, pastries, fruit, and vegetables. It was definitely a lesson in tolerance and understanding that Andy would never forget.

NO HORIZON

Unusually, on December 21, now under operational control of Pearson, C Company were flown 30km east for a new mission. Here, a few miles away from Tahine, they were to conduct a search operation along Highway 20, starting at a small roadside settlement southwest of Dai Ninh called Hiep Thuan. Initially, "Mal Hombre" wanted Nick to hunt down those who had recently been robbing civilians and the trail quickly led south. Nahas followed his instincts toward the Provincial Border with Binh Thuan, while Pearson followed suit, shadowing Nick's left flank along the nearby border with Tuyen Duc. Back in "Lela," Bravo found another elaborate camp complete with sleeping platforms, a 200m trench system, and discarded containers that once held 500,000 units of penicillin.

The steep hills were brutal and machetes left nothing behind to grab or hold. When the guy in front slipped, everyone below automatically braced for impact. But there were still moments of humor. It was so important in places like this for platoon leaders to be aware of their exact location. Like the other commanders, Captain Nahas stayed in regular contact with each platoon by periodic radio checks that often arrived at the worst and most frustrating times. When Ron Newton was asked to report his location, he tried to fob the boss off by saying he was having trouble finding identifiable landmarks. Nick asked if there were any streams nearby, to which Ron responded, "Yes, sir, we are near a stream." Nick then asked, "Well, what direction is that stream running, lieutenant?" Without skipping a beat, Ron sarcastically radioed back, "Charlie six, this is Charlie two-six, it is running downhill, confirm, downhill – over." Nick nearly blew a gasket, raised his voice, and coughed, "Shoot an azimuth and determine compass direction of that damned stream!!!" "Ahh, oh – right, Charlie six, stand by." "Bucky" Cox and "RA" Williams were listening nearby on the company net and fell about laughing. The conversation continued back and forth for another five minutes before Nick realized he was being played!

Soaked in sweat, forearms shredded by razor-sharp grass, "Bucky" and Third Platoon were stoically following an ascending valley track when they came across a fast-flowing tributary of the Dang Ciang River. Everyone froze as splashing sounds emanated from the other side of a dense hedge. "Bucky" gestured toward Sergeant Ted Schnoor to take First Squad around for a better view. Through stifled laughter, Ted explained that it was only a herd of pigs and could he please have permission to shoot a couple for dinner. Of course, "Bucky's" answer was, "Absolutely not," but the decision did not sit well with his boys, who all fancied fresh cooked bacon for supper.

Captain Nahas instructed Cox to recon a decent clearing where all four platoons and the CSF could rendezvous for Christmas.

Leaving his platoon in all-round defense, "Bucky" took sergeants Mike Daly and Paul Cline along with a reinforced squad to make sure the area was also safe for helicopter re-supply.

Working their way up valley, the path terminated at a small isolated farm. From here, "Bucky" crossed another stream and continued along a pampas plateau for another few hundred meters. During a short map check, the NCOs set out their point, flank, and rear security. Suddenly, shots rang from behind and the crack of incoming rifle rounds sent everybody scrambling for cover. Helmets, maps, and compasses all went flying as "Bucky" called for his guys to come on line and attack. However, Paul Cline shouted louder and the team remained in position to defend.

When the gunfire subsided, point security came running over white as a ghost and amusingly reported, "Sir, I was eating a can of fruit cocktail when …!" "Bucky" roared in amusement and the point quickly cut to the chase. Out of the three insurgents engaged, one had been wounded. A quick sweep revealed a concussion grenade and a pair of abandoned sandals. Turning to the guys, Cox proffered, "Fellas, I think we'd have all been dead by now if Ted had shot those pigs." Everyone nodded in acceptance as they processed what had just happened. Later in the afternoon, Captain Nahas arrived with another platoon and asked "Bucky" to come up with a workable security plan that could be implemented by the following morning – which also happened to be Christmas Eve.

That evening, while walking around the perimeter, "Bucky" happily accepted an invitation for a chicken and rice supper from Frank Vinales and Paul Cline. Frank came from a poor Puerto-Rican family in the Bronx and grew up among New York's dilapidated Andrew Jackson Projects. Despite their vastly different backgrounds, he and Paul had formed an unbreakable friendship. Chicken and rice was "Bucky's" favorite but this time Frank and Paul decided to leave out their fresh onion and Tabasco, as they were both suffering from chronic diarrhea. Brought on by a mixture of too much salt, iodine, and Monday-Monday pills, this was by no means uncommon out there on patrol. After dinner, "Bucky" convinced the boys to go ask senior medic Larry Briggs for a course of Darvon. As a hefty prescription painkiller, Darvon was always readily available, with constipation as one of its side effects.

"GOD REST YOU MERRY, GENTLEMEN" – CHRISTMAS 1967

On Christmas Eve, Alpha and Bravo set up their respective perimeters and waited for re-supply. At 1800hrs, First Brigade ceased all offensive operations in observance with a pre-agreed Christmas ceasefire. The plan was for everyone to stay put until Boxing Day. Now joined by the CSF, Charlie Company was also looking forward to a spot of rest and relaxation. Despite the "no move" order, each company was asked to designate one platoon for base security and skeleton patrolling.

As arranged, "Bucky" led his men out on Christmas Eve and 30 minutes later, with Mike Daly on point, they were nervously back on the same trail. Cox pushed Daly's squad out about 30yds and soon passed through the site of his earlier contact. Shortly after 1130hrs, "Bucky" reached a ridge marked on his map as spot height "1059." Here, the narrow saddle was partially covered by trees and waist-high pampas. As left-flank security fanned uphill, they spotted movement ahead and immediately opened up. Everyone dropped to the ground, including Daly's squad, who were now well behind "Bucky."

Kicking up dirt, enemy fire was coming dangerously close as "Bucky" pointed toward a nearby line of trees. Rising to his feet, Platoon Sergeant "RJ" Johnson misinterpreted Cox's hand signal and, believing it was his order to attack, yelled, "Let's go, Third, this is what we're paid to do!" For a split second, it felt more like a training exercise than reality. "Bucky" sent off a quick contact report to Nahas and then told Daly to stay where he was and prepare to defend. Nick offered up artillery support but as Cox followed "RJ" into the assault, he had no time to determine or pass on any useful coordinates.

Stupidly, the enemy had not factored in a decent escape route. The most direct path off the ridge was behind "Bucky" and downhill toward dead ground. But that meant crossing in front of Daly, whom they had not yet seen. Suddenly, shots came from Mike's direction as he began calling, "Maverick, Maverick, where are you? We need your help NOW!"

Leaving the platoon with "RJ," "Bucky" headed back toward Daly, who had two dead enemy soldiers lying inside his perimeter. As predicted, "Bucky" and "RJ's" assault had indeed forced the Vietnamese toward Daly. One, an NVA officer from the 186th Main Force VC, was clothed in US fatigue pants and jungle boots. Incredibly, these boots belonged to a MACV colonel who had been among those killed at Tahine on December 7. Drawn to a holstered, Chinese-manufactured, Tokarev-style 9mm pistol, "Bucky" was astounded that traces of its original packing grease were still on the receiver. Once made safe, "Bucky" presented the pristine semi-automatic to Mike as a memento of his and more importantly C Company's first confirmed kill.

While the platoon was regrouping, "RA" Williams raised his rifle and fired as another figure appeared on the slope above. But the lone insurgent, who was about 200yds away, disappeared into long grass. Dropping his radio handset, Cox popped off a few shots before giving chase, but the man was nowhere to be found.

The boys saddled up and as they were about to continue with their patrol, a message arrived from Brigade. Third Platoon had just been ordered further north, where they were to be picked up by helicopter for another mission. At 1725hrs, Third Platoon emplaned and flew 12 miles northeast across the mountains to provide security for C Battery, 16th Field Artillery, whose 105s were located near a road intersection on Highway 20. Although they looked like tramps, nobody had any idea that the next few days would turn out to be among the best they would ever have in Vietnam.

Dust was still swirling high into the air as "Bucky" wandered into the battery perimeter. A captain dressed in clean combats and highly polished boots approached and asked "RA," "Where's your platoon leader?" Looking like shit personified, "Bucky," who was standing next to his RTO, stepped forward and with a big, toothy grin introduced himself. Comically, the battery commander's jaw dropped as he began to process the filthy, blood-spattered, unwashed forms now surrounding him.

The next four days were spent frolicking in the crystal-clear Da Nhim River, while local women carried on obliviously with their laundry. Nearby, the Montagnard settlement at Dai Ninh was known for its traditional ethnic weavers. But the village also boasted a brothel full of Eurasian prostitutes. Several of the guys fell in love with these women, who had been callously abandoned by their French colonial fathers back in the mid-1950s. These infatuations were short-lived, especially after several troopers contracted STDs. Despite the clap, Dai Ninh was a little corner of paradise, with plenty of Coca-Cola and lukewarm beer known as "Tiger Piss." Quite innocently, "Bucky" talked to the battery commander about a potential night out in Da Lat and was shocked when told that it was only open to officers from the ARVN and NVA! The dream mission came to an end on December 28, when Third Platoon returned to the hunt for 186th Main Force VC.

Just before Christmas, Jim Schlax and his guys were silently waiting in ambush when he heard a vehicle approaching. The three GIs in an M274 Mule were surprised when Jim stepped out looking like a demented scarecrow and demanding to know what they were doing. Jim was even more surprised by their answer: "Sir, we've been assigned to find and bring back a Christmas tree!"

"Are you fucking kidding me?"

"No, the biggest we can find." Jim packed up his ambush there and then and radioed for new instructions. An hour or so later, he was flown to another location, where they were supposed to rendezvous with Alpha.

At 1800hrs on December 24, all battalions from First Brigade ceased offensive operations in observance of the Christmas Ceasefire Agreement. More than two tons of food was distributed locally during this festive period by teams from Civil Affairs. One highlight at Bao Loc was a visit from the Agricultural College, whose students symbolically presented traditional cards in Vietnamese and English during a special Christmas Eve pageant. On Christmas Day, 52 children from a nearby orphanage visited HHC, who hosted them for dinner and gifts.

Because of unusually cold weather up at the Tactical Command Post, "Dee" Dallas took it upon himself to deliver two arctic sleeping bags to "Mal Hombre" and "Fat Cat." A forward air controller at Bao agreed to fly over at low level so "Dee" could personally drop in the goods. Albeit against "Mal Hombre's" field ban on hard liquor, "Dee" cheekily hid a bottle of Jack Daniel's inside one of the bags as a gift for Bob Mairs.

Joe Alexander and his platoon were constantly on duty as LZ or PZ security for most of Alpha's more recent air movements. On Christmas morning, the entire company gathered together and anxiously awaited Bill Norris with his first underslung load of supplies. Geraci was in another chopper with Colonel John Collins from First Brigade. Now aged 47, Collins – known as "Rip" – had served in World War II and Korea, and had been working since July '67 as Matheson's deputy. Two chaplains were also on board along with representatives from the American Red Cross.

Each trooper was given a small seasonal cold pack of desserts, two beers, and two cokes. However, the eagerly anticipated hot turkey dinner looked and tasted like garbage. On the plus side, dressed as Santa, Sergeant First Class Luther Stultz from the battalion's personnel department brought in a ton of Christmas mail. Along with a lady from the USO acting as Mrs. Clause, Stultz made it his mission to deliver packages and donuts to every Rifle company no matter how remote.

Anonymous gift packages were sent in by the "Appreciative American" campaign. Even though the anti-war movement was gaining momentum, many back home still sent cards, letters, and packages addressed to "no name" soldiers. Luckier than most, "Skip" Rattee was over the moon with his presents from home. Although "Skip's" parents Carroll and Rita did not have a lot of money, they still managed to send their son a generous goody bag. Rattee was tucking into his homemade cake when Joe Alexander stopped by for a visit. Even with his mouth full, Carl still managed to greet Alexander in his usual friendly, unintelligible New England way. When offered a slice of cake, Joe politely refused and said, "Wow, your family really keep you squared away, don't they?" As they chatted, little extras were being seamlessly shared among the platoon. Joe was glad to see that Carl was giving away some of his soup and Kool-Aid to those who had not received anything from home. Carl explained to Joe what was what and who had sent it. Until that moment, the lieutenant had not really known much about Carl's family or if he even had a girlfriend. "Skip" was very close with his parents but even tighter-knit with his three sisters Carol, Marilyn, and Pamela, who was only 14. However, "Skip's" girlfriend had dumped him shortly before the battalion left for Vietnam. Quickly trying to backpedal, thinking he was on a much safer subject, Joe inquired about the sergeant's current taste in music. "Skip" liked most things except for The Box Tops, whose song "The Letter" had become a niggling reminder of the "Dear John" he'd received before shipping out. With that, Joe figured it was time to go, but as he turned to leave, "Skip" proffered, "Are you sure about that cake, sir? It's deliciously moist and made with real rum and brandy." Joe figured what the heck and readily gobbled down a slice, quickly followed by another. Several miles from Alpha, across the plateau and hills, Mike Stuart was receiving his pile of gifts from Supply Sergeant Bill Cook. One box provided enough Christmas razzle-dazzle for Mike to line his sandbagged parapet with two fake plastic trees strung with baubles and tinsel.

On December 26, Joe Alexander's men were designated security and reluctantly returned to humping. During one patrol, the platoon stumbled across an adult tiger devouring a deer. Up until that point, nobody really believed the scuttlebutt about wild tigers … but this was not a Sunday visit to the zoo and it put the fear of Christ into everybody. The beautiful big cat leapt up and took off as the point man turned and ran like a lunatic possessed. Flank security opened fire as the panic-stricken beast ran a gauntlet of 5.56 before disappearing into dense undergrowth.

After the ceasefire, patrols from C Company discovered blood-soaked bandages and penicillin wrappers close to where the two insurgents had been killed on Christmas Eve. Coatie Brandon from

First Platoon came upon a hole close to a massive abandoned base camp. Tunnel rat Bill Young was called forward as Staff Sergeant Udo Taring dropped in a grenade. Armed with a pistol and flashlight, Bill lowered himself into the darkness, crawled about 20ft, and then found two unexploded American 250lb bombs! For situations such as this, the Rifle companies patrolled with personnel from A/326 Airborne Engineers. Primary tasks for these sappers were cutting clearings, demolishing bunkers, along with disposing booby traps and hidden ordnance caches.

That night, Lieutenant Jim Moore and his men from Fourth Platoon killed four insurgents, recovering rucksacks and several new AK-47s. All information now pointed toward another massive base a few miles further south, closer to the border with Binh Thuan. Consequently, Bravo, along with the Red Legs and Heavy Mortar Platoon, flew some 35km east in support. The new Tactical Headquarters and firebase was established on Mount Cocora that at 900m would provide more effective cover for captains Nahas and Pearson as they continued on with their search. Alpha was also migrating eastward toward C Co screening a long-distance provincial track below the village of Phu Hiep. Gaffney was happily now in receipt of a new indigenous interpreter and three "Yard" warriors, who were all keen to boost his firepower!

Ron Ford had been the recipient of an anonymous gift package, which contained a small Santa. Hanging from his rucksack, the red-suited decoration had become a potential target. As he was just about to throw it away, a five-year-old Montagnard child came over and expressed interest. The look on the boy's face was priceless as Ron knelt under his heavy burden, gently handed over his gift, and mouthed, "Happy Christmas, kid."

Chapter 7

"Badge of Courage"

The Battle of the Knoll – January 2, 1968

Keeping a discreet distance, Pearson's CSF continued to shadow the far-eastern flank of C Co as it followed a number of blood trails. After another small skirmish, Ted Schnoor was on point when something caught his eye. At the time, Ted was having trouble with his M16 and decided to swap rifles with Private David Wing before he went forward. The sergeant returned with nothing to report and handed David back his weapon. As Wing went to readjust his waist strap, he accidentally caught the trigger. David was distraught as Ted collapsed screaming in front of him. However, Wing was not entirely to blame for the negligent discharge that almost cost the life of his sergeant.

Strangely, by the end of December, 3/506 was redesignated from "airborne" to "airmobile," and a number of non-parachute-trained draftees were sent in to replace those who had been wounded or were coming to the end of their current periods of active duty.

After the New Year's ceasefire, C Company resumed its activities along the border with Binh Thuan as Ron Newton and Jim Kessinger were ordered to patrol further south. Newton's regular radio operator, Howard "Turtle" Wilson, had been asked to remain at the CP coordinating mission traffic, while buddy Gil Bennett stood in. Before leaving, Ron instructed squad leaders Furman

Johnson, Max Cadena, and Louie Wombough to each leave one man behind to bolster perimeter defense. Known as "Sergeant Rock," Johnson was Ron's recently arrived "shake 'n' bake" from North Carolina. Second Platoon had not yet had enough time to get to know Furman, a quietly reserved individual with a two-year-old-son who clearly was his world.

Traveling in light scale to allow for extra ammunition, the men cached their rucks, ponchos, and liners with Captain Nahas. Accompanying Newton were two airborne engineers – Corporal Alan Blair and Private Hans Kletinger from A/326. C Company now also had Lieutenant Steve Williams from the 9th Combat Tracker Team on hand, albeit this time without his dog – which had recently been returned to Phan Rang due to a mix-up with its food.

Primarily for inter-platoon communications, Newton, Platoon Sergeant "Hardcore" Schiavone, and their squad leaders were using the unpopular helmet-mounted FM short-wave radios. After checking equipment, weapons, and noise discipline, they moved out around 0800hrs. The idea was to patrol a couple of miles southeast along the sandy tracks up valley toward the Da Kra River. With Highway 20 still only a few miles north, the elevated hill country was made up of largely uninhabited dense pine and thick bamboo forest.

Second Platoon had not been out long when Ron's point man Corporal Bob Barrett caught a fleeting glimpse of their first bad guy. Newton's boys swept the area before arriving at an intersection between three distinct trails. The enemy understood American tactics well enough now not to hang around and fight unless cornered. Each squad selected a path and patrolled forward, whereupon Max Cadena came across fresh footprints. Johnson and Wombough were called back, as Ron, "Hardcore," and Steve Williams made their way over to the entrance of an enormous bamboo thicket.

A few moments later, Nick Nahas granted permission for Ron to bring the rest of his men up. While moving through the bamboo, Newton took another call from Nick advising that Jim Kessinger and First Platoon were now on their way to assist. The trail seemed to go on forever and one hour later, as they emerged into the sunshine, the point came under fire. Although the encounter was brief, it appeared to be from one or two insurgents using a vintage American Browning Automatic Rifle. Slack man Cadena managed to get off a few shots before the enemy fled into lower ground. Within seconds, Max and his squad were descending a shallow valley while Newton and Wombough buttoned down the rear and flank. But just like before, the individuals disappeared like apparitions into thin air.

Now unsure of his exact position, Ron stopped for a map check. Although able to confirm their last known location, Newton was struggling to orientate himself amidst the rolling green canopy. Ten frustrating minutes elapsed before Ron gave in and called Captain Nahas for smoke. This time, Nick knew Ron was not playing around. Obligingly, the Red Legs based on Mount Cocora placed marking rounds onto two prominent nearby hills. With that, Ron was able to triangulate and by resection determine his approximate position. After registering the grid with Nick, Newton and "Hardcore" joined forces with Kessinger and pressed on.

Within a few minutes, First Platoon spotted and opened fire on two more insurgents. Asking Jim to wait on high ground over to his west and leaving Max Cadena to block, Ron made his way up onto a hill opposite. Kessinger identified one particular thicket as the place where he had seen the two men that also happened to be the same area Max had screened earlier. For the next minute, both platoons poured fire into the target area. Afterward, six of Ron's guys went down to assess but found nothing and as a result Captain Nahas decided to order everyone back to base.

"Hardcore" and Newton were concerned as to where the VC had gone. It seemed highly likely that they were dealing with people who knew the landscape. Reluctantly, Nahas gave permission for Second Platoon to continue. Ron soon came across dozens of fresh human tracks, including one particular section of pampas that had been trampled by at least five elephants. This was not only a game changer but also the first time Newton had actually seen any real evidence of the mammals being used. Up until that moment, he had only ever encountered random piles of dung in the deepest draws and valleys. The guys were of course aware of the tribe who had lived here alongside the Asian elephant for 1,000 years, but these tracks did not seem to support whether these were VC or M'nong.

Tracker Steve Williams knew all too well that the enemy used these magnificent rare beasts as natural prime movers to aid with major construction programs – which was deeply worrying. As a precautionary measure, Ron asked Nick if he could arrange a couple of gunships to fly in and provide top cover. Newton was then instructed to head for the nearest high point and to do nothing more than set up an observation post. Straddling the border between Lam Dong and Binh Thuan, at an elevation of 1,000m, the feature directly in front seemed best served to provide him with a commanding view across the valley.

BONDED BY BLOOD

Before moving out, Jim Odoms, Mike Munson, and Mike Hill from First Squad were covering right flank security when an insurgent appeared out of nowhere and threw at least one concussion grenade. The squad had unwittingly triggered the rear end of a linear ambush intended for the main group. Team leader Mike Stuart was nearby walking slack and closest to the detonation. Flat on the ground, Munson and Hill were shielded from injury by their helmets. There was a brief exchange of fire and the enemy withdrew down into the jungle and away toward the OP target that Lieutenant Newton was now calling the "Knoll."

The blast had knocked Sergeant Stuart to the ground, rendering him momentarily unconscious. A fragment from the grenade, specifically designed for close-quarter fighting, had smashed Mike's helmet down onto his forehead, tearing open an old scar. Blood streaming from his face, Mike rejoined Wombough's squad as the platoon gave chase, until Munson reported seeing more movement in the distance. While he had the chance, Stuart broke out a first aid kit and quickly bandaged his head.

Through binoculars, Newton identified at least eight VC and called in 24 rounds of "Fuck You." Ron was not sure if the insurgents were trying to draw him away from the hill or into something more serious. As the barrage was getting under way, medic Floyd Skaggs set about examining Mike's forehead. Just as Skaggs closed the gaping wound with butterfly strips, an order came down the line to move.

With all three squads assembled, Newton quickly traversed west back to the three-track intersection. With their location now marked and recorded, Newton struck out for the Knoll. Heavily forested, the bi-province feature was part of a saddle that connected into a slightly smaller mount over to the east. Approaching the lower slopes, they reached a fork in the trail where both tracks showed heavy usage. Captain Nahas called to advise that gunships were now hovering near the CP and waiting if necessary to be tasked. Ron decided to place Wombough's squad at the slope's base with Mike Stuart and radio operator Phil Witherspoon.

"Hardcore" and Sergeant Johnson agreed to take First Squad, Steve Williams, the two engineers, plus Doc Skaggs and skirt around to the far side. Radioman Graham Morris should have gone with them but his "25" was no longer working properly due to a broken antenna. Reluctantly, Newton sent Morris to Wombough and prayed that "Hardcore" and Johnson's helmet radios would suffice.

Newton began to ascend the western trail with Bob Barrett and Max Cadena on point. Behind Newton and Bennett were M60 gunner Ed Baker and his assistant Jerry Hill. Leading the rear section, Everette Parham was carrying the thumper with "Ski" Vinscotski, Bob Williams, Bill Bangert, and Sergeant Ron Barnes in trail. Keeping a casual five-meter spacing, 20 minutes later, Newton's team had almost reached the summit when they suddenly came under small-arms fire. Bob and Max engaged and saw two figures fall from nearby trees.

Moments later, a hand-grenade landed behind Cadena. Ron's first thought was, *Shit, that thing looks old* – then BOOM! Shrapnel ripped upward into Max's right leg and backside. Untouched by the blast, Newton found himself laughing absurdly as the ridgeline lit up. CONTACT RIGHT ... Lieutenant Newton had just triggered the 186th Main Force Battalion's first line of defense. The intensity and determined level of response was something Ron had not seen before and the next few minutes felt weirdly surreal.

Sergeant Barnes was able to spot for his guys, who took out another two or three enemy before Louie Wombough was wounded attempting to reach him. As Louie was hit in the hip and thigh, Mike Stuart looked up and saw a couple of Caucasian men nonchalantly directing the Vietnamese response. Mike never found out who these people were but believed they could have been either Russian advisors or American deserters, or perhaps even French defectors from the mid-1950s.

"Bucky" Cox and Third Platoon were digging CP defenses when Ron's voice crackled over the radio. "Bucky" could see the Knoll from Nahas's perimeter and hear escalating waves of enemy mortar and rocket fire. Anxious to get into the fight, leaving their heavy rucksacks behind, Third and Fourth platoons rushed into action.

Back on the Knoll's lower slopes, Third Squad were now heavily pinned down. As Wombough reported his wounds, Newton was busy dodging a wave of grenades before losing communications with Johnson and "Hardcore." Bob Vinscotski and Jerry Hill managed to identify and silence the offending bunker but not before a grenade exploded directly on top of Williams. Under covering fire from Third Squad, Newton managed to extricate himself and move downhill into dead ground. As the lieutenant gave orders to pull back and reorganize, Vinscotski took a bullet in the back and another above his left hip. Jerry Hill grabbed "Ski" and dragged him down into cover of the long pampas grass.

Finally, Newton made contact with First Squad, who were also taking casualties. For a split second, the lieutenant thought about artillery support for "Hardcore" but the risk seemed way too high. Ron called the gunship commander, codenamed Lancer 2, and placed him on immediate standby. Then again, Ron lost communications with the other side of the hill. As Newton pulled

Then-Private First Class John Geraci in 1943. (John Geraci Jr.)

Lieutenant Colonel John Geraci in early '69. (US Army)

The Battalion Command Staff shortly before deployment. (Freeman "Dee" Dallas)

L–R: Major Bob Mairs, S-3, Captain Tom Gaffney, CO A Co, and LTC John Geraci during Operation *Klamath Falls*, December 1967. (US Army)

Captain Bill Landgraf (right) with First Platoon Sergeant Joe Jerviss at the Dragon's Graveyard. (Joe Jerviss)

Battalion Surgeon Andy Lovy at Phan Rang. (Andy Lovy)

Left C Company commander Nick Nahas and his new bride Rosalie in 1964. (Nick Nahas)

Above left Lieutenant Ron Newton. (Ron Newton)

Above Lieutenant Wylie "Bucky" Cox, Jim Kessinger, and Ron Newton. (Ron Newton)

Left Platoon Sergeant Henry "Hardcore" Schiavone at the Dragon's Graveyard with Private John Beatty holding mirror. (Ron Newton)

Lieutenant "Bucky" Cox (right) with
Platoon Sergeant Henry "RJ" Johnson and
"Kit Carson Scout." ("Bucky" Cox
Archive – Author's Collection)

Lieutenant Joe Alexander at Fort
Campbell. (Joe Alexander)

John Gfeller pictured a few years before he
joined 3/506. (Patricia Gfeller Owen)

L–R: Battalion Sergeant Major "Snake"
McCorkle, Medic Timothy Spatt,
Lieutenant Herb Hohl III, and Corporal
James Ellsworth during Operation *Rose*.
(Joe Jerviss)

Members of Third Platoon, A Co seen here at the Enlisted Men's Club in Phan Rang, January 1968. ("Jay" Eckhart)

Sergeants Ron Ford and Biven Patterson. (Ron Ford)

Sergeant Mike Stuart during Operation *Klamath Falls*. (Mike Stuart)

Left Mike Trant at Firebase Bartlett north of Phan Thiet. (Ron Ford)

Sergeant Mike Krawczyk being awarded a Purple Heart by new Battalion Commander Walter Price. (Mike Krawcyk)

Lieutenant David "Mike" Pearson, leader of the Currahee Shock Force. (US Army)

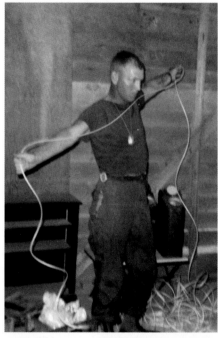

SFC Philip Chassion at LZ Betty, giving a lesson on measuring detonation chord. (Joe Jerviss)

Gear packed and ready, members of Second Platoon C Co wait patiently for airfield transport at Fort Campbell. (Mike Stuart)

Troops from A Co boarding their flight to Alameda Naval Air Station. (Jim Schlax)

Men from C Company waiting to board troopship *General William Weigel* at Oakland Naval Base. (Mike Stuart)

Jerry Gomes (bottom left) with colleagues from the S&T Platoon on their racks.
(Jerry Gomes)

Jerry Gomes seen here with some of
S&T's heavily secured weapons.
(Jerry Gomes)

The *Weigel* passing underneath the
Golden Gate Bridge en route to Vietnam.
(Mike Stuart)

Troops on deck saying goodbye to America. (Jim Schlax)

Lieutenant Jim Schlax on board the *Weigel* en route to Vietnam. (Jim Schlax)

Senior staff, possibly from the 503rd, preparing to receive another rush of drunken troopers dockside at Subic Bay. (Jerry Gomes)

C Co sergeants partying at Subic Bay. (Mike Stuart)

Top Members of Alpha returning to the *Weigel* after a few too many downtown beers. (Jim Schlax)

Above View from USNS *Weigel* after docking at Cam Ranh Bay on October 26, 1967. (Jerry Gomes)

Left The American Red Cross were on site serving donuts to the troops as they disembarked at Cam Ranh Bay. (US Army)

Top Lieutenant Colonel Geraci leads Brigadier General Salve Matheson and George Blanchard in inspection on October 26, 1967. (US Army)

Above Convoy carrying 3/506 leaving Cam Ranh Bay on October 26 for Phan Rang. (Jerry Gomes)

Left Members of C Co on ranges at Phan Rang during Proficiency Training, late October '67. (Richard Pittman Archive © Mike Krawcyk)

General William Westmoreland delivered a welcome speech to 3/506 on November 8, 1967 at Phan Rang. ("Bucky" Cox Archive – Author's Collection)

L–R: Hal Dobie, George Schultz, Andy Daniel (kneeling), Guy Brooks and Chris Adams. (Chris Adams)

The local ARVN secured a landing zone due south of Phan Rang on salt flats near Son Hai for the Chinook carrying Dr Lovy's MEDCAP team and supplies. (Andy Lovy)

The rugged Padaran Hills were home to 3/506 during Operation *Rose*. ("Bucky" Cox Archive – Author's Collection)

C-Ration re-supply during Operation *Rose* and the Dragon's Graveyard. ("Bucky" Cox Archive – Author's Collection)

On November 19, 1968, the VC-friendly coastal village of Son Hai was cleared by C Company and its inhabitants evacuated back to Phan Rang for interrogation. (Mike Stuart)

Chaplain Otis Smith holding Sunday service while at Bao Loc in December 1967.
(US Army)

Trooper from C Co standing watch over a potential exit point from the VC tunnel system at Son Hai. ("Bucky" Cox Archive – Author's Collection)

C Co clearing Son Hai on November 19, 1967. ("Bucky" Cox Archive – Author's Collection)

Right One of several combat assaults carried out by the 117th Army Helicopter Company "Slicks" into the Dragon's Graveyard during Operation *Rose* in November '67. (US Army)

C Co Weapons Platoon Leader Lieutenant Jim Moore dries out his clothing during Operation *Rose*. (Richard Pittman Archive © Mike Krawczyk)

81mm mortarmen Richard Pittman (left) and Willie Moss during a fire mission on Operation *Rose*. (Richard Pittman Archive © Mike Krawczyk)

Richard Pittman giving his best 1,000yd stare during Operation *Rose*. (Richard Pittman Archive © Mike Krawczyk)

Typically, six canteens of water per day were just about adequate for each trooper. Space-saving water bladders (seen here) were also introduced. (US Army)

Members of C Co at Song Mao in early December 1967. ("Bucky" Cox Archive – Author's Collection)

View from helicopter during one of C Company's numerous combat assaults in Lam Dong Province during Operation *Klamath Falls*. (Mike Stuart)

One of the first C-141s to arrive at Bien Hoa Air Force Base spearheading Operation *Eagle Thrust*, which began on December 13, 1967. (NARA)

back, Third Squad were still battling below him against increasing rocket and mortar fire.

Listening to the radio chatter, "Bucky" Cox was doing his level best to reach Newton. Meanwhile, Ron had to do something to ease pressure on the other two squads and ordered Baker and Hill to bring their M60 and follow him back up the slope with Gil Bennett and thumper man Parham.

Still desperately trying to contact "Hardcore" and Johnson, the only intelligible response Newton could make out was Johnson's call sign! Suddenly, "Sergeant Rock's" voice weakened and went off air. There was to be no further communication. Fearing the worst, Ron decided to try to get a verbal message to "Hardcore," telling him to break contact, move back, and allow the gunships to move in. But first Ron had to deal with the problem in front of him. It took ten minutes of crawling for Newton to get anywhere near the southernmost enemy position on the ridge. Finally, Ron and Gil Bennett hunkered down behind a log and prepared to rush. Baker and Hill provided covering fire with Parham as Newton and Bennett dashed forward in small bounds. The others followed but as they closed, a BAR opened up, forcing both men onto the ground. Ron was hit in the heel and Bennett in the buttocks, but as Gil went down, the "25" broke free from its cradle and catapulted forward into the undergrowth. Realizing that Bennett was going into shock, Ron twisted around and ordered him and the others to get back into cover while he tried to find the radio. Scrambling around crab-like on all fours, Newton was struck in the left buttock by another bullet. Adrenaline masked the pain and as Newton turned, he was hit in the other cheek. This time, Ron felt the round rip through muscle and up into his lower back. Suddenly, Newton's VHF helmet radio sparked up and Mike Stuart came on air. Mike thanked Ron for the "distraction" and announced that Wombough's men had all now successfully extracted and were "safely" back with the remainder of Second Squad! Ron's mini-counter-attack had failed and it was now time for him to get the hell out of Dodge.

Ed Baker and the assault team had gone when Ron returned battered and bleeding to the log. The lieutenant caught up with them a little further downhill as they stopped to take a break from carrying Bennett. Realizing that more help was needed and despite his pain, Ron crawled and limped on through about 400m of tall pampas to Mike Stuart, who was then in the process of establishing a defendable perimeter. Stuart immediately sent Sergeant Barnes and Mike Hill to assist with carrying "Ski."

Sergeant Stuart had managed to get Graham Morris' radio working, albeit with a greatly reduced range. By now, Lieutenant Newton was in a whole world of hurt, but he knew that if the gunships were not deployed within the next few minutes, he would be overrun. Ron ordered Stuart to bring in the attack helicopters but due to his radio constraints, Mike suggested Max Cadena might be a better option. Thinking Max had been killed, Ron was overjoyed to learn that he was now also back inside the perimeter. While Ron had been attacking the bunker, despite his own injuries, Max had taken charge of Witherspoon's "25" to establish contact with Captain Nahas, who in turn had called for medivac. Ron told Max that he was heading over to him with the wounded, but neglected to mention that he was also a casualty. Things eased momentarily as the enemy began to redirect its resources against "Hardcore." Cadena had already managed to account for most of Newton's injured, all except for Bob Williams with Vinscotski, Bennett, and Bangert, who were all awaiting urgent evacuation.

When he reached Cadena, Ron immediately contacted Nick with a situation report. The "25" was full of traffic as Nahas and Geraci, who had just arrived at the CP, anxiously inquired about First Squad's status. Geraci desperately wanted to know how far "Hardcore" had traveled but the only positive information that Ron could provide was an approximation from Furman Johnson's penultimate transmission.

Newton was reminded by Nahas and Geraci to utilize his air and artillery assets while he still had daylight. With that, Ron brought in the artillery direct onto the ridgeline, immediately followed by Lancer 2. Ron threw out smoke to indicate his tenuous position but when the helicopters arrived, it had all but dissipated. As Newton popped his last canister, he yelled for more but the plea was swallowed by rotor noise. After a dummy pass, the first gunship came back around and blasted the slope with rockets ... firing in salvoes of twos and fours. Before any adjustments could be dialed in, the first run clipped the edge of Newton's perimeter with 7.62mm tracer – adding two more troopers to his list of wounded.

CHECKPOINT CHARLIE

Around 1745hrs, during their last attack, both choppers were hit by heavy-caliber enemy fire. The lead helicopter began trailing smoke after its co-pilot was wounded in the leg. Now in serious trouble, the only clear area for the pilot to land was at the Charlie CP. The bird came down "hot," spewing fuel, and as the pilot frantically shut down his engines, both gunners leapt out to unstrap their wounded colleague. When the crew reported into Captain Nahas, he noticed that the microphone mounted on one gunner's helmet had been completely shot away!

After the artillery and air attacks, enemy fire on Newton's side of the hill went quiet. The second lull gave Mike Stuart and Max Cadena the opportunity to fully assess and give additional first aid to their wounded. Outwardly, apart from his face, hands, and arms being covered in blood, Mike appeared fine. While Ron was on the radio to Nahas and Geraci, Stuart gingerly began to remove his boss's boot. Growing impatient with Mike's overly cautious fiddling, Cadena shouted at him to, "Forget the fucking laces and just cut the damn thing off!" Seemingly oblivious to the squabble, Ron turned onto his stomach while Mike prepared a compression bandage for his bullet-riddled bare backside!

At exactly 1846hrs, the dust-off flew in and evacuated Ron's three most critical cases, along with Sergeant Wombough. As Third and Fourth platoons were approaching, they saw the helicopter under a hail of green enemy tracer fire. One of Lieutenant Cox's gunners, Corporal Max Ralya, shouldered his M60 and asked for permission to open up on the perpetrators. Believing that the inevitable enemy response would totally crucify him, Cox said no and immediately regretted his decision. As the medivac took off, it was hit multiple times from the ridge. The ship shuddered but thankfully its pilot managed to retain control and banked sharply away down the valley.

Once Cox and Moore had found a defensible area near the base of the hill, they began thinking about how best to deploy. Captain Nahas ordered Third Platoon to find Ron, so "Bucky" started toward where he had seen the medivac land. It was now time for the next pair of gunships to begin their attack runs. Every smoke canister Second Platoon possessed had now been collected and brought to Newton. Ron gave the order "danger close" as he, Max, and Mike Stuart started pulling pins. The tracer rounds seemed to float in mid-air while rockets ricocheted along the ground in front of them. Armed with 48 rockets and four mini-guns, each helicopter packed an incredible punch. The high-pitched scream of their cannons was terrifying as the choppers whipped in low overhead. By now, it was just getting dark when Jim Moore came on the net, "Madman, Madman, this is Ridge Runner, over."

Newton responded, "Hey, babe, sorry I can't be there to greet you, can you see the enemy from your location?"

"Negative on that, Madman, how are you and your heroes doing and where do you want me, pal?" After a few wisecracks, Ron directed Fourth Platoon toward his smoke, prompting Moore to quip, "What's all that red stuff you people are swimming in … Kool-Aid?" When Jim reached the trail junction below the Knoll, Ron told him to continue south toward "Hardcore." However, Newton thought it best for "Bucky" to wait until nightfall before attempting to move across to him. But it was too late. The enemy mortar and machine-gun fire had already forced Third Platoon up onto higher ground and away to the east. This was not necessarily part of the plan but at least from here "Bucky" could act as temporary back-up for Moore.

Ron had a hard job convincing his guys (who all wanted to go look for Bob Williams) that they would be in a far better position by relocating across to "Bucky." Finally, everyone agreed and with his arm firmly wrapped around Private John Beaty, using a battered M16 for support, Newton slowly shuffled off into the night with his men.

The move took much longer than expected and "Bucky" sent some of his troopers down to help carry Ron and the "stretcher cases" back up to his perimeter. Max Cadena was angry and frustrated. This was his second tour and also the second time he had been seriously injured. Back at the company CP, burdened with over 80 rucksacks and a downed helicopter, Nick Nahas made the difficult decision to stay put with First Platoon and relocate at first light.

OBEDIENCE AND DUTY

By 2115hrs, Jim Moore returned with "Hardcore" and what remained of First Squad. With one leg hanging precariously by a thin strip of muscle, Steve Williams was in a terrible state. Covered in blood, a large piece of "Hardcore's" scalp had been peeled back. The guys tried their best to calm him down but Schiavone was in no mood for small talk and muttered at Cox, "Tell the CO that he got his fucking contact!" Head swathed in bandages, he began to explain what had happened …

The moment they came under attack, slack man, Furman Johnson, was hit. "Hardcore" threw out smoke but his grenade failed to ignite. As Furman desperately tried to make contact with Lieutenant Newton, another bullet pierced his helmet and killed him. Overwhelmed by fire, "Hardcore" led his men downhill into a gully. When his own radio ceased working, "Hardcore" ordered Johnny Jackson to go back and recover "Rocks." On reaching Furman, Johnny was hit in the right forearm and shoulder. Turning to Sergeant Ron Marquez, "Hardcore" gave him the good news. Marquez had only taken a few steps before he fell dead under a hail of bullets.

The VC quickly began to move downhill toward a clump of trees on First Squad's left flank. Mike Munson and his crew immediately brought their M60 into action but the enemy responded with machine guns, grenades, and rockets. Luckily, Munson was able to neutralize the Vietnamese machine gun but could not stem the flow of high-explosive projectiles.

Among those now in the gully with "Hardcore" were Ron Kiser, Sergeant John Headlee, Grenadier Len Taylor, the two engineers, and Lieutenant Steve Williams. Seriously wounded by shrapnel, Taylor passed his '79 across to Williams. The tracker had a great view and was able to effectively harass the enemy as they advanced. Moments later, he was hit by a blast from another rocket. As Williams screamed for help, Private Braxton Baston crawled across and applied a tourniquet to his leg. Assisted by Kiser and Allen, Braxton began dragging the wounded toward a thicket, where medic Floyd Skaggs had just established his aid station. While moving, they came under a heavy barrage of mortars that killed Hans Kletinger and badly wounded his colleague Alan Blair. No longer able to walk, Blair was told to wait while the guys went back for more casualties. Meanwhile, in the gully another blast had broken Sergeant Headlee's leg and torn flesh from "Hardcore's" scalp and left ear. Even while Schiavone's wounds were being treated by Skaggs, he directed his other M60 team to cover the hill and trail to their right. When Skaggs was told that "Sergeant Rock" and Johnny Jackson had been hit, he ran forward to help and never came back.

After Jim Moore deposited his medic with the wounded, he went to find Schiavone. As it was getting dark, Jim noticed movement in a nearby half-circle of trees and issued a password. His challenge was met by a blistering response and when the shooting stopped, Moore heard "Hardcore" calling to him from below. As Fourth Platoon apprehensively moved toward the platoon sergeant's position, they came under rocket attack. Moore put up a security perimeter to counter and continued on into the gully. Although several men were still missing, Jim had no choice but to extract back to "Bucky" with what he had.

As Newton and Cox listened intently to "Hardcore's" debrief, they received word that A Co was to be flown in the next morning. Moore got on the radio to Nahas and ordered up a cocktail of artillery, along with a Douglas AC-47 gunship known as a "Spooky" or "Puff the Magic Dragon." Before "Armageddon" was due to commence, "Bucky" made one last desperate call to Nick for another medivac. Much to his surprise, the captain confirmed that a chopper was inbound. An earlier twist of fate had brought the bird into Nick's CP to collect three badly wounded troopers, privates Ortis, Jackson, and Perry, who had all been accidentally injured in a claymore explosion.

After a brief radio conversation, it quickly became clear to Cox that the pilot was not happy about the extra pick-up. By now, it was pitch black and the medivac jockey was refusing to land. Taking out his flashlight, Cox walked out onto the LZ with "RA" Williams to force the pilot's hand. "Bucky's" bold move paid off and less than a minute later, the wounded were en route to Long Binh near Saigon. Mainly due to lack of space, Ron, Max, and Bob Barrett remained behind after electing for a flight the following morning.

Later that night, during one pass, red rain from Spooky ripped through nearby trees. Narrowly averting disaster, Ron screamed into the radio handset for its crew to adjust fire. Temperatures plummeted to just above freezing as artillery began to pound the Knoll. With nothing to keep them warm, Ron shivered as he cuddled up with Max and Bob for an uncomfortable night under the stars.

The next morning, when their medivac arrived from Xuan Loc, Ron said his goodbyes and handed over control to ranking NCO Mike Stuart. On board, Newton felt like he was resting on a bolt, but it was actually a bullet lodged one inch below the base of his spine.

Chapter 8

"The Aftermath"

January 3–8, 1968

Leaving one squad behind, Captain Nahas removed all useable ammunition from the downed gunship and headed south. Immediately upon arrival, Nick ordered "Bucky" to take out a couple of patrols and look for those still missing. The captain had a lot of reorganizing to think about, including getting a helicopter airlifted out by Hook and rucksacks brought up to his new location.

Built to resemble an independent fortress, the assortment of discarded clothing and blood trails leading away from the Knoll suggested more. By early afternoon, Bob Williams' shattered corpse was found where he had died the previous day. The bodies of Furman Johnson, Ron Marquez, and Floyd Skaggs were discovered lying close together. Like Johnson, Skaggs had suffered a fatal bullet wound to the head. "Bucky" had also accounted for Hans Kletinger but the whereabouts of Alan Blair was still unknown.

Heading toward the collection point, Jim Moore stumbled across Johnny Jackson and Morris Allen sheltering in the long grass. The fact that they were both still alive was nothing short of a miracle. Peppered from head to toe by shrapnel, they told Jim about the possible whereabouts of Blair. "Bucky" immediately took a squad and picked up a trail of blood that led him into an isolated thicket. Covered in a shimmering mass of ants, Blair's body was found sitting upright against a clump of bamboo. Fire Team Leader Tommy Williams III, known to all as "TW3," dropped to one knee and gently began to brush away the insects before applying repellent to Alan's face and hands. Etched into memory, the spontaneous reaction deeply moved everyone who stood watching in silent witness.

Before the dead could be flown back to Phan Rang, it was Mike Stuart's task as acting platoon sergeant and now platoon leader to record and pack any personal items belonging to the deceased. Despite previous orders to travel light, Mike was surprised to find a small diary in one of Floyd Skaggs' pockets. As Mike flicked through, he learned that the young medic constantly described a feeling of inadequacy. It was clear by his prose that the doc, like many other volunteer medics, was a hippie at heart. Floyd need not have doubted himself because a few weeks later the self-confessed awkward kid from Ohio was awarded a posthumous Silver Star.

After the bodies were lifted out, Nick Nahas gathered everyone together. In total, six men had been killed and 15 wounded. Nick was a tremendous leader who really knew his boys and now it was time for him to provide solid reassurance. Nick was the coach and Charlie his team, and everyone had to collect their wits, overcome fears, and memorialize these terrible losses for later. However, the toll would soon rise to seven when "Ski" Vinscotski died in hospital from catastrophic internal bleeding.

Tom Gaffney flew in with his men as planned and rendezvoused on the hill with Nahas. Set to act as a blocking force, Alpha had listened remotely to the battle unfold over the radio. Joe Alexander tried to ask "Bucky" about Ron Newton but the best Cox could manage was a smile and a few shattered words of encouragement.

Two days later, Newton was moved to the 36th Evacuation Hospital at Vung Tau. For a time, it looked like he was going to be left with a permanent limp, but like Max Cadena, he went on to make a full recovery. However, "Hardcore" Schiavone's head injuries were deemed so serious that he had to be repatriated home to the United States.

BURY 'EM DEEP — JANUARY 4, 1968

At dawn, Gaffney and Nahas swept upward toward the Knoll. Scattered across the feature were dozens of individual fighting positions that all had to be cleared. "Bucky" was worried by the casual way some people were using their M79s. Moments later, one of John Harrison's men, Sergeant Angel Tirado, was floored by a thumper frag that penetrated deep into his left foot.

On the Knoll itself, there were around 23 bunkers, interlocked into a zigzag pattern, each topped by a 2ft-thick reinforced roof. Most had been torn apart by firepower previously administered by Newton. Those partially destroyed revealed weapons and equipment secreted into walls and ceilings. Although over 30 Vietnamese troops had lost their lives on the ridge, only a handful of bodies had been left behind. However, Gaffney was confident that the numerous blood trails would ultimately lead him to whatever it was the bunkers were built to protect. Covered by a dense canopy of tall trees, running east, south, and west, three deep river valleys lay behind the defensive line.

Leaving C Co to continue with its search on the Knoll, Gaffney sent Jim Schlax and Len Liebler toward the eastern valley. John Harrison was sent to survey the gully where "Hardcore" had fought so valiantly. Sap from a shattered pine tree slowly dripped onto Doc Skaggs' discarded, battle-damaged steel helmet. Piled around bases of splintered trees were heaps of 7.62mm brass and link. First field dressings covered with congealed blood lay scattered among spent 5.56mm, empty magazines, and jumbles of expended thumper shells.

Around midday, as Schlax's platoon were following a valley trail down into Binh Thuan, they came under fire from the high ground on their right. Sergeant Phil Malott was hit in the left ankle. Because Jim did not relish the idea of battling his way uphill, he called in fast air to drop napalm. Apart from the "Bird Dogs," most aircraft were not fitted with FM radios, meaning "Mal Hombre's" platoon leaders were denied opportunity to practice calling up and safely bringing in their own strikes. Consequently, Schlax misjudged the distance and narrowly escaped frying some of his own guys.

Moving southeast through a clearing directly above the valley, Schlax soon fell in behind Liebler, who was now taking shots from a prominent feature a few hundred meters ahead. "Mal Hombre" was in the C&C chopper and told both platoons to sit tight while he arranged fire support. The first marking round landed short and scared the heck out of everyone. After the adjusted barrage, Liebler was told to pop smoke for Jim Pratz, as he brought in a pair of Phantoms to finish the job.

After the final F-4 gun-run, both platoons edged forward to secure. At 1600hrs, Schlax and Liebler were ordered to create a perimeter and begin searching the densely wooded slopes. Their patrols soon revealed multiple signs of recent use, including shelters and caves. Empty French medicine bottles and used bandages were piled high near three marked graves that revealed four NVA bodies. Twenty minutes later, deep in the woods, an arms cache of Chinese weapons – including a Chi-Com PPSH World War II-style sub-machine gun – came to light on a raised platform. Large balls of elephant dung were also found in a series of pens across the plateau. Things were starting to make a little more sense and Gaffney knew it would only be a matter of time before the valley gave up its secrets.

Around this time, Bob Mairs received a report that Jim Pratz had killed three "pink" elephants. Killing an elephant was completely against regulations unless harness scars indicating previous heavy load bearing were visible across the animal's shoulders and back. Mairs flew out to check and found that it was true, but they were only pink after rolling in red-colored mud. Sadly, the beautifully rare creatures had been used and abused by the VC and therefore Jim was well within protocol to have targeted them.

Earlier, John Harrison swept a short distance to the source of a spring, whereupon he walked into a hidden camp, complete with classroom, mess hall, and small bunker system. Over the next four hours, Second Platoon collected in a variety of rockets, grenades, and ammunition, plus food, clothing, and field gear that included an NVA uniform and ID card. His men also found a storeroom complete with wine cellar and food products.

Ironically, many of these items had been donated by American charitable organizations.

Earlier, Ron Ford and Chris Adams were resting when they spotted a thick-set white man reading what looked to be a topographical map. On the count of three, they opened up and the guy took off into the thick jungle. With their water fast running out, Staff Sergeant Pulley sent Adams and some of the others to the nearby stream. Ronnie and Andy Daniel were ordered either side for security and as Ford was heading upstream, he spotted a severed human foot in the babbling brook. While the squad were busy filling canteens, they heard Ron walking toward them singing the Wilson Pickett song "Barefootin'." Having attached the foot to the end of a long stick, Ford was now skimming his "third leg" through the water. Their new gangster boy from Philly, Harold Rodney, stood up and joined in with Ronnie. Everybody burst into laughter and enthusiastically provided vocals for the chorus. At that moment, Andy Daniel came back and after seeing Ron and Harold arm in arm blurted, "Guys, don't expect me to be drinking any of that fucking death juice!" With that, everyone to a man immediately upended their canteens and frantically emptied out the tainted contents.

Meanwhile, Joe Alexander had been sent down the northern slope to a rock-walled passageway. Joe and his men cautiously entered the secluded feature and uncovered another encampment. There was barely enough space for the platoon to deploy when the track widened and disseminated into a cluster of smaller trails. Within a short distance, one path opened out into an assembly area big enough to parade a platoon. Here there was a 4x5m gable-roofed hut complete with tables, chairs, and utensils. A fire-pit connected to a trench chimney confirmed the windowless bamboo structure had been a kitchen. The covered channel coursed outside for some distance before venting through a leaf pile. Remnants of food and empty containers were scattered across the hard-packed floor, along with several large bags of unopened rice. A loaded BAR sat upright in a small opening. Resting on its bipod, it pointed northwest uphill toward the saddle. Ironically, most of these vintage American weapons had been sold to the French after World War II as surplus.

It had always been traditional for Jim Schlax's radio operator, Guy Brooks, to brew water for chow while Jim organized their night defenses. As Len Liebler was handling tonight's security, Jim borrowed a small P-38 can opener that "Brooksie" kept on his dog tags. When Jim tried to return the chain, Guy laughed and said, "Ah, there's no immediate rush, sir, I don't plan to be needing those anytime soon – if you know what I mean?"

FOR THE GRACE OF LUCK – JANUARY 5, 1968

While Harrison's men set about securing an LZ, Lenny Liebler began screening the Central valley. C Co were out patrolling the eastern upper draw when they came across a cache of B40 rockets, explosives, a selection of grenades, and 100ft of electrical cord. Directly below C Co, Joe Alexander returned to the camp he had found previously. This gave way to another settlement closer to the stream source. Joe and John Gfeller ordered their men to drop rucks and begin a wider search. The first decent find was an outside classroom set into a bowl-shaped depression some 15m in diameter. A small hole cut into the canopy illuminated this natural amphitheater with sunlight. Carpeted with a layer of mountain grass, much of the space was taken up by neatly arranged rows of wooden benches, enough to seat upward of 40 people. At its base was a podium surrounded by training aids, including western-made flip-over sandwich boards and a few tables and chairs.

Other similar-but-smaller clearings soon emerged. One such space overlooked the lower reaches and was deemed to be a mortar firing point. Items of NVA and US uniform were collected throughout, along with equipment such as ammo pouches, belts, and helmets. Although it could not be pinpointed, a low humming noise was emanating from somewhere underground. But Joe's men did find a network of bamboo pipes that ingeniously channeled stream water around the site.

Third Platoon had not been patrolling long when they struck pay dirt in the Central Southern valley. Dug into the upper slopes was a field hospital built around another stream. Again, a complicated system of bamboo-piped water was in operation and the entire area encased by more of the same – rendering it completely obscure from above. Hidden in this "forest," the hospital made entirely from bamboo encompassed an operating theater, eight beds, 40 bunkers, six latrines, and four mess halls. The initial search turned up a couple more bodies – all victims of artillery – and a pit partially filled with amputated limbs. A huge haul of French-made penicillin, ammunition, 150lb of dried rice, and fish – along with several hundred bags of salt – all seemed unbelievable. Recovering penicillin was important because it denied protection against amebic dysentery that along with malaria accounted for ten percent of all NVA infiltration losses. Several blood-soaked stretchers, a large roll of white cloth, and a complete nominal roll belonging to C Co were also recovered. All documents found verified that the 186th Main Force VC had broken down into smaller groups as they sought to evade 3/506 and First Brigade.

Over at the Command Post, Captain Nahas asked Mike Stuart why his face and neck were still covered with caked-on blood. Mike said he had forgotten, when in reality it felt to him like a pact with those who had died. Begrudgingly, he agreed to go wash it off and disappeared toward the nearest stream. Mike had not been gone long when someone tripped over a ruck and dislodged a rusted fragmentation grenade.

Nearest to the blast was 19-year-old Private John Carlock from Second Platoon and Company Medic Larry Briggs – who were both thrown backward like rag dolls. "Bucky" ran over and amidst the carnage found "RJ" Johnson also down. Mike Krawczyk was in the process of dressing his assistant Curtis Stephens' right arm when he noticed something was wrong with Captain Nahas.

Initially, Nick thought he had escaped unharmed, but a small piece of shrapnel had entered his stomach, cauterizing the skin as it passed through. Because there was no bleeding, it took some convincing by the other medics before Nick would get on the helicopter to Bao Loc. Shortly after arriving at the aid station, he began to vomit a weird bright-blue liquid. At the time, Doc Lovy was in Phan Rang, and somewhat baffled, the medics decided to book Nick onto the next flight out.

At Nha Trang, the doctors found that a tiny sliver of metal had penetrated Nick's intestines. The blue fluid turned out to be grape-flavored Kool-Aid ingested shortly before breakfast. As a "good deed" after closing Nick's internal wounds, the surgeon also removed his appendix, stating it was surplus to requirements!

Larry Briggs was tragically pronounced dead at the scene, while John Carlock died later at Long Binh. With Lieutenant Roy Somers temporarily running C Co, Salve Matheson arrived by helicopter with First Field Force Commander, General William Rosson. Both leaders were set to join "Mal Hombre" for a somewhat downbeat tour of the hospital complex. The following day, Lenny Liebler's men dug up a row of unmarked graves. Five decomposing bodies were dressed in standard black pajama-style uniform. All had died from wounds relating to either grenade or gunshot. As the VC had no official rank structure and carried no ID, it made it almost impossible for their bodies to be identified. Conversely, a more elaborate marker was found nearby dedicated to a deceased NVA soldier from the province of Thai Binh in Northern Vietnam.

A couple of hundred meters further down from the hospital, Liebler's guys found a sizeable cache of World War II American and Russian weapons, and a US AN/PRC 10 VHF portable radio. During a sweep of the sprawling base camp in an adjacent valley, Jim Schlax and First Platoon came across a rucksack belonging to an NVA junior officer from Second Platoon, Third Company, 186th MF Battalion.

At 0930hrs the following day, as Joe Alexander was patrolling, his point man spotted two complete PRC 10 radios sitting upright in the middle of a clearing. One of the transmitters broke squelch with a 5-5 loud and clear order in Vietnamese on frequencies 38.8 and 39.2. By late afternoon, Alexander and Gfeller were still pondering about the enemy radios when called back for extraction. Further north, B Co had already pulled out from its original mission and was now waiting for the battalion along Highway 20 near the village of Dang Som – 30 miles east of Bao Loc.

Bravo had recently experienced its own tragedy when another accident left Private First Class Oscar Hardison with over 60 percent burns. The 19-year-old from North Carolina inadvertently set off a white phosphorus grenade. With no dust-off available, Hardison had to be flown to Bao Loc via a re-supply chopper and died a few days later at a specialist burns unit in Japan. Just as with C Co the only explanation to probable cause was a rusted safety pin, so clearly things would have to change.

Shortly after 1000hrs on January 8, the Hooks and slicks arrived to shuttle A and C companies plus Red Leg guns back to Dang Som. The enemy was no longer an elusive "super" soldier but an adversary who could be met with and overcome. In total, 57 base camps had been destroyed, 156 insurgents killed, and 77 weapons captured. Along with 100 tons of rice, three tons of salt and 516lb of tea were recovered. Ultimately for 3/506, *Klamath Falls* had been a successful test of sustained operations in a very hostile and unforgiving natural environment which had readily accepted its first down payments in blood.

Chapter 9

"Beer, Bang, and Boom Boom"

Phan Rang – January 9–16, 1968

Driving along Highway 20 toward Da Lat, the drivers were now all too familiar with the 100-mile convoluted route to Phan Rang. The rugged road climbed steeply past quaint houses and spectacular scenic waterfalls before reaching Phan Cam Ly Airfield and the elite National Military Academy.

Originally created as a colonial sub-alpine playground known as "Little Paris," Da Lat was the provincial capital of Tuyen Duc and comparable to Western resorts such as Aspen or Chamonix. Lavish French-style villas plus the former Emperor's Palace and golf course all seemed utterly unbelievable.

Andy Lovy had originally asked to ride with the dust-off, where he felt more effective, but his request was ignored. A couple of hours into the ten-hour trip, a vehicle up ahead lost control and turned over. The convoy came to an abrupt halt and without full radio communications, nobody knew why. The first hint that there had been an accident was when a helicopter landed in the distance. Trapped nose to tail, Doc Lovy was not going anywhere and frustratingly had to sit it out under a poncho like everyone else.

Slowly, the convoy descended, twisting around each new hairpin until the cooler mountain air gave way to the rugged coastal cliffs and raised humidity of Phan Rang. Here at the Eagle's Roost, people could at least look forward to three hot meals a day and partially laundered uniforms. With no perimeter duty or other responsibilities, the stand-down at base camp was a great opportunity to relax and scrub away the layers of orange-colored dirt.

Permission was granted at morning roll call to visit the strip, but everyone had to be back by nightfall. Concerned that his boys might not adhere to these instructions, Tom Gaffney asked "Mal Hombre" if he could arrange transport. Tom wanted his guys to let off steam and still be under a modicum of military control. Before hitting the Officers' Club, Gaffney gathered his platoon leaders to offer advice on the local black market and street gangs. Around each main base was a tinsel town built from packing cases and material pilfered from the Americans. Here, anything and everything was available for US dollars, which ultimately would be used to pay off district chiefs, who in turn used it to buy American arms to sell at hefty margins to the insurgents. Subsequently, use of the dollar was actively discouraged and there were few, if any, legal places to spend it. Although a soldier could request USD for RnR, there were basically two currency options available. Military Payment Certificates – known as MPCs – or the Vietnamese Dong. MPC was the only cash used on base and even though against regulations, it was generally accepted in the local economy.

The "strip" at Phan Rang was just a long line of dusty ramshackle drinking spots and whorehouses, with the most popular being the infamous California Bar. Here you could sit out back and buy drinks for the girls, who invariably would order a "cocktail" known as Saigon Tea. This was overpriced sugar water designed to maximize profits. All the while, girls aged between 16 and 20 would flirt and ask if anyone wanted a room for "boom-boom." Strangely, those hookers who were only a couple of years older seemed unpopular with the younger troopers. Not so fussy, the senior NCOs and officers were always charged at a higher rate. Some even borrowed fatigues from their subordinates to get the cheaper prices – which again could be even less if you paid in contraband dollars. If the madam thought one of her clients was overstepping the agreed time, then she would pound on the door demanding, "You take too long – GI pay more money!"

After returning to camp, Chris Adams, Ron Ford, and Mike Trant headed to the Air Force Snack Bar for a cold milkshake and ice cream. Over the last couple of days, Chris had become more familiar with Mike, who projected a big-town swagger with plenty of mouth. Things were not going well for Trant, especially now he was back in the supply room after a recent breach of safety with Joe Alexander.

The guys decided to pop into the base cinema and found Andy Daniel showing off an expensive new Rolex he had just purchased from the PX. The boys could not believe that their friend had gone and crudely scratched his initials into the backplate! Known as "AJ," Andy was a tall, raw-boned black soldier from Demopolis, Alabama. His father had died a couple of years earlier, leaving him to shoulder responsibility for his mother and younger siblings. Despite all of that, "AJ" was fun to be around and always ready with a cracking joke and beaming smile.

Unsurprisingly, the last two months had left a number of wounded recovering in medical facilities across several provinces. Somewhat unexpectedly, Doc Lovy was denied permission to fly up to Nha Trang and visit Nick Nahas. At the time, Nick was desperate to return and growing increasingly worried that he might get posted back to another unit. However, "Mal Hombre" did allow Andy and Curt Washington to take a jeep to Cam Ranh Bay for other duties. Before returning, Andy and Curt dropped in on the main medical supply depot to collect 50 pocket-sized nylon litters they had recently requisitioned. Andy could see several thousand of these portable carriers stacked high against a wall. When Curt approached the supply officer and pointed toward the pile, he was abruptly informed that they were being held back for units with a much-higher priority. Curt quietly explained their position but still the answer came back as "NO." The two men seethed when they learned that the litters had been stored here for well over six months. Slapping another form on the desk, Washington filled out a second order and pushed it across the counter. For sake of transparency, it was made clear that a copy would be forwarded up the chain of command. Curt then added that if the guy made any attempt to stop them removing the goods, he would simply kick the living shit out of him. With that, the officious "accountant" stepped aside as the two medics loaded up and drove off into the sunset.

Against regulations, Shock Force Platoon Sergeant Phil Chassion took Mike Pearson to the NCO Club for a few beaucoup beers with Staff Sergeant Harrison Cox from Battalion Supply. Halfway through the evening, "Paladin" convinced "Chass" and Cox to come with him to the Officers' Club. By this time, the guys were well oiled but in an affable mood. Quickly rumbled, they politely agreed to move into the back office, whereupon they claimed "squatters' rights" and played poker until sunrise.

Juicy barbeque steaks sizzled at the beach party the next morning as everyone enjoyed "Mal Hombre's" free Red Stripe. A ripple of excitement began to circulate that General Westmoreland, true to his word, was about to announce the long-anticipated combat jump. As the only outfit in First Brigade currently on jump status, naturally the task fell to 3/506. Bob Mairs told an elated but very hungover Mike Pearson that he planned for the Shock Force to act as Pathfinders and go in 30 minutes ahead of the main drop. Pearson was also relieved to learn that Paul Cline and his squad from C Co had also been selected to jump alongside him as security.

Upended into the earth by fixed bayonets, 12 M16s, known as "soldiers' crosses," stood in tribute, each topped and tailed by a steel helmet and jungle boots. The memorial service on January 12 began with the presentation of a posthumous Purple Heart for Winston Hamilton. "Speedy" left a wife and a beautiful nine-month-old baby daughter. Following a prayer of remembrance for the 12 souls, Bravo's Roger Shannon, Erskine Widemon, and medic Robert Davis were presented with bravery awards for their part in countering the ambush that took "Speedy" on December 3.

Afterward, Brigadier Matheson hosted a reception at the club. Throughout the evening, Doc Lovy was overwhelmed by the number of platoon leaders who came over to thank him for the specialist training he had invested into their company medics.

"General Matt's" new aide-de-camp, Lieutenant John McKnight Jr., proceeded to get smashed. As previously mentioned, McKnight's father was a good friend of Matheson's and had been a member of the original Third Battalion during World War II.

Former leader of the 2/327 Hawk Recon Platoon, John Jr. had hosted Pearson back in November during orientation at Chu Lai. John seemed unhappy with Mike's behavior at the club the previous evening and soon turned his vitriolic rivalry toward the Shock Force. "Paladin" listened politely to the lieutenant's rhetoric but when he crossed the CSF line, Mike lost his cool and double-punched McKnight to the floor. Emotions were running high after the ceremony but Matheson did not blame Pearson, whose men he especially adored and affectionately called his "Crazy" Shock Force.

THE JUMP THAT NEVER WAS

At 0600hrs on January 14, razor wire was pulled across the entrance of Battalion Headquarters. "Mal Hombre" gathered the men and confirmed that the jump was on and set to take place 130 miles northwest in the province of Phuoc Long. Shortly afterward, senior officers and NCOs were called to a briefing hosted in the air-conditioned conference room by Bob Mairs, Master Sergeant Billy Wright, and Intelligence Officer Bob Robinson. Flanked by a dry wipe board and lectern, Major Mairs introduced everybody to a small contingent from Brigade who had been assigned to "lob in" as liaison. Projected onto a large screen was a map covering the intended target and although it appeared to be heavily forested, the DZ itself had been logged.

Two days from now, First Brigade were launching Operation *San Angelo* from Bao Loc to act as a blocking force for Third Brigade, then scheduled to attack Song Be City from the northeast. The operation was intended to neutralize the North Vietnamese Army now entering III Corps' Tactical Zone via the nearby neutral Cambodian border.

The 9th NVA Divisional Headquarters was also believed to be located somewhere south of the Be River (known as Song Be), where the US First Infantry had a firebase. Here the rolling wetlands combined with forest and wide streams. Rubber plantations and bamboo were in abundance to provide superb natural defensive obstacles and building materials.

Most hamlets surrounding Song Be had been fortified and their VC/NVA occupiers well supplied via the trail. Over the last two years, bombs and chemicals had driven away wildlife but not much else. At least three enemy regiments were believed to be active here. Most VC had already traded their old SKS rifles for the new AK-47. Further bolstered by Chinese mortars, rocket launchers, and heavy-caliber machine guns, they were almost ready for business.

Planning and intelligence elements from 2/327, along with Brigade LRRPs, had been on the ground for nearly two weeks scouting a new Forward Base Camp. The remote region had been a source of concern since October '67, when VC offensive operations began against the numerous Special Forces camps threatening their lines of supply. Ahead of the Brigade's main helicopter assault, 3/506 was to capture the old base and airstrip at Bu Gia Mop. Situated close to the river, Bu Gia Mop had been overrun two years before and was now being used by the North Vietnamese as a main supply depot and distribution hub. Heavily committed, the NVA callously killed anybody who dared get in the way, such as the "Yard" settlement at Blu Blim.

Back at Phan Rang, Ray Mayfield was attending to paperwork in the A Co office when Gaffney arrived and half-jokingly asked "Bull" to go find him a blond-haired, blue-eyed trooper with no visible scars. Gergen laughed and immediately pointed to Ray. Sergeant Mayfield was not actually aware that Salve Matheson and brigade intelligence were in the building when told to put on a T-10 parachute, reserve, and assorted jump equipment. Walking into the operations room encumbered by gear, Mayfield stood statuesque while Matheson and his staff inspected the equipment.

Afterward, "General Matt" stepped up onto the stage to explain his latest information regarding Bu Gia Mop and the possible presence of enemy anti-aircraft artillery. If that was not bad enough, one of the LRRP teams had reported seeing a stockpile of CS gas canisters during a contact in a nearby village. Looking across at "Mal Hombre," Matheson recommended that as a precautionary measure, everyone jumping should wear a respirator!

Despite this negative intelligence, there was still a positive air of excitement as everyone took turns to gather around the sand table, aerial photographs, and briefing maps. Each platoon leader and sergeant talked to their respective crews about surrounding enemy and friendly forces, objectives, ammo, food, terrain, radio frequencies, weather, flight plans, aircraft loading, jumpmasters, and chalk numbers. January 17 was now D-Day and the jump set for 1030hrs.

Meanwhile, Bob Mairs and "Dee" Dallas boarded a C-130 and flew to Bu Gia Mop to assess despatch timings and inspect the drop zone. One hour later, as the aircraft made its first pass, Bob noticed hundreds of tree stumps covering the ground. While banking for a lower run, their *Hercules* came under fire from the surrounding forest. When a round came through a cockpit window, Bob's pilot decided they had seen enough and turned for home.

Back at base, "Dee" was walking across to the Planning area for a final briefing when two helicopters flew in. A senior staff member from II Corps stepped out and inquired where he might find Colonel Geraci. Captain Dallas escorted the Logistics Officer to the briefing room and introduced him. Thirty seconds passed before conversation escalated to a different, slightly harsher tone. Wondering just what the heck was going on, Dallas looked on as the full-bird visitor picked up a phone, mumbled something into it, then handed it to Geraci. "Mal Hombre" listened intently before ending the conversation with an affirmative, "Yes, sir."

At that point, Geraci was ushered out to the G-4 chopper while Dallas and the remaining command staff were asked to board the other. When both helicopters touched down, a major led everyone to an emergency brigade meeting full of senior Army and Air Force staff. A briefcase containing all of the operational jump orders had just been reported missing. "Dee" bit his lip as Brigadier General Matheson went on to say that it had been left on the seat of a jeep in Phan Rang! Disappointment was palpable as "Matt" explained Westmoreland had decided to cancel and was now detaching

3/506 from Division and reassigning them to the capital of Binh Thuan Province – Phan Thiet. When the G-4 asked if there was anything else that might be required ... Dallas raised his hand and sarcastically piped, "Two boxes of M16 bore brushes, please ... it looks like we are going to have plenty of time for cleaning!"

THEY OWNED THE NIGHT

General Westmoreland decided now would be the right time to employ a bespoke "airmobile" battalion task force under control of General Rosson and First Field Force. Military intelligence from the far northern provinces strongly indicated that over the last few weeks there had been a plethora of enemy movement around Hue. Troubled by anti-war sentiment, particularly in Congress, President Johnson had just launched what in retrospect seemed to be a fairly deliberate campaign to put the war in a more positive light. In his most recent State of the Union Address, Johnson neglected to mention that the situation was probably about to get a lot worse. At the time, the US government was claiming victory with every battle being won and casualty rates on the decline. According to White House spin, the NVA were being pushed back across the border into Laos and Cambodia. But in reality, by January, build-up and infiltration along the Ho Chi Minh Trail into Central and Southern Vietnam had increased from 6,000 to around 20,000 troops per month.

In the South, Third Battalion was given complete autonomy for its deployment across Binh Thuan. 3/506 would continue to support the ongoing Rural Development and Pacification program, as well as security for engineering projects on Highway 1. The concept of pacification had originally evolved around Phan Thiet, where it had proven a successful model. Designed to improve morale in the countryside, this program allowed young ARVN troops to stay at home with their families, thus helping the local economy and still assisting with defense.

That being said, the local population of Phan Thiet were not particularly interested in northern politics. During this last 12 months, the region's main insurgent players had been 482nd VC Battalion, who across their four companies usually fronted around 400 irregulars. Recruiting, training, and duty were supported by local hamlet and defense force leaders, who supplied additional "foot soldiers" when necessary. There were often instances when these part-time citizen soldiers were unavailable to fight due to their existing commitments within the ARVN. Like with most Local Force VC battalions, the 482nd had its own cadre of advisors from the People's Republic of China and NVA regulars assigned to Command and Control, intelligence gathering, recruiting, training, tactics, supply, and communications. Every Main and Local Force unit in South Vietnam had a specific role. Some were being trained to attack cities, while others blocked lines of communication and tied down allied units in the countryside. Up until now, military action had been subordinate to all political goals, but things were changing.

On average, a VC battalion had a full-time cadre of local or regional residents intermixed with NVA non-commissioned officers. The foot soldiers were always part-timers on call for night ambush, training, or as laborers to fast-track the building of base camps and bunker systems. Light mortars, machine guns, and rocket launchers were now a key order of battle. In late January '68, the existing Local Force Rifle companies were restructured, reinforced, and consequently became vastly more powerful. The VC had always been flexible and good at assembling small team "shoot and scoots." But as discovered at the Knoll, their new tactics were well planned, with predetermined secondary fighting positions stocked with ammunition. As the 482nd and other local units tried to tighten their grip around Phan Thiet, ambushes were stepped up, as were targeted assassinations and kidnappings. However, indifference from the urban population and local fishing community still made infiltration and traction difficult.

Just as the battalion was waving goodbye to First Brigade, they learned that a young Vietnamese boy had just handed in the missing briefcase. Everything of "value" had been removed except for the secret jump documents! Operation *San Angelo* still went ahead as planned and 48 hours later, First Brigade discovered a massive base camp complete with stockpiles of food, deep bunkers, and high-speed truck trails linking to the border. Around 35,000 North Vietnamese troops and thousands of tons of equipment had now traveled down through Cambodia. Although most northern routes were losing overhead cover to American bombs and defoliants, it did not slow migration.

The rank and file were also receiving heavy periods of political indoctrination. With one full rest day in every seven at pre-designated base camps, NVA troops received briefings and updates on the route ahead. These ranged from weather conditions, road repairs, and building requirements. Situated along each section were self-sufficient barracks with excellent communications. Fifty thousand teenage boys and girls kept vehicles rolling and also served on road repair gangs as construction and cable workers.

Spaced every three miles, control points guarded cleverly camouflaged truck parks. Fuel, food, and ammunition depots were similarly spread to minimize potential loss. Supply trucks worked in relays along designated sections of road. Most routes also had a layover system much like a regular truck stop. However, despite this incredible infrastructure, motorized losses from US strategic bombing were running at around 50 percent. Troops in North and South Vietnam were now under overall command of the resourceful General Nguyen Giap.

A fluent French speaker with no official military training, Giap had been a history teacher and journalist before becoming interior minister in President Ho's early government. It is interesting to note that Giap had also been instrumental in creating the Viet Minh Army that ended 83 years of French colonial rule at Dien Bien Phu.

Chapter 10

"Living in the Dirt"

Landing Zone Betty and Phan Thiet

In early January '68, as a response to the emerging increase in NVA activity around the Ashau Valley, First Cavalry Division decided to reassemble its widely scattered elements in the Northern I Corps Tactical Zone near Hue. This consolidation pulled Second Battalion, 7th Cavalry, who were part of its Third Brigade, out from Phan Thiet where they had been working for 18 months.

The white-stone, arched main entrance to LZ Betty was connected to the city via a long and dusty road that cut through a cemetery. These burial grounds belonged to Phan Thiet and covered a vast area directly to the north and northeast of Betty. With Ta Cu Mountain to its west, the strategically placed airstrip was originally built by the Japanese using Allied prisoners during World War II.

In the early 1950s, "Betty" became an important operating base for the French, who installed concrete bunkers and built many of the permanent offices and workshops now being used by the Americans. The old minefields, many still uncharted, were another legacy that proved to be a double-edged sword for everyone using the base.

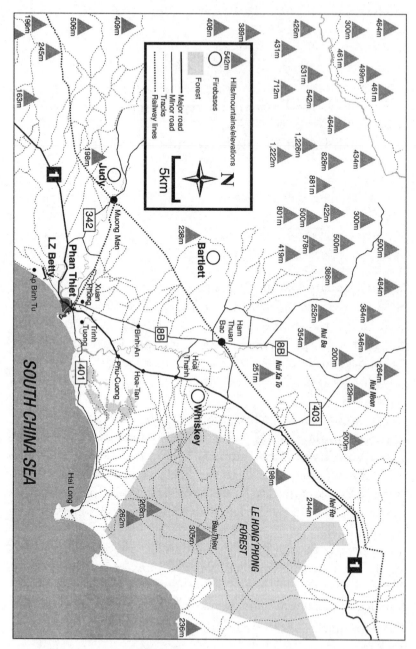

MAP 4: Phan Thiet: Overall Area of Operations From January 1968

Situated about 100 miles east of the capital Saigon, Phan Thiet had a population of around 50,000. At its center was a large square dominated on all sides by colonial-era buildings and flats. Divided by the tidal Ca Ty River, meaning "Billion Fish," the city of two halves was connected by the Nguyen Hoang Bridge.

Residential and business areas were situated in the Southern sector while Phan's administrative heart, rail and power stations, were found across the river in the shadows of a large, ornate water tower, hospital, and cathedral. There were also three ARVN camps, along with local headquarters belonging to government and police, plus a large prison containing hundreds of political prisoners. Nestled along Highway 1, the thriving coastal fishing port was home to thousands of small sampan boats. Renowned as a production center for fish sauce, the pungent odors defined and permeated into every corner of the city.

The rural outskirts opened onto large fields and rice paddies. Made from block or brick/stucco with metal, tile, or thatched roofs, the houses here were more spread out and often surrounded by trees. For the most part, the rural landscape was almost featureless except for an odd pagoda or ancient ruin, with one unpronounceable hamlet looking very much like another. Several main roads, flanked by power lines, crossed south and west. These arterial routes were dotted with stores but within a few steps of leaving any main road, pavement quickly gave way to sandy footpath or cart track.

Unlike anything previously experienced, the land surrounding Highway 1 and railway to Saigon was a vast expanse of dry paddy interwoven with banana plantations, irrigation ditches, and small strips of woodland. Fields encased by solid, thick earth embankments topped by tall hedges were difficult to negotiate. Captain Gaffney said that crossing the Ca Ty River was like a trip to Disneyland – you never knew what to expect. Disneyland also aptly described a small rebel-influenced village called Xuan Phong. The term quickly embedded itself in battalion nomenclature and from then on was used to describe all dusty, sun-baked badland northwest of the city.

TAKING UP THE SLACK

Shortly after dawn, the prime movers began arriving at Phan Rang along with 30 or more additional trucks and tankers loaded with ammunition and aviation fuel. The 70-mile journey south along Highway 1 included an overnight stop and was expected to take a torturous 48 hours. Ahead of the convoy, Mike Pearson and Phil Chassion set off with their Crazy Shock Force as advance guard. Even with "Paladin" and "Chass" on point, Captain Dallas was still concerned about security. "Dee" was apprehensively reflecting on a book he had just finished about the French Indochina War called *Street Without Joy*. Author Bernard Fall had focused heavily on Highway 1, where in the early 1950s a fortified 20-mile stretch had become a focal point for Viet Minh resistance.

The forward air controllers had fighter aircraft standing by while "Mal Hombre" and "Fat Cat" hovered overhead. On days like this, Geraci would sit where he could clearly be identified from the ground. Nobody realized that during these little acts of bravado, the colonel could not actually see a damn thing and was relying entirely on Bob Mairs for visual guidance. But nevertheless, it looked great and promoted confidence. The only tangible threat came from clouds of thick red dust kicked up by the seemingly endless line of vehicles. Eventually, when the elevated towers of Betty finally hove into view, everyone breathed a deep sigh of relief.

While the troops bivouacked out by the airfield, Geraci and Mairs headed for the Officers' Club to discuss handover options with Second Battalion, 7th Cavalry Commander Lieutenant Colonel Joe Griffin and his Executive Major George Burkhart. Subsequently, the headshed were given an aerial tour of Betty that included two forward support bases – codenamed Judy and Bartlett – while Tom Gaffney, Bill Landgraf, and new C Co commander Captain Doug Alitz were introduced to the peripheral defenses. Alitz was enthusiastically looking forward to a more defined role. Totally different from Nick Nahas, Doug was a gung-ho kind of guy who turned out to be a decent leader and was well respected by the guys.

Six observation towers along with dozens of sand-bagged bunkers outlined the perimeter. A few hours later, it was the turn of the platoon leaders to take a terrain walk to the old concrete bunkers up on the cliffs. These French fortifications came with some of the most stunning sea views in South East Asia and it was hard to imagine that there was even a war on.

THE PHONEY WAR

"Mal Hombre" was no longer in command of an independent battalion but leader of a combined multi-unit task force. With a total of 14 to staff both the Logistics and Supply and Transportation Platoon, "Dee" Dallas was daunted by the prospect of servicing this new army that included several 105mm and 175mm howitzer batteries, five M48A3 Patton tanks, plus a selection of self-propelled guns and Quad-50s.

Out in the bay, destroyer USS *Frank E. Evans* dedicated a shore fire control party and air liaison forward control team to the cause. Bizarrely, many of the five-inch shells being used dated back to World War II and would often explode in mid-air before reaching their targets. The colonel also inherited a number of indigenous units, including two battalions from the 44th ARVN Regiment, two companies from the Mobile Strike Force, known as "Mike," and a mixture of regional and popular forces whose collective loyalties were at best questionable.

Army pay for the ordinary South Vietnamese soldier was one-sixteenth that of the average GI and went part of the way to explaining their poor motivation and commitment. Unsurprisingly, the ARVN were very class conscious and a soldier could not progress further than his social standing or family background would allow. Peasantry formed the backbone while most of its officers were drawn from urban privilege. Paradoxically, most peasant soldiers did not want to die preserving the lifestyle of this ruling elite. By comparison, most local VC were compensated not only financially but also with food and protection for their families. However, those "Hanoi loyalists" among them served freely to further their own extreme political beliefs.

The ARVN had been dying at a rate of 2,000 per month and things did not seem to be getting any better for them. America was fighting for what it believed was a world free of enforced rule or ideas. But the war "Mal Hombre" came to fight in late 1967 had already begun to lose much of its original logic and approach.

FORWARD INTO BATTLE

Dedicated rotary support came from Major Ronald Baker and the 192nd Assault Helicopter Company in the form of 21 UH-1H troop-carrying Hueys called "Polecats," seven UH-1B gunships known as "Tiger Sharks" led by Captain George Verner (codename "Baron 42"), plus two CH-47 Chinook heavy lift transporters. Medical and communications back-up was supplied by the 568th Clearing Station along with their two medivac helicopters. The 192nd, whose motto was "We bow to none," were also supplying general support to local ARVN and MACV bases in several towns and cities as far away as Bao Loc and Da Lat.

"Dee" Dallas and John Boes spent their first day deciding where to set up, what they had to work with and how best to re-supply 1,800 people. Going by previous experience, the team calculated an emergency basic load of ammunition needed for a rifle company in the field and kept these wrapped and ready to go on a moment's notice. A helicopter re-supply point was set up adjacent to the cemetery where it would not interfere with regular air traffic. However, one of "Dee's" guys, Staff Sergeant Richard Allen, almost passed out when a warrant arrived from the gunship boys immediately requesting a starter pack of one million rounds of 7.62 link and 200 rockets!

A plane landed carrying the II Corps Logistics Officer, who promptly made his way over to the supply compound, where he deposited two boxes for Captain Dallas. When "Dee" returned, he was somewhat puzzled by his mysterious packages. Everyone looked on with interest as "Dee" carefully opened a box and began to laugh. Inside were the M16 bore brushes he had jokingly ordered back at Phan Rang! It was reassuring to know that despite all current uncertainties, senior management had not completely lost its capacity for humor.

The team soon had a mess hall up and running, along with a freshwater purification unit vital to keeping men moving in the stifling heat. With daily supplies coming in by sea, the two Hooks were also put to good use flying in fresh milk and other perishables from Phan Rang and Cam Ranh Bay. After several nights spent sleeping in a tent out by the runway, Andy Lovy and Curt Washington were allocated rooms in one of the base buildings. The fact that Headquarters Company had taken all the available mattresses seemed immaterial when Andy discovered that a shower block and clean lavatories were now easily accessible. Shortly after moving in, Lovy took over the aid station previously used by 7th Cavalry, nestled between the Supply Team and Tactical Headquarters.

Once settled, Andy drove down to Phan Thiet with a couple of his medics to see what he could do for the local kids. With Doug Alitz now running C Co, not surprisingly his previous role as civil and military operations officer had temporarily landed on the doctor's shoulders. After a brief introductory visit to the regional MACV office at Nga Bay, Andy headed off to a nearby children's hospital to say hello. Although Phan Thiet appeared to be cosmopolitan, it also reflected a tremendous intervention by American culture – which Andy was vehemently against.

Wisely, Bob Mairs decided to establish a secondary Tactical Operations Center in a buried, empty CONEX container. Adding steel plates to reinforce the roof and sandbags covering all external walls, Bob's "emergency office" could withstand almost anything. Not so wisely, "Fat Cat" was nearly buried alive when the shaped charge he had placed to blow the original hole spectacularly malfunctioned.

Now at the end of their respective tours, "Bull" Gergen and C Company's Ben Patterson became the first seniors to re-up. Gergen took some extra leave before flying down to Bien Hoa for his new job as command sergeant major with 2/327. Until Captain Gaffney could find a permanent replacement, Ray Mayfield, Tom Gentry, and Jim Goree from Intelligence would all be doing short stints as acting top kick. When Brigade was forced to move back north to Phu Bai in February, Gergen and his new boss Lieutenant Colonel Charlie Beckwith made for a terrifying combination. The standard 12-month tour sometimes made continuity and cultural understanding difficult, which is why many volunteered to return with outfits such as Special Forces or MACV.

Alpha Supply Sergeant Bill Norris had ordered Mike Trant to assist in the erection of a number of enormous circular supply tents. By now, Norris' constant bullying was once again having a serious effect on Mike's mental health. When word went round that Lieutenant Harrison was looking for riflemen, Trant jumped at the chance and applied.

Keeping the machine armed, fed, and watered soon became a matter of routine. The company supply sergeants were now able to set up their own specific requirements so that logistics knew how many "arrow" lifts would be needed for each platoon. When out on operations, every soldier carried up to five days' rations and was re-supplied according to the prearranged platoon schedule. Many would eat everything they could at re-supply to leave more carry space for ammunition and water. Because of his enhanced workload, Captain Dallas never found time to inventory the base ammunition dump. Consequently, it went completely unnoticed that the ARVN against all safety protocols were negligently stockpiling fused heavy-caliber shells together with bags of detonating chargers.

OPERATION *McLAIN*

At 1900hrs on January 19, 3/506 officially took over from Second Battalion, 7th Cavalry. With the change of ownership came a change of operational title, from "Byrd" to "McLain." From now on, each Rifle company had its own area of operations in which to conduct daylight search and destroy, reconnaissance, or cloverleaf ambushes by night.

Initially, Alpha had the combined rotational mission to not only secure LZ Betty with elements from the CSF but to patrol by helicopter combat assault. Due to the old minefields, Gaffney decided it would be stupid to move on foot directly outside the perimeter. Over the last few months, the airfield had been regularly targeted by mortar fire from the 482nd VC, who were now operating out of a secret base camp a few miles away to the east.

Around this time, a LRRP team from First Brigade made a sizeable find near Phan Rang. The patrol followed blood trails that led them to a group of huts, tunnels, and caves. Clothes covered with dried blood lay scattered on the ground, and there was a pervasive smell of fish sauce. Elements of 3/506 were called in to search the area that was confirmed as another hospital complex.

Before pushing the button, Gaffney created an emergency fire-plan and had Joe Alexander test fire and zero the battalion's heavy mortars from their new home across the airfield at Tower 4. Set on high ground, crucially the coastal outpost covered all vulnerable western and northern approaches to Betty. Joe's nearest neighbors were an engineer company, tank platoon, and aviation fuel depot. The Military Affiliate Radio System was also close by and known as MARS. Staffed by volunteers, the radio shack used amateur civilian operators from all over America to connect troopers via radio with their families back home.

Some of the boys from Second Platoon had been given the afternoon off and were down at the Beach Club when "Weapons" dropped their first test shells. Thinking they were coming under attack, the boys tossed their sodas into the sand and ran for cover! While on the beach, Ronnie Ford was forced to confront his grenadier Guadalupe Aguero after a challenge was made to his authority in front of the squad. Ron and Guadalupe – known as "Ese" (slang Spanish meaning "Hey You") – were good buddies but insubordination was something that Ronnie would not tolerate. Although small in stature, the "Texican" was a tough kid and it took everything Ron had to kick his ass. After the brawl, Ron's Saint Christopher medallion was missing and he ordered "Ese" and the boys onto their hands and knees to search. Ron was secretly relieved that nobody argued and equilibrium was quickly restored to his small but perfectly formed team of bandits.

Operations got under way with Lenny Liebler's men manning the coastal perimeter towers, John Harrison designated as Immediate Reaction Force, and Jim Schlax out on patrol. Joe Alexander's mission was now to provide an early warning system and fire coordination for the task force. Joe was working alongside elements of 4th Battalion, 60th Artillery Regiment, who in a dedicated ground support role were equipped with 40mm M42 Dusters and Quad-50s. On moonless nights, their searchlights were set to refract off low cloud, illuminating the perimeter.

Two platoons from Alpha would always be on continuous daytime airmobile operations, often alongside the Currahee Shock Force or B Co. Elements of First Platoon Bravo under Joe Jerviss were ordered to help two CIA men extract a compromised, middle-aged French informant. With Jerry Gomes from Transportation as his driver, Joe followed the agency men in their jeep for a couple of miles to a small hamlet off Highway 1. En route, Jerry hit the charred remains of a body lying arms outstretched, as if begging for earthly release.

Arriving at an upmarket property, First Platoon stood guard as the CIA dashed inside with two of Joe's troopers. After changing into combats and a steel helmet, the man was brought out and ushered nervously aboard the truck. Gomes and Jerviss returned to Betty without ever knowing their charge's name or how close he was to being murdered. Afterward, Bravo were airlifted out by Hook to take over Nui Tio Ha, the twin-peaked firebase codenamed LZ Bartlett. Twelve klicks due north of Betty, at 349m, the 105mm artillery base known as "Titty Mountain" stood beneath an impressive range of hills.

Here at Bartlett, Bravo prepared to conduct a series of small independent ambush and recon patrols. During a brief handover from 7th Cavalry, the nearby mountain of Nui Ong was identified as being where the real action could be found. Joe Jerviss jokingly told his opposite number, "OK, we'll operate like you, then – sit around smoking, drinking, and topping up our tans," which did not go down well. All bunkers and buildings were made from discarded "105" ammunition boxes and there was even a small chapel. Jerviss' hooch HQ immediately filled with smoke the moment he walked in. The outgoing platoon sergeant had very thoughtfully left him a "booby-trapped" smoke grenade as a welcoming present.

Mike Pearson and the Shock Force were tasked with a similar mission over at LZ Judy. Located 10km northwest of Betty, Judy overlooked the town of Muong Man where E Battery, 5th Battalion, 27th Artillery Regiment were operating their fire support base. Shortly after the CSF arrived, 20 men from the Provincial Reconnaissance Unit flew in without their CIA advisor. These South Vietnamese Special Police fought under the Phoenix Program. Designed by the CIA, Phoenix was created specifically to identify and destroy VC political infrastructure. The Shock Force often teamed up with local units like the PRU when carrying out ambush duties. Intelligence-based collaborative missions such as these regularly snagged lead elements of larger forces. However, some of the things Captain Pearson had said to these Vietnamese made him unpopular and before long a rumor started up that they were planning to kill him.

The CIA guy, who called himself Mr. Billings, eventually rocked up in a chopper to airlift his team into the field for a 48-hour patrol. By nightfall, much to Pearson's frustration, the PRU had consumed all of their rations and were talking about going home two weeks early for the Tet holidays. Tet, meaning "first day of spring," was the premier Buddhist vacation period in Vietnam and marked each Lunar New Year at the end of January. Although fireworks had been banned, the sacred, ethnic three-day festival was meant to be a time for family reunion, happiness, and prosperity for the coming year. A 48-hour ceasefire had been agreed in advance and most indigenous troops were now looking forward to some quality time off with their families. Comparable to having Thanksgiving, Christmas, and New Year all rolled into one, ironically Tet was also a time to pay off debts, forgive others, and make friends with old adversaries.

THE DISTRACTION OF KHE SANH

First Lieutenant John Ross had only just been assigned to A Company as executive officer when he became separated from the Command Post. Captain Gaffney was doing his best to guide the lieutenant but for obvious reasons was reluctant to give grid coordinates openly over the radio. Finally, Jim Schlax got a call to go out and found Ross walking along a dusty road close to the minefields. Jim smiled when a grateful but still somewhat naive Ross inquired what the hell was wrong with the captain. Despite the unnaturally calm feeling preceding Tet, Jim explained that the enemy was out there somewhere and still listening.

At dawn on January 21, a base close to the Laotian border and Northern Demilitarized Zone at Khe Sanh came under intense artillery bombardment. Hitherto unknown to the American people, Khe Sanh soon came to overshadow all international news. The 325th and 304th NVA had up to 20,000 soldiers at their disposal against 5,600 American and South Vietnamese troops. Symbolically, the assault in '54 at Dien Bien Phu had also been led by the 304th and this jingoistic fact was not lost on the press.

In early '68, the US 3rd Marine Division were using the base as a means to block infiltration through the DMZ to Route 9 and the Ho Chi Minh Trail. The siege became one of the most controversial battles and brought with it serious debate in Congress on America's overall military strategy. Khe Sanh soon grew into a distracting symbol of US presence and effort. After President Johnson gained assurance as to Khe Sanh's "importance," its defense became his top priority. The month-long siege eventually sucked in most of the available B-52 bomber force, First Brigade, and several other American divisions – leaving Hue wide open for the NVA to exploit. General Giap cleverly made no attempt to disrupt water supply and allowed in just enough aircraft to keep Khe Sanh's defenses functioning.

Westmoreland told Lyndon Johnson that this could be a decoy for a major enemy strike. However, the president was now so preoccupied with the siege that he paid little heed to Westmoreland's warning. With its emphasis on tactics and mind on Khe Sanh, the US main command believed that a countrywide attack could never succeed and therefore was unthinkable.

While the siege was unraveling 400 miles away, Doug Alitz and his Charlie troopers were comfortably settling into their role as security for 27th Combat Engineer Battalion. Although predominantly the main mission fell to C Co, elements of Joe Alexander's platoon were also occasionally tasked. The length of road being covered was huge and stretched from its southern border with III Corps to Phan Rang. While aircraft traversed the skies above spraying defoliant, armored bulldozers known as "Rome Plows" cleared away all potential cover from either side of the road. Occasionally, one of Alitz's platoons would get lucky and pull detail closer to the coast. This usually meant setting up camp on some unspoiled golden beach under a cool breeze. There was no better duty and the guys made the most of these impromptu mini-vacations.

Sergeant Mike Stuart had been leading Second Platoon for the last three weeks when Doug Alitz mentioned Charles Arce from HHC would be taking over. On Arce's first day, he had the guys patrolling with Mike on point. The sergeant became agitated when Charlie ordered him to cut back on pace. But this was not the jungle and to Mike's experienced way of thinking, speed was of no tactical consequence. Arce had been a liaison officer or LNO and was not the kind of replacement leader everyone had been expecting. Stuart had been on a short fuse since being blasted by the concussion grenade and was now suffering from severe migraines that brought on temporary loss of vision. In fact, it was getting so bad that Mike knew, once back at Betty, he would have to go and seek medical attention ...

Chapter 11

"We Stand Together"

January 22–February 1, 1968

With Joe Alexander now on standby as Immediate Reaction Force, the remainder of A Company were assigned to the towers and numerous perimeter bunkers alongside the CSF. Reinforced by sandbags, each emplacement slept five men, with the roof doubling as an observation post and defensive position. Bunker guard duty was considered boring and easy, and at that time provided many opportunities for mischief.

Lieutenant Harrison's platoon had managed to smuggle in several cases of beer and by sunset were on top of their bunkers drinking and cooking up a C-Ration casserole. Twilight signaled playtime for the large Tokay Gecko, whose piercing, high-pitched call sounded like "FUCK YOU" – which in turn gave rise to the nickname "F.U. Lizard." After a few beers, Ron Ford thought it would be entertaining to orchestrate an inter-platoon grenade-throwing contest against the lizards. Of course, Ronnie had his secret weapon, Mr. Biven Patterson, who outclassed everyone with his powerful pro-pitching arm. As the competition got under way, someone in a distant bunker decided to burn off a magazine of 5.56 and in doing so kick-started a chain reaction across the base.

In a matter of seconds, the entire perimeter lit up, including the towers! Ron and Biven were relieved when everyone slipped back into uneasy silence. The CP rang wanting to know what was going on. Ford told Harrison that both fire teams were responding to incoming fire but the "enemy" had now withdrawn! Although no individual was charged, Gaffney decided to issue a "bunker ban" on all alcoholic beverages.

"Mal Hombre" gave Andy Lovy a huge amount of leeway when it came to dishing out his medics, but things did not always go according to the plan. One medic in particular, Sergeant Robert Childress, was a militant and active promoter of "Black Power" and had upset every platoon he had ever worked with. Finally, at the end of December his latest tenure with Alpha came to an abrupt stop when he was removed and charged with offenses pertaining to hatred and mutiny. Racial harmony was paramount and derisive behavior such as this would not be tolerated. At the court-martial on January 21, Andy stood for Robert as a witness. Lovy always believed that more questions could have been asked regarding Robert's background and home life before "Mal Hombre" decided to sentence the 18-year-old to six months' hard labor at Long Binh Jail (LBJ).

Tom Lundgren was one of Doc Lovy's "contract" medics who bounced between companies covering when others were sick, injured, or on leave. Lundgren always joked that Lovy provided the childhood that he had missed – complete with live ammunition!

Initially, Lundgren was assigned to the "Beach Club" as a lifeguard, although he could not actually swim. Access from Betty was via a cleared path through the minefield. Vietnamese barmaid Goldie was always on hand serving beer and soda, along with her infectious smile enhanced by a string of gold fillings. Armed with his M16, it was Tom's job to look after any off-duty swimmers. It was a dream gig that involved much drinking and fun, although several murder attempts by the VC were foiled during his tenure. Shortly afterward, Tom was assigned to a coast guard cutter whose role was to assist the Navy against maritime arms smuggling.

He also got to spend a day on a fast patrol craft for a "mission" along the coast. These shallow-drafted vessels were formidably armed with twin Browning .50-cal guns and a rear-mounted 81mm mortar. The commander of this particular "swift boat," PCF-19, was a goofball and keen to show off his skills. After a while, he cut engines at a distant beach and drew Tom's attention toward two houses. The lieutenant wanted to demonstrate accuracy of his mortar and selected one house as a target. Tom was horrified when a shell went through the roof and exploded. Gleefully, the commander pointed out that they were a force to be reckoned with. "But, sir," protested Tom, "someone lives in that place and you've more than likely just fucking killed them!"

"Ah, so what?" came back the arrogant and ignorant reply. "It's an enemy structure and therefore a totally legitimate target!" Ironically, a few months later, while on night patrol up on the DMZ, PCF-19 was sunk by unidentified aircraft.

WHAT'S KEEPING YOU?

Jim Schlax and Lenny Liebler were on their seventh combat assault and being flown 15 miles north to screen the outlying areas around Bartlett. Joining them was a platoon from B Co who flew out from the forward base to act as LZ security. Thrown together at very short notice, the mission had no time for a full briefing. As per procedure, Schlax usually assigned each of his two M60 teams to a rifle squad, whose sergeants would then add the names to their own nominal roll. But on this occasion, Corporal Clyde Schaffer and privates Rich Easter and Dave Johnson were accidentally omitted from their host squad's paperwork. Not long after landing, Third Platoon came across one of the large French colonial-style houses that proliferated Bihn Thuan Province. Orders came down from Gaffney for Lieutenant Liebler and Ed Bassista to go inside and search the place. Much to their surprise, they were greeted at the door by an immaculately dressed Vietnamese couple. The gentleman was wearing a pressed white suit and his wife a gorgeous blue silk dress. Her perfumed smell was exquisite and contrasted heavily with Lenny and Ed, who standing in the hallway carrying rifles and paraphernalia of war seemed totally out of place.

Courteously, the man gestured for something to drink. Len and Ed nodded as a crystal decanter half full of top-quality French brandy and four matching tumblers appeared. Eyes lit up as drinks were poured and glasses lifted in toast to Vietnam and friendship with America. It was like the guys had been transported back to another place in another time … reminiscent, they thought, not of colonial France but rather Victorian England. Ten relaxing minutes went by before Gaffney's impetuous voice came crackling over the radio to enquire what was keeping them. Looking at Ed with that *Oh, fuck* expression on his face, Lenny told the captain, who was overhead in a helicopter, that they were currently experiencing "language" problems. Not at all happy with the answer, Gaffney ordered that they get on with the job. Before saying goodbye, Ed and Len eagerly nodded acceptance as the Vietnamese couple offered them another round!

Back at the helipad, jokingly known to all as "Can Do," Jim Schlax did a quick headcount before the penny dropped that Schaffer and his gun team were not present. Captain Gaffney was furious and the young lieutenant knew he was in deep shit. There was no way around it; First Platoon saddled up, got back on the helicopters, and returned to look for the missing men. It was getting dark by the time Jim and his troopers began their search. Schlax was frantic with guilt and despite obvious risks started yelling into the night. The following morning, Third Platoon had flown back to join the hunt while Gaffney hovered overhead scanning for a sign. The search party that now numbered around 80 men continued looking until a radio message changed everything. At 1620hrs, Clyde Schaffer and his team reported into the Tactical Operations Center at Betty. The three men had spent the last 20 hours walking through bandit country and even stopped several times to ask for directions! When the search teams returned to base, Schlax felt like clobbering and hugging the "missing" men all at the same time. Gaffney chose not to punish Jim, figuring that he had learned another valuable lesson.

These regular screening patrols were never wasted. Recently dug graves, fresh trails, caches of weapons, ammunition, abandoned equipment, and rice were all indicators of a possible enemy build-up. Air assaults carried out by A and B companies over the previous week had by pure chance missed the 482nd VC Battalion's new headquarters east of Dai Nam. Less than three miles from Betty and surrounded by a system of bunkers, their cleverly hidden Disneyland base was situated north of Phan Thiet.

One of Lovy's youngest medics, Al Thompson, had only recently turned 19. Al was now attached to Bravo after two monotonous months of guard duty with HHC and a recent assignment to Jim Schlax. Thompson still felt like a kid trying to do a man-sized job but he knew it took maturity to become effective. Out to prove his worth, shortly after arriving at Bartlett, Thompson inadvertently "volunteered" for an eight-man night reconnaissance patrol. Local intelligence suggested the VC were using a nearby gully as a possible transit route toward Phan Thiet. Shortly before dusk, the men moved down Bartlett's scree-covered hillside. With no visible trails, they carefully picked through what seemed like endless wait-a-minute brush. As per SOPs, Thompson accompanied one of the radio operators and quietly followed him down into the creek toward a central cluster of rocks. As everyone gathered on top of the largest boulder, a strange low murmur revealed an approaching enemy. Dumbfounded, everyone sat motionless while a split column of silhouetted insurgents passed by on either side. Whispering a weird kind of cadence chant, the enemy platoon disappeared into the night completely unaware they had been compromised.

During the early morning hours of January 28, members of Dave Pearson's Shock Force and Vietnamese Provincial Reconnaissance Unit ambushed around 50 VC in the same area. One person was seen running away on fire, while another was blown to pieces by a thumper round. The gun battle left ten insurgents dead, including a woman. Documents, medical supplies, equipment, and around a dozen large bags of rice were recovered. During the clean-up, a young nurse was found hiding and seemed relieved to defect under the policy of "Chieu Hoi" or "open arms." This program had been established to give members of the NVA and VC opportunity to return to the Southern flag. As with this case, any defection usually brought valuable information that would often lead to hidden weapons, ammunition, and supplies. Many former VC went on to become what were known as "Kit Carson Scouts" and handed over locations of hundreds if not thousands of booby traps and base camps. This term was originally devised by the US Marine Corps in homage to legendary frontiersman and Civil War officer Colonel Christopher "Kit" Carson.

In the first instance, Americans were encouraged to treat defectors differently from regular detainees or POWs. Respect was to be shown and a receipt issued for any weapons brought in under "Chieu Hoi." Individuals would then be taken to the Provincial Headquarters in Phan Thiet for processing. A substantial bounty was awarded to each defector and over the next two years around 17,000 insurgents turned against North Vietnam. Working as an interpreter, a bilingual scout could earn up to $300 a month compared with an ARVN colonel, who took home around 70 bucks.

All offensive operations came to an end at 1800hrs in accordance with the Tet holiday agreement. During the 36-hour ceasefire, Phan Thiet was placed off limits to all American troops. Worrying reports began to filter through regarding locals being cajoled into giving gifts to the Viet Cong and forced into flying National Liberation Front-style flags. From their hilltop home at Bartlett, despite a ban on all pyrotechnics, B Company sat and watched the "Year of the Monkey" fireworks over Phan Thiet. Celebratory ARVN tracer fire arced into the night as Joe Jerviss sat and discussed Vietnam's uncertain future with his men.

NO ORDINARY WAR

Doctor Lovy was ordered to relocate his aid station to a large corrugated Quonset hut a few hundred yards away opposite the 568th Clearing Station. The unexpected move was not only isolating but would seriously interfere with Lovy's own response times for incoming casualties. It made sense to keep these two facilities separate but when voicing concerns to Houston Hauser,

Lovy was told his building had already been requisitioned for General Rosson.

At 0800hrs, Rosson flew into Betty from Nha Trang to discuss possible defense options for Phan Thiet. Afterward, the general and "Mal Hombre" visited LZ Judy for a short meeting with Mike Pearson. "Paladin" then took Bob Mairs into Muong Man. Nestled on a hill alongside the Ca Ty River, Muong Man was an important rail hub and Mike recognized its potential to the VC. As a precaution, Major Mairs arranged for an artillery observer to be flown in from Betty for the next few nights to keep an eye on things. Mike was right to be concerned because the following evening it came under attack from Company 3, 482nd VC Battalion. Muong Man's attack coincided with a countrywide uprising directed against hundreds of vital government installations and bases.

Later that evening, "Fat Cat" asked Pearson to have two-dozen men prepared and ready for a 30-minute Quick Reaction Force back at Betty. John Harrison's platoon was out hunting deer when news arrived that the holiday ceasefire had been terminated. The company, less Joe Alexander, was immediately sent out to Chuo Thiem Lam. Both the village and its nearby pagoda were beyond the cemetery along Highway 1. Harrison's idea was to screen for a few hours before returning to base around lunchtime. Second Platoon set about checking houses with a "Kit Carson" interpreter who called for occupants to step out and be identified.

Everyone was on edge and at one property, despite numerous calls, there was no response. Before he entered, Ron Ford ordered Aguero to launch an M79 round through one of the windows. The blast badly injured several Vietnamese civilians hiding inside. Ron's gunner at the time, Corporal Francis Edwards, flipped out, stuck the muzzle of his machine gun into Ford's face, and threatened to kill him if he did the same thing again. Edwards was not a very popular individual within the outfit and many like Ford and Adams disliked him intensely. Ronnie got angry and told the corporal that he did not care but did give a fuck about his squad ... and that until whoever attacked Muong Man was found, then hard entries like this would surely continue.

When the scout received no response from the next house, Harrison decided to send Ronnie in first. Apprehensively, Ford entered with his M16 switched to full "rock 'n' roll." Suddenly, an old man appeared and in that split second, Ron blasted the terrified pensioner to death. Badly shaken, Ford watched Harold Rodney drag the body outside to be searched. Captain Gaffney absolutely did not want anything like this to happen again and ordered that a softer approach had to be taken with all future entries.

Around 50,000 enemy troops were believed to have been involved across the country. The main attacks occurred in Saigon and Hue, where the old citadel was captured. However, more than 30 Provincial capitals were also targeted, with initial exceptions being Phan Thiet and Phan Rang. Most available South Vietnamese forces were withdrawn into the towns, where fierce urban fighting quickly broke out. Small groups of VC penetrated Saigon but luckily the US commander of II Field Force, General Fred Weyand, had kept two American battalions in reserve. Except for Hue, many towns were regained within a week – although Phan Thiet would be an altogether different story ...

THE FIRST ATTACK ON PHAN THIET

The 482nd VC Main Force Battalion opened its offensive against Phan Thiet with a fusillade of mortars against the airfield. The Navy responded quickly while Bravo and CSF were recalled back to Betty from their forward firebases. Over the next month, Phan Thiet would come under several ground assaults all aimed at demolishing its Provincial Command infrastructure.

During the early hours of January 31, keeping its 4th Company in reserve, the 482nd began its war with a number of coordinated attacks. Initially, Company 3 was to gain control of Phu Khan Hamlet, situated due north of Betty along Highway 1. A few kilometers to the northeast, companies 1 and 2 advanced down Highway 8 to storm the now virtually empty ARVN bases at Trinh Tuong, Cao-Thang, and Dinh Cong Trang.

Homebase of 44th ARVN Infantry Regiment, the northernmost camp at Trinh Tuong was temporarily defended by a small element of Regional Force and a platoon of local artillerymen from Phu Trinh. Outnumbered and outgunned by B40 rockets, the 50 defenders eventually managed to repel Company 2 with assistance from an ad-hoc relief force. The same thing happened to Company 1 at Dinh Cong Trang. Overall, the reactive and swift ARVN counter-attacks wiped out the 482nd's deputy battalion commander, two company commanders, and two platoon leaders.

Back at Betty, "Mal Hombre" mobilized his helicopter attack wing while Jim Pratz took to the night sky in his "Bird Dog." Flying over the city, Jim put in an urgent request for Spooky. Forty precious minutes ticked by before the AC-47 finally arrived. By 0500hrs, faced with advancing and growing relief forces, companies 1 and 2 began to withdraw into the heavily populated Cho Go slum area, banana groves, and Disneyland paddies northwest of the city.

Those from Company 2 that made it to Cho Go were heavily shelled and bombed by Navy and Air Force alike. Demoralized, the VC quickly dissolved into the hamlets of Xuan Phong and Phu Thien. Here, the villagers were forced from their homes and sent south across the Nguyen Hoang Bridge into the city. The chaotic expulsions allowed insurgents to blend in and use the refugees as a shield.

As further reinforcements arrived, government troops were able to move into the two villages and regain control. By then, most of Company 2 had either gone to ground or simply crossed the bridge and disappeared into hamlets around the estuary. Still intact, Company 4 came out of reserve and gathered together the remnants before heading northwest to their Battalion Headquarters at a school near Dai Nam. With the 840th Main Force Battalion now moving in from the north, 482nd VC planned to re-equip and reinforce by absorbing their regional guerrilla companies.

THE TURKEY SHOOT

By 0900hrs on January 31, Gaffney marched A Co northward through the cemetery to intercept Company 3 and the tattered

Over Christmas '67, "Bucky" Cox was given a special security mission near Dai Ninh. Members of Third Platoon are seen here bathing in the nearby Da Nhim River. ("Bucky" Cox Archive – Author's Collection)

Visit from "Santa" on Christmas Day to Bao Loc, 1967. L–R: SFC Luther Stultz, Brigadier General Salve Matheson, and Lieutenant Colonel John Geraci. (US Army)

A representative from the USO handing out donuts to a member of First Platoon Alpha on Christmas Day. (Jim Schlax)

Known as "Hippy," Wayne Johnson was in Mike Stuart's squad and carried the M79. (Mike Stuart)

Members of Alpha's Weapons Platoon on Highway 1 before the Tet Offensive. Sergeant Carl "Skip" Rattee is seen holding bananas. (Joe Alexander)

A platoon summiting somewhere in the Central Highlands, '67/'68. (US Army)

Members of C Co on patrol near the Provincial Borders between Lam Dong and Binh Thuan. (US Army)

Burdened by his "25," a radioman from 3/506 struggles to cross a small jungle river during Operation *Klamath Falls*. (US Army)

"RJ" Johnson and "Bucky" Cox survey their domain while waiting for nightfall in the Central Highlands. ("Bucky" Cox Archive – Author's Collection)

Substantial cache of rice slung ready for extraction by Chinook, near Bao Loc, December 1967. (US Army)

Charles Jackson from First Platoon, B Co cooling down while on patrol in the Central Highlands, December 1967. (US Army)

Two weary troopers out on patrol during Operation *Klamath Falls*. (US Army)

The infamous California Bar and strip in Phan Rang. (Mike Stuart)

Mid-January '68, jumpmaster briefing in the conference room at Phan Rang. L–R (foreground): Mike Pearson and Phil Chassion. (US Army)

Aerial view looking west across Phan Thiet toward LZ Betty (obscured by cloud), LZ Judy, Muong Man, and Ta Cu (694m). (Bill Robie)

Downtown Phan Thiet looking northwest across Ca Ty River, bridge, and Highway 1. (Bill Robie)

Trucks carrying B Co leaving Phan Rang for Phan Thiet on January 17, 1968.
(Joe Jerviss)

Sergeant Jeff Cunningham making final
checks at Phan Rang before the motor
march to Phan Thiet. (Richard Pittman
Archive © Mike Krawczyk)

Driver Jerry Gomes from the S&T
Platoon (bottom left) en route to Phan
Thiet. (Jerry Gomes)

Captain Doug Alitz assumed command of
Charlie Company in January 1968.
(US Army)

Mike Stuart outside one of the
French-built concrete bunkers at
LZ Betty. (Mike Stuart)

These original French interconnected terraces at LZ Betty faced the eastern end of the
runway and formed the operational offices for TF 3/506. (US Army)

Left View west from
one of the 34ft watch
towers at LZ Betty
toward Ta Cu
Mountain and LZ
Judy. (US Army)

Lieutenant General William Rosson with Lieutenant Colonel John Geraci. (US Army)

A UH-1H Huey delivering a squad from 3/506 during one of many combat assaults around Phan Thiet. (US Army)

Above Troops from B Co at the Pick-Up Zone before flying to reinforce Alpha on February 2, 1968. (US Army)

Left Lieutenant Jim Schlax from A Co with his "Kit Carson Scout" Bong. (Jim Schlax)

One of many typical hamlets encountered in the area known as Disneyland. (Richard Pittman Archive © Mike Krawczyk)

Richard Pittman and Clyde Braughton from C Co take a break from security duty along Highway 1. (Richard Pittman Archive © Mike Krawczyk)

During the first week of Tet, the enemy attacked the airfield with mortars. One of the rounds overshot and landed close to A Company but failed to detonate. Mike Trant (standing front right) and his colleagues are pictured where the dud came down. (US Army)

By way of commemorating C Company's first serious contact, the guys had Mike Daly's 9mm Chi-Com pistol engraved and dedicated to Captain Nahas as a leaving present. (Nick Nahas)

Members of C Co waiting their turn to be airlifted back to Phan Thiet before the Tet Offensive. (Mike Stuart)

View from the eastern side of the Van Ta House toward the shack that became Lieutenant John Harrison's command post during the battle on February 2, 1968. (Ed Blanco)

Damage inflicted by Second Platoon Alpha to the eastern side of Van Ta House during the battle. (Ed Blanco)

Pictured in April 2021, Mr. Van Ta's daughter Ngo Thi Don, now aged 79, sitting on the porch opposite where Andy Daniel died on February 2, 1968. (Steve Broering)

Left 2nd Lieutenant John Harrison, SSG Ray Mayfield, and medic Private First Class John Melgaard receiving their Silver Stars from Major General Olinto Barsanti while Lieutenant Colonel John Geraci proudly looks on. (US Army)

Below Radio Operator David Stiles (left) and Emmett Clark from Second Platoon Alpha clearly showing helmet damage received during battle at Van Ta House. (US Army)

Bottom Lieutenant Colonel Geraci with Captain Gaffney and Alpha HQ following the battle at Van Ta House. (US Army)

One of many dead insurgents left behind on the soccer field during the first attack on Phan Thiet. (US Army)

Jerry Gomes outside what was left of the Civilian Provincial Hospital in Phan Thiet. (Jerry Gomes)

Above C Company moving past a huge bomb crater in Disneyland during early February 1968. (Richard Pittman Archive © Mike Krawczyk)

Left Doc Lovy (holding paperwork) overseeing wounded troopers being unloaded from a medivac chopper on the helipad at Phan Thiet. (US Army)

Liston Green from C Co taking a break while on patrol in Disneyland while an air strike is carried out in the middle distance. (Richard Pittman Archive © Mike Krawczyk)

Third Platoon C Co Radio Operator Richard A. Williams. ("Bucky" Cox Archive – Author's Collection)

Geraci shaking hands with Lieutenant General William Rosson. Also pictured are Lieutenant Colonel Robert Elton (left) and Major General Olinto Barsanti. (US Army)

Elements of 3/506 moving through the ruined streets of Phan Thiet during mid-February 1968. (US Army)

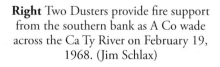

Right Two Dusters provide fire support from the southern bank as A Co wade across the Ca Ty River on February 19, 1968. (Jim Schlax)

Forward Air Control "Bird Dog" spotter plane circling above C Co in Disneyland during February/March 1968. (Richard Pittman Archive © Mike Krawczyk)

Joe Alexander and his men crossing the Ca Ty River on February 19, 1968. (Jim Schlax)

By early March, the Currahee Shock Force was reorganized into a full LRRP reconnaissance role. (US Army)

On March 12, 1968 at LZ Bartlett, A Co held a memorial service for those killed during the Second Battle of Phan Thiet. (US Army)

In early June 1968, Bob Elton, Nick Nahas, and several others attended a "welcome ceremony" held near Da Lat's main market place. (US Army)

Lieutenant Donald Whiteman with "Kit Carson Scout" near the MARS Shack at LZ Betty. ("Bucky" Cox Archive – Author's Collection)

Above Phan Thiet, April 16, 1968: Captain Bob Robinson (left) updates Lieutenant Colonel Robert Elton on the current tactical situation. (US Army)

Right C-130 Hercules aircraft lined up at Cam Ly Airfield after delivering 3/506 in preparation for Operation *Banjo Royce*. (US Army)

Memorial service led by Bob Elton and Mike Pearson at LZ Betty on June 1, 1968.
("Bucky" Cox Archive – Author's Collection)

C Company platoon leaders, L–R: Bob
Roos (2nd Ptn), Gordon "Gordy" Gant
(3rd Ptn), and Dave Rivers (1st Ptn).
(David Rivers)

L–R: Colonel John Collins, Robert Elton,
and "Snake" McCorkle during the change
of command ceremony at Bao Loc on
June 18, 1968. (US Army)

remnants of Company 1. When Alpha arrived at Phu Khan, they began receiving fire from a bunker up on the highway. Moments after First Platoon were sent to engage, a white flag appeared. Gaffney was livid when the occupants turned out to be ARVN.

Two hours later, Alpha made contact with the first VC, who as expected had gone to ground inside the cemetery. The difference in fighting spirit between companies 1 and 3 would soon become apparent. Tom deployed his force in a "company wedge" with First Platoon at the tip. As Jim Schlax swept in, a VC appeared, raised his hands, and promptly surrendered. However, a few minutes later, another stepped out but this kid had no intention of giving up and, as he lifted his RPG, was shot dead by Corporal Marshall Nelson.

Within a few minutes, Gaffney took off through nearby brush and collided head-on with the enemy. Using a technique learned from the Chinese in Korea, Gaffney tore into the exhausted VC, inflicting heavy casualties. Acting as slack, Lieutenant Harrison and his radio operator Hal Dobie cautiously followed point man Andy Daniel as he pushed through a thick hedgerow in chase. Halfway across the narrow field, an insurgent sprang from an opposite hedge and began firing. "AJ" for some reason did not engage but stood motionless as the individual ran toward him. Harrison could not believe what he was seeing and yelled several times at Corporal Daniel to shoot.

As Harrison raised his rifle, Ron Ford was on the other side of the hedge when a bullet hit Aguero's hand. "Ese" screamed, dropped his M79, and fell backward onto Ford. Chris Adams had just bent down to pick up a magazine when the thumper landed beside him. In a split second, he grabbed the launcher and fired at the shooter, who was still loosing off maniacally with his pistol. At such close range, the 40mm round had no time to arm and struck the Vietnamese between the shoulder blades as he turned. The guy fell and then stood up. Dumbfounded, the boys wondered if he was high on drugs before everybody opened up. Ron emptied about 18 rounds into the Hanoi loyalist as Adams reloaded and fired again. The man, who probably weighed less than 90lb, crumpled as his head fragmented into a red haze. Afterward, as the smoke cleared, Harold Rodney went over and lifted up the body by its ragged, blood-soaked collar and joked, "Come on, man ... pull yourself together!" It was so ridiculous that Ford and Adams began laughing. When the boys recovered the pistol and presented it to "Ese," they were amazed to see that one of their rounds had actually penetrated the barrel! Later identified as the VC province chief, everyone agreed he had been one brave bastard.

Lieutenant Harrison chewed Daniel out for not firing. Although he had done the same thing once before, "AJ" never provided clear reason as to why he froze. Traditionally, after each contact a point man would be rotated, but John decided to leave Andy up front as they moved toward their next objective. After returning to base, Platoon Sergeant Jim Bunn had a more understanding exchange with Andy – just to be sure that it would never happen again. "AJ" revealed that he had recently developed a liking for glue and agreed to stop. Recreational drug use was difficult for Bunn to comprehend but boys like "AJ" were ultimately the reason why he came back for a second tour.

By 1400hrs, A Co had counted 13 Vietnamese dead and captured their company commander as well as his political officer. Without decent leadership, the enemy began to unravel as Gaffney called in the Tiger Sharks. As the gunships approached First Platoon, the lead chopper dipped its nose and fired two rockets at the trailing squad. Lieutenant Schlax turned to see several, including Mark Jones, blown off their feet, but luckily everyone was OK. The gunships killed another 40 stragglers as they withdrew toward the pagoda at Chuo Thiem Lam. Captain Gaffney was surprised when Baron 42 refused to engage, claiming that pagodas were off limits! Over the radio, Tom explained that he was unconcerned about damage and that his men were already smashing the building with thumper and M72 LAW. With that, George Verner relented and gave the order for his pilots to go in.

At the same time, Gaffney passed coordinates to his new artillery observer. The guy went off to relay Tom's instructions back to the Fire Detection Center or FDC. Moments later, a barrage of 105mm rounds came in from Judy and landed among the company. Gaffney was furious as he yelled, "Check fire, check fire – you dumb shit, what did you tell them?" The FO explained that he had under-adjusted Gaffney's coordinates. When the observer continued to question Gaffney's experience, Tom blew his stack and ordered the young officer to get the fuck off his battlefield.

On his first strafing run, one pilot was hit and wounded by machine-gun fire coming from the temple. The same gun was also targeting Ford and Adams when they heard an M79 being fired from behind the structure. Two seconds later, a thumper round landed between Ron and Chris but failed to explode. Staring open-mouthed, the friends were unsure if the gleaming warhead was actually VC or US. Before they had a chance to get angry, a couple of 60mm mortar rounds exploded behind them, killing an ARVN soldier and seriously wounding another.

Still on duty northeast of the city along Highway 1, another tragedy struck C Company, but this time it was the turn of Fourth Platoon. Known to all as "Brad," mortar-man Sergeant Clyde Braughton was accidentally shot by his friend Mike Herrington. That morning, while breaking down their overnight defensive positions, "Bucky" Cox heard a gun go off. He turned to see "Brad" fall backward and Mike holding a Colt .45 pistol. Immediately, "Bucky," Jim Kessinger, and Mike Krawczyk ran across to assist. The round had hit "Brad" square in the solar plexus. Unable to cannulate due to venous collapse, the on-scene medic was forced to find alternatives and eventually got an IV started in "Brad's" foot. While waiting for the chopper, Jim Kessinger held "Brad's" hand and did his best to prevent him from going to sleep. When eventually the medivac arrived, as Braughton was being loaded the medic signaled for a surgical procedure known as a cut-down. A short while later, Doc Lovy came on air to apologize for the delay and advise that "Brad" had died before he reached the clearing station. Sergeant Herrington was saddened beyond words as "Bucky" quietly nominated two friends to keep suicide watch on him.

In the inquiry that followed, it transpired that "Brad" had checked, cleaned, and reinserted the magazine on Mike's pistol before handing the weapon back "made safe." Without thinking, and quite negligently, Mike racked the slide toward him expecting it to lock, but a broken sear allowed the working parts to slip with disastrous consequences.

By midday, around 25 wounded civilians were brought into the clearing station by helicopter. Doc Lovy and his team were working with two 568th doctors, Pat McMann and Jeff Carr. Both were hoping to get everyone treated and expediently returned to the Provincial hospital in Phan Thiet. But over the next few hours, more injured Vietnamese arrived. The hospital happened to be next to Dinh Cong Trang Camp and it soon became apparent that Dr. Carr's casualties were going nowhere.

Within 30 minutes, the medics had more casualties than they could handle and with the two medivac choppers now so overstretched, it was almost impossible to get one booked for Vung Tau. "Mal Hombre" came over to see what was going on and immediately turned over his C&C.

Just behind Battalion Headquarters was a tall antenna for the LORAN aircraft navigation system. The beacon's red flashing lights acted as a warning for any helicopter or fixed-wing night activity. The mast also provided the enemy with a perfect aiming stake when targeting Betty with their mortars. That evening, while Lovy was making his rounds, a massive explosion rocked the building. The recently allocated Quonset hut had taken a direct hit. Debris flew through the clearing station windows, plunging everything into darkness. Using flashlights, the medics quickly ran round checking on their confused and frightened patients. Badly wounded by shrapnel, the Medical Platoon Sergeant Richard Clark was carried in from across the street. As he was being set up for IV and prepped for surgery, Clark regained consciousness long enough to explain that Sergeant Charles Martin was still trapped in the rubble. Andy ran over and found Martin dressing his own wounds and wondering what all the fuss was about.

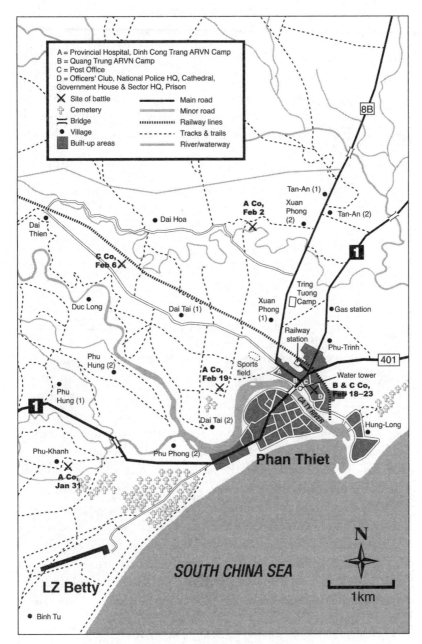

MAP 5: Phan Thiet: Tet Offensive, February 1968

TIME MARCHES ON

Ironically, in the midst of all this action, Expiration of Term of Service or ETS dates for some senior NCOs began to arise and a number of "irreplaceable" squad leaders returned to the States. Shortly before Staff Sergeant Mike Daly was due to go home, C Company held a collection and purchased the 9mm Chi-Com pistol he had recovered back in December. Ultimately, the idea was to engrave and present it to Captain Nahas when he got out of hospital. Doctors at Nha Trang had begrudgingly permitted Nahas to return under stipulation of light duties for four weeks. With a few hours to spare before catching his plane, Nick arranged to meet up with an old friend. Jay Hadlock had been a platoon leader with Nick in Germany and was now the MP company commander at Nha Trang. While Nick and Jay were out enjoying a few drinks, the VC struck and everything changed.

Jay handed Nick a pistol as they leapt into his jeep and headed for the CP. Nick could not stop laughing as he thought about his "light duty" profile recommendation. Jay's guys were already getting ready to join the fight when he and Nick pulled up outside. None of the MPs had fired a shot in anger since arriving in Vietnam and were clueless as to how much ammunition they needed or the most efficient way to carry it. Nick did his best to put them right but they were just not used to fighting like regular professional infantry.

Hadlock was proud of the steel plates welded onto his vehicles. However, he had overlooked the radiators and tyres. Consequently, within the first hour every jeep was out of commission. Nick found out later that if he had remained in hospital for just one day longer, he would have been evacuated to Japan to make way for a tidal wave of expected casualties. Against all odds, Nahas managed to catch his flight and upon arrival at Betty was given a warm welcome by "Fat Cat." Knowing that Nick was now available, Bob grasped the opportunity and immediately made him his temporary assistant at TAC Headquarters.

He immediately made his presence felt. When things were going hot and heavy, helicopter pilots did not want to take off while the artillery was firing – which caused unnecessary interruptions. As the choppers were located close to the beach, one of Nick's first decisions was to have them fly out directly over water when the big guns were in action … it seemed a simple solution and he wondered why something like that had not been implemented before.

Phan Thiet was now in the process of being reinforced by South Vietnamese troops belonging to Third Battalion, 44th ARVN Regiment commanded by Major Vo Khan. Khan also had M-113 armored personnel carriers from Fourth Squadron 8th Cavalry and a platoon of civilian irregulars at his disposal. More critically, the tri-unit Reaction Force promised from the adjoining province had already suffered casualties during a clash along Highway 1. By the time Khan reached the city, his APCs refused to go any further until first light. Rightly or wrongly, this decision from the squadron commander left Major Vo Khan dangerously exposed as he bravely continued his advance into the city center.

Augmented by 450th Local Guerrilla Company, the 840th MF was also closing in. Supported by artillery and heavily staffed by NVA regulars, the 250-strong force set about attacking both the police station and Officers' Club. However, 100 determined Vietnamese policemen and a platoon of militia were not planning to give up easily. Enemy shells hit the sector Command HQ and nearby residential area. Although parts of the city were now in flames, the initial enemy assault failed to achieve most of its crucial early goals. However, Hanoi's real objective was to demonstrate total military stalemate and weaken faith in government, while at the same time assessing revolutionary strength and resolve inside the city.

Chapter 12

"Blood Trail 556"

The Battle of the Van Ta House – February 2, 1968

"Mal Hombre" and "Fat Cat" flew out early to Judy in Hooks to personally oversee the artillery airlift and Shock Force personnel who were supporting A and B companies. Because of the worsening tactical situation in Phan Thiet, it was a slow process and crucially the last two 105s along with Mike Pearson's jeep did not leave until evening.

By this time, as if to taunt, the surviving VC commanders were monitoring radio frequencies and constantly cutting in with sarcastic messages. Intelligence sources had received reliable information from captured fighters as to the probable location of the 482nd Battalion Headquarters near Dai Nam. Hopeful for results, Alpha and Bravo companies along with Jim Kessinger's platoon were flying in to search the hot spots west of Highway 8, hoping to strike at the enemy from its rear and flank.

Meanwhile, back in Phan Thiet the insurgency had now gained several solid footholds along the northern bank. Trenches had been dug in the park opposite the burning railway station in preparation for another series of attacks against the prison, Officers' Club, and Provincial hospital. Under cover of darkness, those locals who could extricated themselves quietly from the battle area along with the fishing community, who sensibly took to their sampans and headed out to sea.

The morning at Betty started with an intelligence briefing confirming that VC Headquarters and quite possibly the restructured remnants of companies 3 and 4 could be within Gaffney's search area. Joe Alexander and Fourth Platoon were being held in reserve out by the "Can Do" pad, bombed up and ready. As the first choppers lifted off with John Harrison's platoon, Joe's men shielded their faces from the rotor wash.

As they passed over the bridge and water tower, the roads below appeared packed with people. Thick black smoke could be seen rising from the burning gas stations along with strings of ominous yellow and green enemy tracer arcing toward the helicopters. A few minutes later – just before 0800hrs – Harrison, Gaffney, and the command group landed near Xuan Phong – followed a few minutes later by Schlax and Liebler.

The battle in Phan Thiet could clearly be heard as Alpha regrouped. Much to the amusement of Andy Daniel, Chris Adams doused his face with precious water in an attempt to flush fine particles of red dust from his eyes. As Chris blinked away his last droplets, a sniper took a potshot at Sergeant Bob Bell and hit him in the leg. After Bob was lifted out, Alpha cautiously began its approach to target, one kilometer away to the west. With Harrison and his men leading, Staff Sergeant Stacy Raynor's Third Squad were out front with Andy Daniel on point and Willie Pitts as slack. Each heavily loaded with 40 magazines, grenades, and 100 rounds of M60 link, the men were already soaked with perspiration.

Staff Sergeant Raynor was still settling in after being transferred from Third Platoon on January 5 to replace Joel Keefer. From his position on left point, Adams turned to check on Ronnie Ford. Joe Stephenson and James Philyaw were in trail and all nodded acknowledgment. Sergeant Harvey Mathis' squad held center while the rest of Raynor's guys – who now included Mike Trant – covered right. Mike's posting had come through the day before and he was over the moon to be working alongside his buddy Ford.

February 2 was also Phil Chassion's first mission with Alpha since taking over as first sergeant. Instructed to act as Phil's RTO/ liaison for the operation, Ray Mayfield found him surprisingly uncommunicative and surly. But "Chass" was a quiet kind of leader and not always easy to read. Every building and hut was carefully checked with a soft entry, but unsurprisingly most by now had been abandoned. Progress was slow and against protocols, "Chass" decided to drag Mayfield away from Company Headquarters forward between platoons.

Crossing over a dusty track, an old lady surprised everyone when she stepped out of a mud-walled shack, squatted, and began to urinate. Mike Trant looked on and wondered just what the fuck she must have been thinking. Soon, larger properties began to appear, mainly of a 1940s stuccoed style solidly constructed by the French. At this point, Lieutenant Harrison decided to change from Gaffney's original approach plan and dropped down into the Song Ba Thien riverbed. Lined by tall hedges and trees, the dry creek meandered west and afforded a far safer approach than any of the surrounding cart tracks or roads. As the company began to close, Captain Gaffney ordered a change of formation. However, it was almost impossible for Alpha to remain formatted as Harrison navigated his way through the dense undergrowth. But this turned out to be a blessing and when Second Platoon again changed course, it confused the waiting enemy.

Anticipating a more obvious approach, the 482nd VC had sited a large number of bunkers in a right-angle pattern along two cart tracks. Approaching a line of trees that obscured him from view, Harrison emerged between two houses before hinging right through 90 degrees into a deep ditch.

Using the dry streambed, Ford, Philyaw, and Adams continued forward as far as they could go without breaking cover. John Harrison and Sergeant Raynor quickly found themselves facing the rear of a single-storey gabled shack set onto a solid base. The concrete structure sat within a 4ft-high barbed-wire enclosure in the shadow of a thick bushy tree. As the men approached, they noted what appeared to be a lean-to built onto the back. Oddly, there were several large piles of soil around, indicating recent excavation. Over to John's right lay 100m of "open" ground sloping gently up toward a beautiful, whitewashed, stucco, upmarket-looking colonial property originally built by a wealthy rubber plantation owner. The guys were puzzled by heavy iron bars that blocked each shuttered window.

Halfway up the bleached grassy slope was a second barbed-wire fence partially hidden beneath a vine-covered hedge. Between these two fences was a raised base from an earlier building and beyond that a large pigpen adjoined to the house, which was owned by the Van Ta family. Mr. Tran Van Ta was headmaster of a nearby school where 482nd VC had their main headquarters.

Captain Gaffney asked the company to hold while he figured out his next move. With Second Platoon now out of sight, Jim Schlax swung his men into a defensive line and waited. Mayfield and Chassion were only a short distance behind Harrison when movement in the ditch stopped. After listening to Gaffney's last radio message, without saying a word, "Chass" got up and impatiently walked toward the rear of the house. Ray looked on quizzically as "Chass" straddled the wire fence and continued toward a large haystack. Following along behind, Ray inquired if Phil had checked out a nearby cattleshed. Saying nothing, "Chass" struck out and disappeared behind the property. Under the cool shade of a banana tree, Ray waited patiently by the stack expecting Phil to return.

Lieutenant Harrison and his point team were cautiously approaching the shack. Corporal Francis Edwards' M60 squad were back in the ditch with the rest of the platoon – watching and waiting. When nothing seemed to be happening, one of the new guys, Ed Blanco, left Edwards and moved up for a closer view. He was surprised to see a nervous-looking Vietnamese man stripped to the waist and wearing pants that were far too big for him. "AJ" Daniel had stopped the individual, who at that moment appeared to be in the process of frantically changing clothes. Sergeant George Schultz was standing next to "AJ" muttering that something did not seem right. But the man – along with his wife, two kids, and disabled mother – nervously argued they were refugees. Hal Dobie interrupted the "interrogation" with a radio report from Dave Stiles, who was at the other end of the ditch with Jim Bunn and medic

John Melgaard. Stiles stated that a random US ammunition box had just been spotted and they were moving across to investigate.

While they were waiting, Raynor told his squad to grab a quick bite to eat. Chris Adams had just opened a can of peaches when Harrison called them forward. Still preoccupied with the Vietnamese couple, Harrison casually directed Daniel and Pitts toward the elevated four-pillared front entrance. At the same time, Raynor took Mike Trant and headed for the near side, intent on rendezvousing on the porch with "AJ" and Willie. Dodging past an old oxcart through a gap in the fence, Stacy and Mike reached the house and continued moving left.

Adams, Stephenson, Philyaw, and Harold Rodney followed on behind as Ron Ford made his way toward the courtyard and some heavily laden fruit trees. Harrison turned and asked Ford where the hell he thought they were going. With a cheeky grin, Ronnie told Harrison that he intended to set up "security" in the orchard and carried on walking. Still deep in stilted conversation with the Vietnamese family, Harrison had no time to argue, waved his hand, and left Ron to get on with it.

The fruit trees not only offered respite from the sweltering midday sun, but also something sweet to nibble on. Positioning the others along a hedgerow, Ron and Chris passed by the terracotta-and-white-tiled porch shortly before "AJ," Willie, and Stacy arrived at the pillared entrance. Raynor had deposited Mike Trant a few feet away on the corner to provide cover with Stephenson, who was now neatly tucked into the bushes opposite.

Ronnie lazily took a bite out of a juicy "star fruit" before looking around for somewhere comfortable to rest his aching back. Through gaps in the dense foliage, Ford could just make out the old cart track that ran behind the house back to Xuan Phong and Highway 8. With Gaffney's words still fresh in everyone's minds, Andy Daniel politely knocked on the louvered wooden doors and walked in. Just as Ron flexed to sit, the bucolic silence was shattered by a burst of automatic gunfire from inside. One by one, like falling dominoes, bunkers hidden along the cart track beyond Ford and Adams triggered into action.

Instantly, Ron and Chris swept up their gear and sprinted for their lives. As Sergeant Ford passed by the front door, Raynor and Pitts came crashing out. Everyone except for Adams converged on Trant, whereupon they realized that "AJ" had not made it off the porch. In a moment's hesitation, their point man had been shot in the thigh while bolting for the exit. Willie had dropped his rifle in the struggle and to make matters worse, Mike was now on the verge of panic after a succession of stoppages seized his weapon.

Two hundred and fifty meters away, First Platoon came under ferocious fire from the bunker system's northern edge. Private Reg Jackson and "Mac" McDaniel were hit. As medic Mark Jones and rifleman John Matkin pulled "Mac" into a nearby outbuilding, they were targeted from some nearby trees by a sniper. While examining "Mac's" leg, Mark flinched every time a bullet whipped through the mud walls. Despite the growing gravity of their situation, "Mac" thought this was hilarious and said that if Jones did not stop dancing and start bandaging, he was going to bleed to death!

A few minutes earlier, Schlax had ordered his radio operator Guy Brooks to coordinate with Platoon Sergeant Tom Gentry, who was at the rear of the column. Jim was attempting to swing his guys around to face the enemy bunkers and needed Gentry's immediate assistance. But at that crucial moment, "Brooksie's" radio failed. Guy took it upon himself to leave Jim and crawled away through the long grass to personally relay his lieutenant's order. When Brooks thought it was safe, he stood and began to run along the column. The radio on his back made for an obvious target and within two seconds Guy was struck in the chest by a bullet. Doc Jones slithered out and frantically began working on his buddy's collapsed lung … but Guy died before Mark could relieve pressure.

Now unable to raise Schlax, Gaffney asked Harrison to send a runner. By then, Gentry had come across to Jim with his radio and together they managed to communicate their unstable situation back to Gaffney. Jim was told to clear out the snipers and await further orders. No doubt First Platoon's initial radio problems only added to the confusion and probably influenced Gaffney's later decision to call in B Co for support. Later, when the radio was repaired and returned to Schlax, Dennis Carbary volunteered to take "Brooksie's" place. Back in the rear, Third Platoon were completely removed from what was happening. "Jay" Eckhart was last man in Liebler's column and spent the day monitoring radio traffic while watching Alpha's rear.

DYING IN THE DIRT

From his haystack position, it quickly became clear to Ray Mayfield that heavy gunfire was coming from behind the house. Looking for better concealment, Ray crawled away from the straw into an old foxhole on the other side of the fence.

Meanwhile, Raynor and Ford were desperately trying to get "AJ" off the front porch. It was then that Trant decided to mention his rifle was not working properly. Not able to believe what he was hearing, Ron cleared the weapon several times but still it would not cycle. Snatching it back, Ron was frantically fiddling with the breech when Mike revealed it had been working OK on automatic! Through gritted teeth, Ronnie tossed the M16 back and hollered, "Then shoot the fucking thing on automatic!"

Sheepishly, Mike nodded and followed Ron as he crawled around the corner toward Andy. Then the shit really hit the fan as rounds poured into the courtyard from multiple directions. Although "AJ" was no more than ten or 12ft away, they felt the incredible weight of automatic gunfire directed toward them.

Andy was sitting on the top step leaning against a column, jungle fatigues soaked in blood. From below the louvered front windows, Ronnie screamed for Andy to roll down toward him. Ford shouted again and again, but seemingly ignorant of Ronnie's pleas, "AJ" took out his canteens and casually began to drink. Blood was now beginning to drip down the steps and within a minute, Andy stopped responding. Green tracer was bouncing off every surface when "AJ" got hit again. Ford realized that if he and Mike made it up onto that porch, the only thing that would be taken would be their lives. It was heartbreaking but they had absolutely no choice but to scuttle back and regroup.

As Ron and Mike returned to their colleagues, they came under fire from the garden. With his M16 locked on full auto, Mike let rip at a small well house and heard John Harrison shout, "Our guys are in there – stop shooting, what the hell's wrong with you?!" With a *For fuck's sake* look on their faces, Ronnie and Mike felt helpless as they tried to figure out what to do next. The well was protecting Chris Adams, Philyaw, Rodney, Craig, and several others. A few minutes earlier, Chris ran for Harrison but the green tracer forced him to divert.

Trying to crawl toward Harrison, Mike, Ron, Stacy, and Joe Stephenson were turned back by enemy fire coming from inside the Van Ta house. After weighing up their options, they decided to skirt around the pigpen and into a nearby cattle shed. In a ditch behind the gabled shack, John's radio operator Hal Dobie nudged his boss and pointed up at the trees disintegrating above their heads. But this particular heavy-caliber green tracer seemed to be coming from a house overlooking the rice paddy directly behind them. Up until that moment, John had not paid much attention to the property that was clearly fortified with more enemy bunkers.

Miraculously, the solid garden shack sat in relatively dead ground protected from enemy fire. From here, Harrison decided to establish a CP and began to reorganize his immediate assets such as M60, M79, and LAW. The young platoon leader was half-expecting the enemy to withdraw as they had done before with C Co at the Knoll, but this felt different.

With explosions all around and sweat seeping into his eyes, Harrison tried to remain calm. Using every available 66mm light anti-tank rocket and thumper round, John tried and failed to breach a hole through the side of the Van Ta house. But at least his rockets and grenades kept people away from the windows. A door near the pigpen began to make more sense to John as a potential point of entry. Harrison and Bunn followed the ditch around to where Raynor and Ford were still sheltering. The dry watercourse made a perfect conduit as it conveniently connected into the main channel and skirted back to Harrison's CP. Unaware of the "natural trench system," when Raynor's men heard the lieutenant calling they immediately began to make their way across.

Harrison and Bunn had worked out that they could use the shed to stage for an organized assault. The lieutenant ordered Bunn and Stiles to take Raynor's team back and do whatever it took to get inside. Once in, they were to fight their way through to reach "AJ." Leaving Harrison, they crawled back to the shed. Jim Bunn knew Stacy and Ron would follow him without question and quickly outlined that they were going to move out in pairs at five-second intervals. After a quick kit check and confirmation, Bunn and Raynor stepped out into the unknown.

WOUNDS THAT NEVER HEAL

Over by the CP, Corporal Edwards heard Vietnamese voices coming from the lean-to. When battle commenced, the refugee family had vanished down into a shelter. With everything that had happened in the opening moments, crucially nobody noticed where they had gone. Unaware that they were hiding inside, Edwards ran over and fired into the opening, tragically killing the young couple and one of their children. The other son escaped unharmed but his blind and deaf grandmother was not so lucky. With the palm of her hand and several fingers missing, the old lady was in a terrible state. As he wrapped the mangled mass in a field dressing, Eddie Blanco could not believe what Francis had just done.

Ray Mayfield was still monitoring radio traffic while waiting for Chassion when Jim Bunn suddenly appeared in front of him. In that instant of recognition, Bunn was shot in the chest and fell, whereupon he was immediately struck again. Everything happened so quickly that Ray had no time to react or see if the shots came from the house or a nearby sniper.

After hearing the gunfire and seeing Bunn go down, Ford was braced and getting ready to move when Trant grabbed hold of his collar. Mike dragged Ron back as Raynor came diving through the door shouting it would be suicide to continue. Stacy got on the radio with Harrison, who immediately requested they return to his

CP. It was only as the adrenaline began to dip that Ronnie realized what Trant had just done. Mike shrugged, looked at his watch, and noted it had been less than ten minutes since "AJ" was hit – it was his first day back in the field and the previous problems with Norris no longer seemed such a big deal. But enemy fire began to build and the guys soon found themselves pinned down and unable to move in any direction.

Harrison was trying to raise Stiles when Mayfield cut in and told him that he had his eyes on Bunn, who was not moving. John knew it had been a mistake to let his platoon sergeant lead the assault and another not to have immediately appointed a replacement, but it was way more complicated than that. Consequently, evacuation of casualties and re-supply was initially overlooked while Harrison focused on neutralizing all enemy bunkers.

TWENTY MINUTES TO LIVE

The cattle shed was raked from south and west with crossfire. Again, luckily most of the bullets were high but everyone did their best to dig scrapes into the compacted dirt floor. Thankfully, that extra five inches was just enough to keep Ron and Mike alive. Earlier over by the CP, a bullet had torn a chunk out of Stiles' helmet. Luckily, Dave was unharmed but kept grabbing at his head and then looking disbelievingly into his hands. Ron and Mike were opposite him in the shed lying nose to nose, and found this odd behavior hysterical. As they lay laughing absurdly, several insurgents tried approaching from the house but Joe Stephenson held them off through a small gap in the wall.

Lieutenant Harrison received word that satchel charges and rockets were now on their way from Third Platoon. Beyond the front porch, about 200m away, John noticed more muzzle flashes from another line of bunkers coming from what turned out to be the local girls' elementary school. Fearing an RPG attack from the Van Ta house, John instructed Blanco and his gun team to cover one half of the property from a large window inside his CP. While Francis Edwards made ready, Blanco dragged across a black lacquered table to support their gun. Cradling his M60, Emmett Clark, followed by ammo carrier Laris Sutton, came running through a side door. The pair landed on a full grain bin positioned directly underneath a smaller window where they could overlap with Edwards and Blanco.

Badly wounded, George Schultz was struggling to move as Chris Adams crawled out under fire toward him. A nearby oxcart was being systematically ripped apart by gunfire as Chris took hold of Schultz's 782 gear. Every pull on the webstraps brought excruciating screams through George's blood-clenched teeth. It was tough on Chris, who was only small, but he quickly relinquished grip as Dennis Craig and Doc Melgaard took over. Craig and Melgaard dragged Schultz across to the CP as it began to receive more accurate enemy fire. Once inside, Melgaard patched Schultz's sucking chest wound and managed to get the bleeding under control. As George's ammunition was being redistributed, against Melgaard's sage advice, he would not stop talking.

Ed Blanco brought in the elderly Vietnamese woman for more treatment. Melgaard did what he could and afterward led her confused and sobbing back to her underground hiding place. Carrying Schultz's rifle, Chris Adams made it back to Jim Philyaw at the well house. While Jim concentrated on lobbing thumper rounds, Chris and the others fired everything they could spare into the orchard and trees. Suddenly, an elderly man appeared carrying a white flag. After the shelter incident, Harrison ordered his guys to hold fire as the pensioner disappeared into the smoke. Mr. Ta's wife also made a successful break for safety but two of her cousins who were also inside at the time were not so lucky. One, a young woman, appeared on the porch and glanced down at "AJ" before falling mortally wounded.

DANGER CLOSE

The moment the first aircraft became available, Jim Pratz sprang into action to brilliantly coordinate Harrison's targets with his waiting pilots. Recommending approach and direction, Jim's marker rockets had only just begun to smoke over the cart track when the jets throttled up for their first attack run.

"Fat Cat" and "Mal Hombre" were overhead in their chopper trying to ensure that the airspace was now clear for incoming planes. Like Jim Schlax the month before, this was the first time Harrison had ever called in a full-on strike and he was understandably concerned. John's nerves quickly turned to anger as he told everyone to get off his "freak." The battalion net was now his and he alone would be making all further decisions. Win, lose, or draw, the headshed and Gaffney acquiesced and prayed their lieutenant was up to the task.

The enemy had to expose their positions in order to engage and fast air would be there to hammer them into dust. Before releasing smoke, John contacted Pratz to confirm color and his actual location. He then ordered everyone to prepare for impact as the first bombs fell beyond the Van Ta house. Cigarette in hand, Harrison was fighting back and now turned his full attention toward the enemy positions immediately behind him. Major Pratz calmly discussed what was needed and where. But here, due to the close proximity, more accurate "high-drag" ordnance was required. Pratz was so concerned about range that he issued a verbal warning to the jet jockeys. It was not easy to see and report each 750lb strike so John left the relative "safety" of his CP to spot. The last bomb was double "danger close" and scored a direct hit. Concussion caused John's nose and ears to bleed and the CP was peppered with debris.

As the F-4 Phantoms flew over at treetop height, Raynor and Ford marked their position with smoke. Even at 400mph, the jets were taking enemy anti-aircraft fire but still kept coming. Everything continued to shake as rubble came cascading through the bamboo roof onto Ford and the others trapped inside. Ronnie told Stiles to confirm their position and smoke color to the "Bird Dog." Procedures like this were imperative to keep the VC from deploying the same color of smoke. But things would have to get worse before they could get better. John Harrison knew that if he tried to flank the house then there was a good chance his platoon would be annihilated. More aircraft were needed, so Harrison and Pratz began stealing assets from the Navy and Marines. Over the next two hours, dozens of Phantoms and F-100 Super Sabres pounded targets south and west.

About 350m away, across the big paddy, were more houses and huts. Harrison had the fast jets take them out one at a time and when they were no longer available brought in the Tiger Sharks. The 105mm guns were only just coming on line under control of new super professional Forward Observer Bob Richardson.

John loosed off with a LAW and silenced an enemy machine gun firing from across the paddy. Moments later, a figure was seen running from the property and Harrison ordered Sergeant Charlie Hayes to take him out. Suddenly, a young woman came into view and Hayes looked toward Harrison for permission to shoot but John held back. Picking up the dead man's weapon, the girl ran back inside. Cursing, John got on the radio and called Pratz, and a few minutes later the Phantoms came back and bombed the house.

Ronnie, Mike, and the others were now in the ditch and making their way around to where Adams, Philyaw, and the rest of the platoon were waiting. Along the way, David Stiles happened to spot Ray Mayfield and stopped to speak with him. When Ray explained that he thought Bunn was dead, in a futile act of contrition, Dave became angry and lobbed his last remaining grenade at the Van Ta house.

Mike Trant got spooked and briefly found cover inside another outbuilding. When Mike made his way back to the platoon, he found Harrison chewing Ford out for walking away earlier. Sporadic gunfire was still emanating from the Van Ta property and more surprisingly from the bunkers beyond. John's words were cut short by a heavy burst from Edwards and Blanco, who had seen VC firing from a second-floor window. Harrison was about to learn one more valuable lesson when he ordered up napalm in a final attempt to finish the bunkers.

Two jets came racing across the paddy and released their canisters. One of the high-speed strikes flared off across the front yard, splashing Andy Daniel with un-burnt jellied gasoline. The oxygen vanished from the surrounding air as ignition took place behind the house. The heat generated was so intense that it actually scorched the faces of those not quick enough to look away! With most of the visible enemy bunkers now neutralized, Major Pratz and Bob Mairs agreed to divert aircraft returning from other missions. Eventually, Doc Melgaard got the all-clear from Gaffney to evacuate Schultz. With help from sergeants Arthur Henry, Gary Gressett, Larry Rincon, and Ulysses Pulley, George was carried to a PZ in the rear. After waving goodbye, the men had not gone far when they were surprised by a hidden enemy machine gun. In that moment, Henry, Gressett, and Rincon were all hit.

With a little help from Mark Jones, Melgaard treated the injured NCOs before assisting them to safety. Gary Gressett had taken a bullet in the hip and as he waited for the next medivac, Captain Gaffney came over and inquired how successful he thought Harrison's air strikes had been.

A detail from Third Platoon led by Ed Bassista was working hard relaying rockets, ammunition, and water. Chris Adams and Dennis Craig were now part of a re-supply group shuttling back and forth from the battle when they heard Corporal Roland Barbosa and Clyde Schaffer calling to them from the bushes above. While the gear was being collected, the boys were able to exchange quick updates regarding their respective platoons.

FOREVER BROTHERS

Although Andy Daniel was now lying on his back, everyone thought he could still be alive. In an earlier attempt to reach "AJ," Harrison's left ear had been creased and the three-pronged flash eliminator torn from his rifle. Raynor took a headcount before John ordered him to take his squad and try again. Everyone was terrified by the prospect of charging across open ground. Thankfully, Stacy could not levy the same obedience as Bunn and when he gave the order to "advance," Ron Ford and the boys stayed where they were. Losing patience, Harrison – perhaps more through tunnel vision than anything else – personally took control. As the thumpers and machine guns began laying down fire, in a bizarre moment of inner calm, Ford turned, put his lips to Mike's ear, and said, "It was nice knowing you, buddy," to which Michael reciprocated, "I can't wait till we're back on Rush Street getting drunk and laughing about this day – you know I love you, man." As Harrison was about to give his command, Mike remembered the hedge directly in front was threaded with barbed wire. Trant screamed out several warnings to Harrison, who after a brief but agonizing pause called off his assault with a resonating, "STOP!" Relief was tangible and for a moment everyone withdrew from the world, looked up, and gave thanks to Trant. A few minutes later, just as the sun was going down, Jim Kessinger and his platoon arrived.

Bill Landgraf never actually made it to Harrison, after being pinned down for several hours by mortar and B40 rocket fire. When Doc Melgaard returned to the CP after evacuating Schultz, he found Emmett Clark sitting against a back wall awaiting treatment. A blast from an enemy projectile had come through the window, forcing dirt into Clark's face and temporarily blinding him. By early evening, the order came from Gaffney to withdraw. Not convinced that Bunn, "Chass," and "AJ" were actually dead, Harrison was loath to leave and forced to comply.

WE'RE NOT DONE YET

When Captain Gaffney asked Harrison for a full debrief, he looked like a zombie with a thick crust of dried blood around eyes, ears, and neck. Tom listened intently and every now and then sympathetically interjected with a soft, reassuring comment. John told Tom that as soon as his platoon had settled into a dual perimeter with B Co then he was going back. He did not ask, he did not suggest, but told the captain of his intention to recover those left behind. Supporting the decision, Gaffney asked Third Platoon for volunteers but with one caveat – that all squad leaders and married men would be excluded. Everyone unanimously elected to go but only a handful – including Joe Klempin, Tom Paulson, Ray Bennett, Ron Gehr, and French-Canadian Paul Clement – met the criteria. First Platoon also contributed a few volunteers, including John Matkin. But Harrison's first priority was to lead Bob Richardson onto high ground and point out all specific areas in and around the property that he wanted targeted on command.

Harrison whittled numbers down to around 20 but left Hal Dobie out in favor of carrying the radio himself. Among others chosen from Second Platoon were Chris Adams, Laris Sutton, Dennis Craig, Doc Melgaard, and Ron Ford, who was to be John's assistant. Ronnie's biggest worry was that if something should happen to Harrison, would or could he be man enough to step up and take control? Ronnie was beyond disappointed when he found out that Ed Bassista had been among those precluded. Having Ed by his side would have meant everything, but Gaffney had spoken and that was all there was to it.

Ray Mayfield went along simply because he knew the easiest route to Bunn and rough whereabouts of Chassion. An initial plan was agreed that once on site, one man would go out with Ray to check before dragging each body back to "safety." In light order, the guys drew basic load and after checking noise discipline headed off in single file.

Under ambient half moon, it did not take long for Harrison to locate and follow the riverbed back around to his shack CP. Apart from rustling banana leaves, the Van Ta house seemed relatively quiet. However, silhouettes could be seen further south moving around the paddies. A heavy smell of cordite and unburned napalm still permeated as Harrison sent Adams and a couple of others out to ensure flank security. Together with another trooper, Mayfield began moving on Andy Daniel, whose left leg was dangling over the porch steps. After checking for booby traps, they carefully pulled "AJ's" body down and dragged it back to the CP. Imbued with confidence, the two men retraced their steps to get Bunn. A sweet smell of incense wafted out as Ray passed underneath each barred window. Bunn was up ahead still lying in the same position. Within a stone's throw of the body, Mayfield suddenly heard voices coming from behind a door and froze. Slowly, they turned around and with hearts pounding, made their way back to the courtyard, where Harrison instructed Sergeant Joe Klempin to assist. After a quick whispered discussion, Mayfield decided to follow the same approach route he had walked earlier with Chassion.

Vietnamese voices were still audible as Klempin climbed over the fence and crawled across to Bunn. Covered by the others, Joe carried out a thorough fingertip search before crossing Jim's legs and easing him over. It was no easy job to get Bunn's body across the barbed wire, but once free of encumbrance, Joe manhandled him into the nearby ditch.

The guys returned and found "Chass" entangled in another obstacle not far from where Ray had last seen him. Just like before, Klempin checked and recovered the body while his two colleagues stood watch. The barbed wire sprang noisily back and forth as Joe worked to dislodge Phil's lifeless corpse. Once all three were confirmed deceased, Harrison pulled in security, did a quick headcount, and began extraction. John had pre-assigned six men to each trooper and hauling them without body bags was going to be difficult. Supporting head, torso, and legs, three crossed rifles were employed to carry each man. As Ronnie and Paul Clement turned "AJ" onto his front, a heavy metallic taste of coagulated blood filled their nostrils and mouths.

Quickly, the men came under what appeared to be targeted enemy mortar fire. Protected by an embankment, the chunks of shrapnel span harmlessly overhead. As per his previously arranged fire-plan, Richardson brought a powerful barrage of artillery onto the house. Picking up pace, Ron could feel "AJ's" head bouncing along the ground and began murmuring a mantra of heartfelt apologies to his dead amigo.

Thick cloud began to cover the moon and as Harrison became disoriented, he called Gaffney and requested three tracer rounds be fired into the air. Tom did not object and 20 seconds later, a trio of shots burned brightly from the Alpha perimeter. Taking a quick prismatic heading, with Spooky now circling overhead, Harrison's final approach toward safety was scary and tense. It was 15 minutes to midnight and the long, hard, violent day was thankfully drawing to a close. Approaching B Company, Joe Jerviss walked out to greet them. Joe wanted to help carry "AJ," with whom he had played basketball at Fort Campbell, but Ron Ford angrily warned him off. Three dead and eight wounded had left everyone exhausted and Ronnie later apologized to "Pineapple" for what he had said.

Although George Schultz made it to a hospital in Japan, he died three weeks later from acute infection. John Harrison, Doc Melgaard, and Ray Mayfield were all subsequently awarded Silver Stars by General Barsanti for their contributions. However, without Harrison's incredible management, no doubt these would all have been posthumous.

Chapter 13

"Into the Sunrise"

February 3–5, 1968

Major Houston Houser previously ordered "Paladin's" Quick Reaction Force into Phan Thiet. Three hours later, one of Mike's junior NCOs returned to Betty and broke the news about Philip Chassion's death. "Paladin" was heartbroken and it would be another three days before he summoned the courage needed to write Phil's widow Joyce back home in Clarksville.

Wrapped in ponchos, the dead were lined up awaiting collection as a lone supply chopper approached. Standing over Andy's body in the early morning sun, Ron Ford was suddenly overcome by a deepening sense of guilt. Did he do enough? Could he have shown more courage? These thoughts were still swirling as the young fire team leader helped load his friend onto the helicopter. Survival is ten percent knowledge and 90 percent luck, and Ron now began to wonder when it would be his turn. Andy had a huge impact on Ron and Chris Adams, but only time would quell those unanswered questions. Joe Jerviss felt the need to come forward and help move Jim Bunn. Placing a hand on Jim's chest, he whispered that they would meet again before carefully placing him next to Andy and "Chass."

Alpha was still maintaining its section of perimeter when gunfire erupted from a distant tree line. Jerviss was in the process of burning trash after the "arrow" re-supply when a bullet struck his heel. As "Mal Hombre" was still on the ground, Joe was flown out in the C&C for treatment. Miraculously, it was only a light flesh wound and less than two hours later, "Pineapple" was on his way back.

The guys from Bravo who were over on the northern perimeter traded shots as Alpha stood to. John Harrison thought to hell with the VC and elected to wait until his hot chocolate had boiled. A few minutes later, John actually began to feel sorry for the attackers because he knew Gaffney was on the radio dialing up a shit storm. Sure enough, the Tiger Shark pilots followed fast air with their own crazy ballet of destruction as the perpetrators were blown to shreds.

By 0900hrs, Alpha dragged itself back to the battle area. As they aggressively searched, the excessive number of fortifications became more apparent. Unlike the day before, all properties left standing were deemed "hard" entries and posed a different sort of danger for each team. Harrison's platoon flowed forward in open column with point, slack, and entry group in the center. In quick succession, the obstacles were cleared as John rolled through with ruthless efficiency.

Calls from a "Kit Carson" interpreter for anyone still inside the Van Ta house were met with eerie silence. Two water bottles belonging to "AJ" were still on the porch as John ordered Jim Philyaw to launch a thumper round through the nearest window. Jim's projectile struck one of the metal bars and exploded, injuring him, Laris Sutton, and the lieutenant. Earlier, Harrison narrowly escaped after shrapnel from another ricochet bounced off his thigh. This time, a small chunk had penetrated John's left bicep, rendering his arm useless. Being left-handed and therefore no longer able to operate his rifle, John discussed options with Doc Melgaard but flatly refused evacuation. Gaffney took further convincing but eventually agreed for him to remain on duty until evening.

When the entry team moved inside the Van Ta house, they found it empty and dark. Strands of sunlight radiated through damaged shutters, allowing some illumination. Chris Adams was drawn to a pair of chopsticks on the mantel over a fireplace.

A few minutes later, as they were leaving, Chris stooped to pick up an identity card by the front door. The encapsulated document belonged to 71-year-old South Vietnamese man Nguyen Bon. His address was a hamlet where the 482nd VC had begun their first attack on the city. Chris wondered if Nguyen had been the individual who left under a white flag during the battle. With the house clear, someone brought up a potplant and left it in mute tribute on the spot where "AJ" had died.

To deny the Americans a body count, the two reinforced VC companies had already recovered most of their dead. It transpired that the bunkers situated across the other side of the rice paddy were created as a secondary ambush site directed at any relief force that might have flown in to assist. When inspected further, the "shelter" at Harrison's CP was found to be a tunnel that linked into the trees behind. Once the area was declared secure, "Mal Hombre" returned with General Rosson. Harrison and Gaffney brought him up to speed while "Fat Cat" surveyed and sketched the area. The major used his drawings to debrief Rosson, who struggled to comprehend orientation or salient terrain features. Before packing up, Staff Sergeant Fellmann from Third Platoon was appointed as Harrison's new platoon sergeant.

WHEN CAN WE SLEEP?

Back at Betty, members of Charlie Company unloaded "Chass," Bunn, "AJ," and "Brooksie" from the helicopter. Placed in bags, all four bodies were then stored temporarily in the "death tent." Doc Lovy was still in surgery when General Rosson flew in to check on the wounded. Rosson entered the clearing station and a few minutes later demanded to know who was in charge. Having been working all night, Lovy was in no mood for a visit or for his "no gun" rule to be flouted. When the general refused to remove his sidearm, Andy abruptly explained his breach of protocol. Annoyed by Andy's tone, Rosson walked toward the drape that served as a partition to the death tent. Although obscured from view, Andy politely refused Rosson's demands that the bodies be removed. The general continued to argue and brushing his comments aside, Andy muttered, "Sir, those souls will be taken care of the second we have finished with the living!" The head of II Corps continued to push for satisfaction while Andy juggled multiple procedures. "Sir, with all due respect, I knew all of those men personally and they will be dealt with in the appropriate way as soon as we are able." The general grew angry and bellowed, "Son, I am giving you a direct order, so take those troopers to the morgue NOW."

Stepping away from his patient and quite within his rights, Andy ordered two MPs who were stood outside to come in and physically remove Rosson. As they ushered the spluttering commander outside, Andy added, "Oh, and shoot him please if he makes any attempt to come back in!" After surgery, Andy personally washed and identified each soldier before they were transported to the refrigerated facility next to Battalion HQ.

By mid-afternoon, Alpha and Bravo returned to the highway and patrolled slowly south beyond Trinh Tuong Camp. Reaching the recently wrecked ARVN artillery compound, they turned west along the railtracks to Ap Dai Tai – where Gaffney and Landgraf set up a defensive perimeter for the night. Bolstered by two Local Force companies, the remaining VC had withdrawn south to the soccer ground. Despite their costly and unsuccessful attacks against government Army bases, the 482nd had still managed to gain several isolated footholds. On a dawn low tide, they crossed onto Phan Thiet's northern bank to strike out at Trinh Toung, Dinh Cong, and the business sector. Two hours later, another enemy platoon forded to attack and capture the main police station and administration block. Continuing toward the Anh Dao Hotel, the 482nd ran into unexpectedly strong resistance from MACV, whose offices were nearby.

Spearheaded by APCs, the 44th ARVN Regimental Task Force finally came around to launching its own attack. The primary target was the sports field where heavy overnight clashes had already been taking place. Afterward, the dead were collected and laid out on the pitch in long rows. Meanwhile, a Civilian Irregular Defense Group

(CIDG) from Loung Son, National Police, Mobile Strike Force Command, known as "Mike Force," and 127th Regional Force Company were moving in to clear the city center.

Despite this pincer movement, many VC managed to escape back across the river and disappeared into Disneyland. Intelligence received from prisoners gave away the 840th MF Battalion as they prepared to withdraw northeast toward Le Hong Phong Forest. Subsequently, the Navy was able to target and inflict severe damage on the 840th as they retreated.

A DIFFERENT ENEMY

Meanwhile, several civilian Chinese Nationalist medical teams from Taiwan had been working tirelessly at the city hospital. As a non-communist state, Taiwan was against Ho Chi Minh and consequently pledged support to South Vietnam. After the 482nd began to threaten the hospital, one of the Taiwanese doctors made his way to Betty. Here, he explained to Andy Lovy that the VC had murdered staff and patients alike and he was now in desperate need of assistance.

"Mal Hombre" immediately granted Andy permission to take two trucks carrying medical supplies and water along with eight medics and a small security detachment. So far, Southern Phan Thiet had seen very little fighting; however, beyond the Nguyan Hoang Bridge, detritus of battle lay scattered everywhere. A passing Special Forces officer confirmed with Lovy that government troops had just cleared the hospital and it was safe for them to enter.

Upon arrival, Lovy's team were immediately swamped by the overflowing humanitarian emergency. Dozens of staff members quickly came out of hiding and began to make themselves known. One exhausted anesthetist joined Andy and Curt on a surgical ward. Two-and-a-half hours later, after one amputation and ten surgeries, the next patient had multiple penetrating shrapnel wounds to his abdomen.

A bowel resection was something new to Andy and as he concentrated his thoughts, the anesthetist calmly mentioned that there was trouble outside. Just as the firing started, one of the Taiwanese surgeons arrived and took over the delicate procedure.

Before his radio stopped working, a member of the security team had managed to send a distress message back to Betty. Meanwhile, part-timers from Loung Son CIDG who were over at Provincial Headquarters kindly diverted some of their men to protect the hospital. A two-man relief force was now on its way in a jeep mounted with a 106mm recoilless rifle. When Harrison Cox and Cliff Darmer crossed the bridge, they were immediately flagged down by MACV and temporarily redirected to engage a nearby enemy stronghold. When eventually Sergeant Cox walked into the hospital's main entrance, everyone cheered and headed for the trucks. But due to ongoing air strikes, it would be another ten minutes before they were actually able to make good their escape.

Swamped with over 500 casualties, two surgeons from the nearby ARVN military hospital also put in a request for assistance. Andy and Pat McMann answered their call and alternated in surgery for over six hours. It was immediately clear that a North Vietnamese Army officer with pus pouring from multiple abdominal punctures needed urgent intervention. With everything he had learned from the Taiwanese, Andy successfully managed to carry out his second OJT life-saving bowel resection. Conversely, a few days later, when the Viet Cong attacked, they showed no mercy to any of the helpless South Vietnamese patients.

After being held downtown, an influx of wounded insurgents began appearing at the clearing station. Despite what had been done to the ARVN patients, Lovy and the other doctors remained impartial and treated everyone, VC or otherwise, with equal compassion and care.

When C Company returned from babysitting the Rome Plows, Mike Stuart was sent to Lovy for tests. As the company prepared for deployment into Disneyland, Virgil Craft refused Stuart's request to go back into the field. A few days later, against his wishes, Mike was on his way home.

THIS IS 3-3 WAIT – OUT

That evening, with no immediate alert status to speak of, some of the Alpha guys were allowed to visit the enlisted club for drinks. The tented facility served cans of beer at 25 cents from a wood-paneled bar. After sunset, "Jay" Eckhart wandered over and found Bob Hill sitting alone at a small table. Drink in hand, "Jay" sat and began to speculate about the latest news. Confident and funny, Bob hailed from Casper, Wyoming where his old man owned a bar called "The Alibi Lounge." Being interested in rodeo, of course Bob's nickname was "Cowboy." When Hill's squad mate "Pete" Knight showed up, he immediately launched into a rant about his new assignment to Staff Sergeant Carl Yoshida as radio operator. "Pete" thought the merger between Third and Fourth platoons was totally "unsat" and undermined morale, especially for guys like him who were not part of John Gfeller's clicky inner circle. Lean, lanky, and outgoing, "Pete" from Michigan could be assertively outspoken but always hated being contradicted by "Jay." Both kids were certain that they knew everything. Of course, "Jay's" more "scientific knowledge" pissed a lot of people off, but unfortunately nothing Knight ever said was based on accuracy – at least not from "Jay's" understanding. As "Pete" paused for breath, "Jay" offered a neutral opinion, but "Pete" went off like a firecracker, thrusting his finger into Eckhart's face and shouting, "Peabody, if you utter another fucking word, I'm gonna beat you into a small box!" With that, "Jay" got up, shook his head, and walked out. Those few choice angry expletives ironically turned out to be the last "Jay" ever heard from "Pete."

Ronnie Ford and Chris Adams were walking back and close to Battalion Headquarters when a truck trundled past transporting a group of rear-echelon types. Looking over the tailgate, the men shouted abuse that Ronnie was simply not prepared to take. As the vehicle slowed to avoid a pothole, Ron spat, "Let's get those leg fucks," and charged off. As he clambered into the back, Ford began punching and then suddenly realized he was on his own! One guy went down and as another came in hard, Ronnie caught him under the chin. The powerful uppercut launched the man head first over the rail. At that point, Ron jumped down, saw the guy was unconscious, and ran back to Chris demanding to know why they had not joined him.

Immediately, Ford went to see John Harrison and explained what had happened. The battalion closed ranks as a CID team arrived to investigate. Although the victim had suffered a severe head injury, thankfully he was stable in hospital. Naturally, Lieutenant Harrison was sympathetic to the circumstances. Unable to join the dots, the CID left empty-handed. Harrison could be arrogant at times but he always made damn sure his boys were looked after and they respected him for that.

Exhausted and sleep-deprived, Bob Mairs flew up to Nha Trang in hope of obtaining permission for a special localized B-52 strike. He wanted this mission to go in west of Phan Thiet, along ingress routes now being used by the NVA. Stinking of sweat and looking like a bum, Bob literally had to fight his way into First Field Force Headquarters. However, even though they were relatively accepting of his idea, the pristinely dressed senior staff still had to get permission from Province Chief Lieutenant Colonel Nguyen Khac Tuan.

After the initial meeting, not one person bothered to offer Bob a shower or somewhere to sleep. Luckily, a friend in Special Forces stepped up and got him sorted out. The following morning, Tuan and his deputy, Major Tran Van Cha, who had led the initial ARVN relief force on Trinh Truong Camp, denied the request. The Vietnamese said that a strike like this would endanger their ancient city but "Fat Cat" suspected there were probably more conspiring factors sympathetic to the enemy behind their decision.

Chapter 14

"Death Patrol to Disneyland"

The Battle of Phu Bon and Beyond – February 6, 1968

Over the previous two days, Charlie Company had experienced only light contact during their Disneyland deployment. After breakfast, A and C companies were gathering in preparation for the next helicopter assault. Alpha flew out ahead of Charlie in staggered slicks across the river. By 0930hrs, both companies and a platoon of ARVN were set down two kilometers northwest of the Van Ta house ready for another Search and Destroy.

The mini task force patrolled south, stopping shortly before midday. One hour later, as their government troops continued south, Gaffney and Alitz screened eastward either side of the railway embankment. During February, it was rare to advance through any remote settlement where inhabitants were still present. Gunfire erupted up ahead as the ARVN came under fire from a cemetery near the tiny hamlet of Phu Bon. Out there, most burials were above ground and these large mounds made for superb defensive obstacles.

Captain Alitz ordered a quick right turn and skirted around the village. "Bucky" Cox was now leading Fourth Platoon and drifted across the tracks onto point. After the Knoll, "Bucky" had handed over control of his beloved "Third" to Milton Menjivar from B Co. "RA" Williams was still by "Bucky's" side and as they shared a joke, the platoon began drawing fire from a nearby banana grove.

Bullets followed "Bucky" and "RA" as they threw themselves into the nearest ditch.

Under a blanket of covering fire, everyone was able to scramble safely into cover. There was some debate as to which direction the shots had come from! For a few seconds, "Bucky" argued with his squad leaders before "RA" drew attention to the plumes of dirt kicking up behind them. After several successful barrages from Forward Observer John Barber, by mid-afternoon "Bucky" had managed to safely extricate his men and rejoin the company. Moving into Phu Bon, Captain Alitz ordered the ARVN up onto point. Until now, the battalion had not worked this closely with any government troops. The South Vietnamese had not been gone long when things started to heat up. Moments later, unwilling to fight, they came running back "di-di," fast-dragging their wounded.

Unaware that two companies of VC were lying in wait, Fourth Platoon sucked it up and advanced toward the gunfire. Cox immediately delivered a situation report to Alitz as Platoon Sergeant Carl Thanheiser, known to all as "Terrible T," crawled toward their wounded point man. As firing increased, "Bucky" sought cover in a nearby grove, but soon began taking shots from inside the plantation. One gunner came rushing forward and hit the ground, convulsing for air. It looked to Cox like the kid had been hit but thankfully it was only a sucker punch from the heavy stock. Suddenly, "RA's" radio antenna shattered. As they broke in different directions, splinters of wood peppered across Cox's right arm. With "RA's" radio temporarily down, Captain Alitz sent Mike Krawczyk across for a situation report.

With Cleo Delong away in Taipei, the communications team was already short-handed. Leaving his radio, Mike took a deep breath, crawled over the bank, and began to work his way toward "Bucky." The volume of rocket and gunfire became so intense that Mike could reach no further than the edge of a dry riverbed. As Krawczyk pulled the pin from one of his grenades, a nearby trooper mouthed the word "FRIENDLY." Mike apologetically acknowledged and carefully replaced the pin! Leaving chaos behind, Mike returned on his belly to Alitz, only to be told that radio communication had just been restored.

The worsening situation forced Alitz to send Menjivar's platoon to relieve pressure on "Bucky's" left flank. Paul Cline, Jeff Arthur, Bob Baldwin, and their squad were selected to lead. As Paul broke cover, a burst of machine-gun fire ripped through his legs and sent him sprawling across the dirt next to a large tree.

Although seriously wounded, Cline encouraged Arthur to drive home his assault. But as the men continued forward, they met with more automatic gunfire and rockets. As Baldwin turned for cover, an insurgent rose up and fired a B40 at point-blank range. From his position along the riverbed, Cox looked on in horror as Bob's severed head was thrown high into the air.

Cline's decimated squad were forced to withdraw, dragging Bob's decapitated body behind them. From that moment, C Co poured everything they had into the enemy bunkers. Several from Fourth Platoon were hit as they attempted to reach Paul, now being used as bait. Eventually, best buddy Frank Vinales grabbed a light armor weapon and bravely crawled out. At that moment, the weight of fire dramatically increased and as Frank launched his rocket, he was hit twice. Realizing their jeopardy, Paul grabbed Frank and rolled onto him like a human shield. Frank could feel bullets impacting into Cline's body as his friend's life ebbed away.

By now, the enemy had brought their heavy mortars into action. On Cox's specific instructions, John Barber slowly began to "walk in" his 105mm artillery rounds at 25m intervals toward the VC battery. Although he could not see where they were landing, Lieutenant Cox could feel the shells getting closer. Suddenly, another mortar barrage came raining in, wounding Jeff Arthur and several others. However, one of the 105s landed close to Company Headquarters and by some miracle did not explode. Captain Alitz immediately overruled Barber and in doing so allowed the enemy opportunity to adjust fire onto Alpha.

Assisted by an engineer, Mike Krawczyk decided to move the shell to a safer distance. Wrapping the warm warhead in a towel, Mike gingerly carried it across to an old farmhouse. Rigged with

C-4 and a one-minute fuse, they quickly retired back to the railway embankment but nothing happened. While walking back to reset, there was a blinding flash and the building vanished into a cloud of debris.

BOMB ALLEY

Shadowing C Company along the embankment, Len Liebler reached an isolated cluster of houses. Each property was surrounded by a small hedge and separated by paddies. Skirting around a bomb crater, Liebler headed for the house to his left while First Platoon moved toward another further ahead. Rounding the property, "Jay" Eckhart's squad was just about to come on line when Lenny ordered a halt. "Jay" knelt and waited patiently while the building was searched. Bemused, "Jay" watched some of Schlax's men about 50m away as they staggered their advance around a patch of open ground.

Out of nowhere came a deep "thump" and then someone shouted, "MORTARS!" The first shell struck about six feet away from Ralph Burdett. The blast wave pushed "Jay" over and when he sat up there were people running toward Burdett, Roland Barbosa, and several others. Burdett was worst hit and suffered a compound fracture to his right forearm along with deep penetrating shrapnel wounds to both thighs.

It was only then that an intense pain manifested in "Jay's" right armpit and crotch. Through shouts of "Spread out" and "Take cover," Eckhart went looking for medic "Joe" Ramos and found him sheltering in the bomb crater. "Jay" stripped off his shirt and dropped his pants. "Joe" examined what appeared to be two small puncture marks but after poking around with a Q-Tip, was unable to find even the minutist fragment of shrapnel.

Back in Phu Bon, as the first casualties were being brought in, Mike Krawczyk immediately called for medivac. Krawczyk and a couple of others ran over to the hovering chopper and started grabbing litters while fighting off the ARVN, who uninjured were frantically trying to clamber aboard. As the Huey settled onto the ground, it trapped Mike's foot under one of its skids. The RTO was stuck fast and desperately tried to convey his predicament to the confused crew chief. Eventually, after much hand gesturing and shouting, the Huey lifted just enough for Mike to pull free!

As Third Platoon withdrew, they brought Bob Baldwin's remains to the CP. It was a shocking sight, as not only was the head missing but also one arm and a shoulder. Returning to the CP, Mike Krawczyk looked on in disbelief at the twisted flesh and bone that had once been a human being. Mike quickly came to his senses as more wounded, including several senior NCOs and Lieutenant Arce, arrived for evacuation.

PREVENTITIVE MEDICINE

At the clearing station, senior medic Charles Martin received news that two of his guys were among the 17 casualties being flown in from Phu Bon. At the time, Tom Lundgren and Al Thompson (who was awaiting reassignment) were available and immediately volunteered to assist. Captain Alitz also asked for water and Al went across to their supply room. After a blazing argument with Bill Cook, Thompson eventually walked out with everything he wanted.

On the dust-off pad, M16s locked and loaded, Tom and Al waited nervously for the inbound chopper. A litter crew sprang into action, unloading the wounded as Tom and Al stepped aboard. On the LZ, multi-colored tracer arced overhead as the two medics waited by Doug Alitz's Command Post. After nightfall, a trooper led them to their assigned platoons. En route, they could clearly hear a nearby VC giving withdrawal orders in Vietnamese.

Upon reaching "Bucky" Cox, Tom was told to dig into the rock-hard ground. As Thompson continued on, Frank Vinales was crawling toward the perimeter. Not long after Frank made his way to safety, "Terrible T" took Lundgren and went out to find Lieutenant Menjivar, who had been wounded earlier. After Thompson discovered that his services were not actually needed, he bedded down in a ditch with a radioman and waited.

In the early hours, Captain Alitz asked "Bucky" to take some men and recover Paul Cline's body. After "Bucky" asked for volunteers "RA," Squad Leader Joe Vogel, "Terrible T," and a couple of others stepped forward. Cox only needed a small team, believing it would be easier to control should things get sticky. From his night defensive area north of the railway, Joe Alexander wished "Bucky" luck as they passed through. Every distant dog bark sent them into a cold sweat as they silently made their way toward the large tree. Once Cline was located, Cox and Sergeant Vogel crawled forward, carefully attached a rope, and pulled. Thankfully, there were no booby traps and the team safely made their way back to Alpha. Cline was one of the finest squad leaders Lieutenant Cox had ever worked with. Anger, sadness, and irony all flowed through "Bucky's" mind as he sat quietly with Paul's body on the canvas stretcher. Charming, funny, and fearless, Cline had been on borrowed time since he arrived in Vietnam and sadly his day had come.

Ed Bassista's squad collected Bob Baldwin and brought him back to Alpha for extraction. Bending toward the shoulders, "Jay" Eckhart almost vomited when he realized that there was nothing to grab hold of. At dawn, Mike Krawczyk was waiting at the PZ when he noticed Cline's bullet-riddled body next to Baldwin's. Peeling back the poncho, Mike knelt for one last look at his comrade. As Krawczyk stood, "Terrible T" limped over and gently replaced the cover. Without a word, they put Cline on the chopper, collected up their gear, and flew back to base.

At Betty, the decimated company was reorganized and placed into reserve. For his actions on February 6, 1968, Paul Cline was recommended for the Congressional Medal of Honor, although later downgraded to a Distinguished Service Cross. For risking his life trying to save Paul, Sergeant Vinales won a Silver Star, but the notification came as bittersweet. Before moving out, Alpha was raked from a nearby set of bunkers manned by Vietnamese Provincial Force. Gaffney was furious and threatened to add them to the 13 enemy bodies they had left behind at Phu Bon.

As Alpha returned to base, Joe Jerviss was leaving for RnR in Hawaii, where his family had been living since October. After arriving at Hickam Air Force Base in Honolulu, Joe eagerly processed through Fort DeRussy. However, an unexpectedly frosty reception from his wife Josephine revealed something was not right. Thankful to be with his kids, Joe brushed it aside. Later, when he showed Josephine the bullet that had been removed from his heel, she threw it into the garden and scowled.

Shortly after Joe left for Hawaii, Mike Trant was told to prepare for five days in Hong Kong. Full of anticipation and excitement, 12 hours later, Mike was looking down on thousands of neon lights as his plane came in to land. After finding a nice hotel, he headed out to find some decent food and strong beer. Mike's hearing had been troubling him ever since the battle on February 2 and the Marines with whom he happened to be drinking suggested a visit to the nearby military hospital.

The British doctor who examined him expressed serious concerns but Michael was not about to let partial deafness ruin his vacation. Luck was on his side when later that night he bumped into a gorgeous 19-year-old Chinese girl who called herself "Charene Greenwood." Miss Greenwood was a high-class hooker and invited the intrepid trooper back to her fashionable apartment. What started off as business turned into something quite different as Charene took a shine to him and invited Mike to stay for as long as his leave would allow.

Meanwhile, back in Phan Thiet, Doc Lovy had sent a team to investigate a serious outbreak of dysentery. Water stored in the ornate tower by Nguyen Hoang Bridge supplied most of downtown with its potable supply. Several decomposing bodies were pulled from the structure, forcing Lovy to immediately shut it down. Before Andy could establish any interim measures, the local black-market price for drinking water instantly soared by 1,000 percent!

Over the coming days, Disneyland continued to be heavily targeted with air strikes and artillery. At 0630hrs on February 8, A and B companies left Betty by truck in preparation for a coordinated attack alongside Mike Force and a mechanized company from Third Battalion, 44th ARVN. After a relatively peaceful day in

Phan Thiet, enemy mortars landed on the ARVN fuel depot and set fire to over 600,000 liters of gas and diesel.

With 3/506 pushed to its physical limits, these missions were conducted without any break or respite. On a typical night defense, one third of a platoon would be on guard and radio watch while the remainder slept. On this particular night, Joe Alexander was given a nudge around 0145hrs to get ready for his two-hour radio shift. All stations changed operators at the same time. As Joe shook himself awake, he found several ugly-looking bugs crawling across his arms, but could not muster the willpower needed to flick them away.

Feeling for his M16 and red-filtered flashlight, Alexander sat down and raised the handset to his ear. The proper procedure for all oncoming operators was to enter the net with an "all stations" coded check, but the radio remained silent for several minutes. Joe's judgment seemed slow to evolve as he broke silence and called network control over at the CP. It took several attempts before a reply came back but nothing was heard from the other call signs. Eventually, all but one station entered as Joe tried to remain focused. When net control anxiously demanded a radio check, Alexander thought to himself, *You gotta be kidding ... we just did that a few minutes ago.* A quick glance at his wristwatch revealed that the lieutenant had been comatose for almost two hours!

The next eight days saw smaller elements searching for pockets of resistance around Phan Thiet. Doug Alitz and his troops went north to help clear the highway between Bao Loc and Da Lat. The short break came as a welcome respite from Phan Thiet's extreme heat. On February 12, the battalion's order of battle underwent a drastic reshuffle when all Fourth platoons were merged to become one composite "Third." The incorporation also meant that every rifle squad would now have its own dedicated machine-gun team. During the shake-up, Ed Bassista moved across to First Platoon, where he took over from Sergeant Keith Rowell. Keith was from Amarillo, Texas and although a couple of years older, immediately gelled with Ed as a serious fighting partnership.

Two weeks prior, John Gfeller and Tom Gentry, who had recently been appointed as Alpha first sergeant, tried to figure out how best to assimilate. For instance, in Alpha's reconstituted Third Platoon, it meant Joe Alexander would be taking over command from Len Liebler. Although across the battalion, platoon leaders and their sergeants provided most input, it came down to the company commanders to make any final decisions.

Salve Matheson's supply officer, Californian Lieutenant Colonel Robert Elton, codenamed "Spider," took command of 3/506 on February 14. Somewhat against his wishes, "Mal Hombre" was being promoted out to assume duties as a MACV senior advisor in the Mekong Delta. Before he handed over to Elton, John summoned Doc Lovy for a formal meeting. Andy was not in the least bit surprised when Geraci told him about the court-martial paperwork he had just received from Rosson. John explained it had always been his prerogative to initiate such matters and was surprised to learn that everything in Rosson's statement was true. However, he also understood the pressure that Andy was under at that particular time. Geraci had "power of reprimand" and due to the mitigating circumstances was happy to let Andy's potentially career-ending escapade go with just a written warning. That same afternoon, former Deputy Commander of First Brigade Colonel John "Rip" Collins took over from Brigadier General Matheson. After 13 months in command, "General Matt" was finally moving to the III Marine Amphibious Force at Da Nang, as Lieutenant General Robert Cushman's Army Advisor.

The handover ceremony took place in Phan Rang beneath a constant stream of helicopter traffic. A color guard from each unit stood at attention while "Matt" and "Rip" awaited the arrival of Major General Barsanti. Saying goodbye was always going to be difficult but knowing Collins was taking the reins made things much easier for the "old man," who delivered a beautiful, heartfelt speech before departing.

Chapter 15

"Take it to the Bridge"

The Second Battle of Phan Thiet, February 18–23, 1968

Despite losses of around 450 personnel, the 482nd and 840th VC battalions had successfully restructured for another attempt against Phan Thiet. MACV intercepted a radio transmission that revealed the forthcoming attack and alerted 3/506, 44th ARVN, and local militias. Early on February 18, the two enemy battalions, along with their supporting units, advanced across the railway toward Quang Trung Camp and Provincial Command Compound. Before both locations could be assaulted, the 840th first needed control of the nearby police station and prison whose liberated inmates it was hoped would provide another 500 fighters. Luckily, things did not go quite according to plan and several delays allowed time for Central Command and its adjacent Provincial Military HQ to be reinforced.

Another assault came from the southwest via three more insurgent companies designated 430th, 480th, and 889th. Thankfully, these local units were quickly blocked by artillery and a determined counter-attack from the ARVN that almost destroyed the southern shoreline. Now able to protect and keep the Nguyen Hoang Bridge open from both ends, the South Vietnamese dug in and waited for back-up. Faced with overwhelming rocket fire, police and ARVN guarding the jail fled, allowing the 840th to take control. Reconnaissance aircraft and Forward Air Control were quickly on station and began circling the night sky looking for targets. Spooky gunships were soon unleashing death onto places such as the soccer stadium where a large number of VC had been reorganizing. Red rain pushed them toward the Ca Ty while five-inch Naval Artillery roared into action. But despite such efficient harassment, the Vietnamese still managed to regain control of northwest Phan Thiet. Shortly after 0700hrs, attack helicopters neutralized another assault taking place on a small hamlet called Nhoa Hai. Afterward, the Cobras were re-tasked to strafe the soccer field where again more insurgents were gathering.

Captain Landgraf and his men departed Betty at 0800hrs on the 18th, primarily to join with South Vietnamese troops and recapture the hospital. Passing a long row of abandoned shops, Bravo crossed over Phan Thiet's prefabricated bridge into the unknown. During training, 3/506 had never remotely considered the prospect of having to fight a large-scale urban battle. But nevertheless, weighed down by heavy rucksacks, here they were. By now, most of the 106s previously belonging to "Weapons" had been brought out of storage, remounted, and distributed among the Rifle companies with both good and bad results. Consequently, a number of 106 experienced troopers, such as Joe Alexander's radioman Ernie Ladd, were reassigned to help out.

Known as M50s, a handful of Ontos light tanks had also been attached for the battle. Moving as a linear force, Landgraf was planning to fight northeast toward the railway. Lieutenant Joel "Joe" Noah had only recently taken over Third Platoon from Don Love and was still getting acquainted with his men. Previously, Noah had led the Supply and Transportation Platoon and was more at home dealing with trucks than grueling house-to-house fighting. Sure enough, it did not take long before Bravo was forced to stop outside of the girls' elementary school and call for air support.

As the Cobras were still busy, Landgraf and the 44th ARVN had to sit and wait their turn. Sent as a QRF to protect Provincial Chief Lieutenant Colonel Nguyen Khac Tuan, Jerry Gomes and his colleague Tony Martisauskas – known to all in the S&T as

"Alphabet" – drove the CSF from Betty to Khac Tuan's compound. By nightfall, the perimeter came under heavy rocket attack and Shock Force trooper Gary Curtis was badly wounded in the face by shrapnel. A Quad-50 held off the enemy until 2200hrs, when Captain Landgraf arrived to reinforce. For two hours, allied artillery pounded everything surrounding the cathedral as flares lit targets for Spooky. Despite this, the compound still came under another blistering attack from mortars and recoilless rifles. Although B Co and the CSF held off the infantry, a small number still managed to get close enough to lob hand-grenades into Landgraf's perimeter. Three hundred meters northeast of Bravo, the 44th ARVN were also being hit hard. But by 0700hrs, the enemy broke contact and withdrew to a secondary line of pre-dug defensive bunkers.

DANGEROUS STREETS

Joe Jerviss had just got back from Hawaii and was being briefed by First Sergeant Roberts outside the Orderly Room. As Jerviss stood in earnest conversation, he glanced down and noticed the partially covered body of Corporal George Fuller. Roberts explained that Fuller had just been brought in from Phan Thiet after being crushed by a collapsing building.

Passing by the Provincial HQ Compound, Jerviss could see dozens of VC bodies scattered around its walls. Before reuniting with Herb Hohl, radio operator Mike Shepherd quickly explained to Jerviss that Captain Landgraf was preparing to attack in a three-pronged sweep toward the ruined railway station. First Platoon would be advancing along Highway 1 behind a rolling barrage of air and artillery. Stephen Cook and Second Platoon were to break right toward the prison, while "Joe" Noah took the left flank with the ARVN. Right from the outset, it was bunker to bunker and alleyway to alleyway. Upon reaching their first obstacle, Jerviss instructed one of his corporals, Charles Jackson, to roll in a grenade. For some reason, Jackson bowled overarm and the device bounced off a lintel, causing everyone to dive for cover. Jerviss was in the middle of chewing Jackson out when he noticed dozens of Viet Cong darting back and forth across the highway up ahead. Marshall Hill was immediately sent out onto the road with his M60 and within minutes had mown down over 30 insurgents.

Moving from building to building, Jerviss pleaded with his gunners to keep their bursts short. Those who ignored the order soon found themselves under direct enemy counter fire. But when tracer rounds preceded incoming rockets, the gun teams soon eased up on their triggers. As the only qualified anti-tank man in the platoon, Jerviss clambered onto their recently acquired jeep and brought its 106 to bear on a number of ground-level enemy positions.

As Sergeant Joe Savage was telling "Pineapple" he had seen the ARVN executing insurgents, Lieutenant Ashland Burchwell arrived and asked for directions. The new Civil & Military Operations Officer wanted access to an alleyway further along the street, where he had hoped to encourage surrender. Jerviss thought he was certifiable and told him so, but it made no difference.

The week prior had been quiet enough in Phan Thiet for Burchwell to implement a new civic action program. While working with a team from 245th Psy Ops Company, he had seen a marked increase in defections. Fluent in Vietnamese, Burchwell had come to 3/506 in January and perhaps encouraged by his recent success believed he could make a difference. Despite "Pineapple's" continued warnings, the lieutenant walked away and disappeared from view. Moments later, a burst of automatic gunfire demanded everyone's attention. As Jerviss turned around, the officer's lifeless body was being carried toward him on a door.

At that moment, a journalist who had been given prior access decided it was too dangerous and headed for the incoming medivac. Soon afterward, word arrived that the hospital was still in enemy hands and Third Platoon were encountering formidable resistance. Over to the east, a company-sized force of VC had been sent to distract and delay the ARVN, allowing their Provincial HQ attackers time to withdraw beyond the railway and to regroup for another assault.

By 1930hrs, another large gathering was disrupted on the soccer field. Unable to penetrate that far, Third Platoon managed to spring several successful ambushes along the railway tracks. Hohl and Jerviss had been lucky compared to Second and Third, who had so far incurred around a dozen wounded, including Lieutenant Cook.

Now working with Herb Hohl's First Platoon, Al Thompson came across a small library in a ruined house. Leafing through student textbooks covering everything from French to Geometry, he noticed a paperback copy of Ernest Hemingway's *For Whom the Bell Tolls*. Famously set in the Spanish Civil War, its irony was not lost on the young medic, who only a few hours before had eaten lunch next to a smouldering rebel body.

Shortly after first light, Captain Landgraf realized that he had lost a folder containing his radio call signs, frequencies, and authentication codes! Thankfully, after a frantic search among the rubble, it was located and returned intact. Not far from Landgraf, the eastern ARVN quadrant came under heavy fire from a group of fanatically naive teenage reinforcements. At the same time, dozens of previously hidden enemy mortar teams sprang into action only to be silenced by the Air Force. Prior to resuming its attack, Bravo was joined by C Company for a collective push. Because of snipers, the company became so strung out that Doug Alitz and Mike Krawczyk actually ended up on point!

Once again, "Joe" Noah and his men from Bravo ran into heavy resistance and took more casualties, including sergeants Vince Parkhurst and Albert Woods, and Private Daniel Bodin, who were all killed. Only a few hours earlier, Parkhurst had wished Woods a happy 21st birthday before a Chinese-made rocket cut him in half. ARVN troops reached the hospital and cleared it of the last remaining VC. By nightfall, B and C companies had advanced little more than 400m and did not yet realize that the enemy, low on ammunition, was now moving westward toward Alpha. The withdrawal was mainly due to Gaffney's men unwittingly blocking a vital re-supply from reaching Phan Thiet. When orders came on the 23rd for Bravo to withdraw, Herb Hohl and Joe Jerviss regrouped outside the Post Office across from the watertower. Just as Jerviss was taking roll call, a couple of Aussie SAS troopers came by ahead of a platoon from the Civilian Irregular Defense Group. Much to Joe's amusement, the guy in charge was maniacally waving his pistol as if the hero in some big-budget war movie. Leaving behind a pervading smell of 289 barbecued enemy bodies, Jerviss wished the Australian warrant officer luck before setting off on foot with his men for Betty.

Chapter 16

"Red Sand"

The Battle of the Ca Ty River – February 19, 1968

On the evening of Sunday, February 18, Captain Gaffney called a meeting to brief his seniors about ongoing operations in Phan Thiet. Supported by two M42 Dusters, Alpha was about to be deployed as a blocking force for Bravo and Charlie. Instructed to flank the city via the Ca Ty River, Gaffney and his men were then to circle two miles northeast and hopefully stop the enemy from making good their escape. After being bombarded for the last couple of days and low on ammunition, it was clear that NVA/VC forces were already in the process of withdrawing.

Early the next morning over at the outpost, Joe Alexander's jacket was damp with sweat as he took roll. Carrying more ammo than food, Third Platoon had been packed and ready for almost eight hours. With Sergeant Carl Yoshida and his First Squad leading, Joe wheeled around and set off along the perimeter track. Halting just outside Betty's main gate, Alexander nervously waited near the ammo dump for Gaffney to arrive.

The company had not been on Highway 1 long before turning onto a dirt road lined on either side with abandoned houses. Up ahead, the tide was out, making Ca Ty easily fordable. With each Duster weighing over 20 tons, the tank commanders were concerned that the soft, sandy riverbed would be unable to support their vehicles. Frustrated by this unexpected refusal, Gaffney tried to argue but the Duster guys would not budge. Five minutes later, Lieutenant Colonel Elton accepted their offer of an opening barrage. It was a disappointing start but the mission would have to go ahead with or without this crucial mobile support.

The Dusters fired over 200 shells into dense trees that obscured the opposite bank. Afterward, Jim Pratz made a low pass to seed with smoke. Shielded by a white screen, Joe Alexander followed Harrison and Schlax down into the knee-deep water. When Joe reached the other side, Jim was already waiting with his pocket Minolta ready to catch Alexander's moment for posterity. After a few minutes, Sergeant Yoshida came back and rather worryingly reported a number of hastily abandoned enemy positions.

Alpha's beachhead was on the southern tip of a small peninsula bound on either side by water. No more than a mile away was Route 88, a football stadium, Cho Go slums, Highway 1, and the bridge. Third Platoon moved cautiously through Harrison and settled into a semi-circular security position. Following his recent losses, John's platoon was acting as drag or reserve for the mission.

THE POINT OF NO RETURN

Jim Schlax and Tom Gaffney were now over to Alexander's right facing a dusty, open paddy and cemetery. Gaffney told Schlax to peel off and scout around the burial ground. Keeping the river to his right, Jim began moving north. From here, it was just possible to see Phan Thiet's white-topped watertower. The abundance of small buildings and terrain obstacles quickly forced Schlax to move away from the meandering shoreline. Shoehorned into a dense strip of banana trees, Jim decided to retrace his steps. Passing an old shack, the lieutenant was now slightly in front of his men as they moved into a small open field. Up ahead, a glimpse of steel helmets filtering along a ditch caught his attention. Before Jim even had a chance to speak to radioman Dennis Carbary, the enemy opened up.

When Schlax dialed in the contact, Gaffney ordered him to hold and await further instructions. Placing his rifle on the ground, Jim turned to signal everyone behind to seek cover around the shack. As he went to pick up his M16, Jim felt it vibrate as a burst of enemy machine-gun fire ripped into the concrete hard earth. Scrambling on all fours back to the hooch, Jim and Dennis found it difficult to determine any solid targets for Gaffney.

Word arrived that Doc Jones was dealing with a casualty but nobody seemed to know just who exactly had been injured. Not wishing to move until the individual had been identified, Schlax walked around the hooch hoping to gain a better view. Suddenly, a searing pain erupted as a high-velocity bullet penetrated his right leg. Ed Bassista was only a few feet away and ordered his machine-gun team to engage. As the M60 burst into action, everyone followed suit and within seconds First Platoon was pouring everything they had into the line of trees.

Moments later, Doc Jones reported in and as he began to explain it was just a false alarm, he looked down and saw blood on Jim's fatigue pants. Had the bullet been one inch higher, then Jim would have almost certainly bled to death before Mark arrived.

Once he found out what had happened, Gaffney ordered First Platoon back to his CP. Nobody could have known that they were on the extreme right-hand edge of a much larger system of over ten heavily defended bunkers. Gaffney got on the radio to Joe Alexander and ordered, "Alpha 3-6, this is Alpha 6 – move to the left flank abreast of Alpha 1-6."

While waiting at the CP for his medivac, Jim handed over temporary control to Bill Griffin, who had recently replaced Tom Gentry as platoon sergeant. After Gaffney's suppressive barrage, Joe Alexander called up Gfeller to confirm he had understood the captain's instructions. When the answer came back in the affirmative, Joe began to slip his platoon westward toward the cemetery.

Meanwhile, Gaffney radioed back to Betty and told First Sergeant Gentry to send out John Ross. Although West Point-trained, the green exec still had no operational experience, but by default was now the only ranking officer available to take command of First Platoon. Waiting to be reassigned, Len Liebler overheard the conversation, grabbed a handful of gear, and ran to the chopper that had just delivered Schlax.

TIME FOR TRUTH

With instructions to link up with Joe Alexander, Bill Griffin, Mark Jones, and First Platoon headed back out toward the cemetery. Two or three choppers were now overhead wanting to know what was going on. Their very presence meant that Gaffney had to hold his next intended fire mission.

As Tom was trying to push forward with his plan, an unexpected message came through on the radio, "Alpha 6, this is Eagle 1, do you need any help down there?" Somewhat taken aback, Tom thanked the assistant divisional commander for his concern and politely pointed out that he was doing just fine. Eagle 1 was quickly followed by Colonel Elton, "Alpha 6, this is 'Spider,' is there anything we can do to assist?" Feeling agitated by the constant interjections, Tom sarcastically told Elton, "If you really want to help, then why don't you go ahead and 'nuke 'em'?" Unimpressed by Tom's flippancy, "Spider" fell momentarily silent.

With the overhead airspace now clear, Gaffney began to call artillery onto an old colonial property that was seen to have a North Vietnamese flag flying from its roof. Gaffney knew that the graveyard was large enough for both First and Third platoons to regroup but Colonel Elton and Bob Mairs seemed to have other ideas. Tom lifted the barrage and ordered both platoons to move, but then asked them to hold while Len Liebler made his way across to Griffin. Once Lenny was in position, Tom could then start implementing his next phase.

From the C&C, "Fat Cat" thought he saw enemy troops retreating and ordered Tom into an immediate all-out, full-scale linear assault. Everyone heard the major say, "They are running in the open – attack now – attack now!" Inevitably, Joe and John responded as they had been trained, but due to the proliferation of burial mounds, thankfully it was difficult for them to actually stay on line. Glancing right, Joe noticed First Platoon moving in behind as he stopped to cross a low dirt retaining wall that opened onto a latticework of dusty rice paddy. There was no obvious retreat to be seen as Joe began to process what lay ahead of him.

IF HELL HAD A FACE

Over on the far left, Gfeller issued a nod of reassurance to Alexander as they slowly continued with their advance. Directly in front at about 40yds were four or five widely spaced farmhouses all merging into the same banana plantation encountered by Schlax. The grove curved around to Joe's right for about 100yds and concealed more bunkers. Adjacent to Gfeller and "Frenchy" Coulon's Second Squad were a number of grassy mounds harboring at least three more hitherto unseen positions.

Immediately, Gaffney realized what had happened and he ordered Joe to get everyone back into the graveyard. But as Alexander went to take the receiver from his temporary radio operator Frank DeJesus, the entire front erupted with ferocious gun and rocket fire. Immediately on Joe's left, Walter Patterson and James Webster were hit. Gfeller began shouting instructions and then sprinted toward the two downed troopers. Ignoring pleas to remain still, Webster rolled over and sat up. Swiveling to look at Gfeller, Webster took another bullet and died instantly.

Now flat on his stomach, Joe looked on as his platoon sergeant hero fell backward as if swept by some invisible hand. A few feet from Gfeller, "Skip" Rattee took a bullet to the left arm and was now lying arched against his rucksack. In an effort to protect "Skip's" injured arm, medic Jose Ramos decided to cut away the straps. While searching for scissors, Ramos had inadvertently left Rattee exposed. "Doc, I'm too short for this shit," were the last words "Skip" uttered as another round flipped his head sharply sideways. It was only then that Ramos decided to drag "Skip" back behind the berm, but it was too late.

Against his growing instincts, Ramos leapt forward and returned to Gfeller and "Frenchy." Twisting toward John, Ramos told him that Carl was dead, but as the platoon sergeant turned to respond, brain matter exploded from his right temple. Feeling enemy rounds now tearing away at his own rucksack, Ramos fell into a hysterical panic. It was either fight or flight. Completely overwhelmed, Ramos chose the latter and with a profound sense of guilt, abandoned his responsibilities and crawled back behind the earth wall, baked rock hard from decades of blazing sunshine.

NOWHERE TO RUN

Alexander had been trying to reach Gfeller when a ricochet clipped the top off his index finger. From the corner of one eye, Joe could see "Pete" Dozier, Joe Reed, and their two M60 crews over on the right courageously returning fire. At one point, Corporal Reed – with complete abandon – rose up and continued to blaze away at the grassy mounds. As the gunners withdrew, Reed grabbed hold of a wounded comrade and dragged him back behind the relative safety of the embankment.

On the right flank, both Carl Yoshida and Henry Parker's squads were taking a beating. Parker had been hit and his Fire Team Leader Sergeant John Colone shot in the upper thigh. A second bullet splintered against Colone's rifle and blasted shrapnel upward into his chest and arm. Don Marshall was applying a tourniquet when he fell mortally wounded across his sergeant's body. Extricating himself from beneath Marshall, Colone began to crawl toward the berm. Inching across bare open ground, John was struck again in the buttocks and neck.

Now completely pinned down, Alexander began directing fire and trying to organize a withdrawal. Enemy machine-gun bullets kicked up dirt and buzzed inches above his head as he attempted to crawl back behind the dike. With rounds getting closer, as Joe clenched for what he thought was inevitable, the crew stopped to reload. Within seconds, the enemy gun was back in action and a bullet struck the front lip of Joe's helmet. Deflecting upward, the round grazed Alexander's forehead and left a large tear in the steel. Again, the firing stopped only to resume a few seconds later.

More rounds passed over Joe's right shoulder and gouged into his left hip. All he could do now was pray that the end would come quick. Unable to lift his chin more than half an inch from the ground, Joe's mind inexplicably began to drift. There was no anger but instead a myriad of warm thoughts directed toward family, church, high school football, and Sharon Horton. Lamentably, Sharon had been Joe's platonic girlfriend back then and her unexpected "arrival" in his consciousness came completely out of nowhere.

At that moment, the enemy gunner refocused attention toward Gfeller and the others from Second Squad lying out on Joe's left. With renewed motivation, clearing Sharon from his mind, Joe exchanged rounds for several minutes until another enemy bullet went through his upper right arm. Fifteen minutes had elapsed since the first shots and the platoon was now facing the distinct prospect of annihilation.

Behind Joe was the ancient retaining wall. Assuming he could reach it without being killed, he figured it might be possible to consolidate. Luckily, most of the guys who had been stuck in "no man's land" were already beginning to crab their way backward toward the same location.

Seriously wounded and unable to move from behind his radio, Frank DeJesus wanted to push the "25" across to Joe so that he could contact Gaffney. Having none of this, Joe instructed DJ to keep it as a shield and carefully move back toward him. It was only when DJ reached Joe that they discovered the device was already full of bullet holes! With Joe and DJ still exposed, the indirect fire ordered earlier by Gaffney now rendered movement impossible. Right from the get-go, Gaffney had hammered into his troops not to run out and extract wounded while under fire. But despite repeated attempts, he could not stop Joe's guys from going after their injured friends.

Thinking he was escaping certain death, Jose Ramos crawled along behind the berm. Passing Tom Vaughan's contorted body, Ramos kept going until he found "Pete" Knight dead and still attached to his crackling "25" ... then everything went black.

"V" IS FOR VALIDATION

Elton and Mairs were now asking Gaffney to withdraw across the river, but a change in tide meant it was clearly too deep. Although he already knew this, Tom sent John Harrison and elements of Second Platoon to determine if a crossing might be possible. Tom was not about to leave his wounded behind and happily passed on Harrison's negative findings to "Spider." Back at the river, two boats came chugging into view and opened fire on John. Grabbing a couple of 66s, Harrison engaged and killed 11 insurgents. As each craft exploded, a cacophony of enemy gunfire erupted from a small boathouse further downstream across the river.

Lenny Liebler had located Joe and for all the right reasons tried to take command. Joe was also in no mood to abandon his men and flatly refused. A few minutes earlier, Len had stopped "Pete" Dozier from Joe's Fourth Squad as he walked by in shock. Dozier made it clear that there were still more wounded lying out in the open. Liebler then asked Gaffney if he could take some of his guys and sweep around to look for them. The captain denied his request, believing that without effective close air support it would be suicidal. At that moment, most of the air assets were heavily engaged in Phan Thiet and would not be available for at least another 30 minutes.

Suddenly, Doc Jones came in from the right, where he had been impressed by Sergeant Tyson, who although wounded was tending casualties while directing machine-gun fire. Although the cry of "Medic!" seemed to be coming from all directions, Mark made for Joe, who was still dangerously exposed in the open. The lieutenant could not believe what he was seeing and told Mark to get down behind the dike. But seemingly unconcerned, Jones insisted that Alexander remain still while he checked him over. The next artillery barrage exploded so close that Jones was forced flat onto the ground. Mark continued treatment and insubordinately refused every direct order from Joe to get under cover.

Jose Ramos did not know how long he had been out, but awoke facing skyward with a smashed helmet and a gunshot wound to his leg. Unaware of Ramos' current location or situation, Joe and Mark discussed their limited options. Alexander had no choice but to order Jones on but as badly as he wanted him to say "yes," he realized he also had every right to refuse. With rifle grenades exploding all around, knowing there were many others desperate for assistance, Jones crawled away into the exposed paddy. Rightly or wrongly, Mark accepted the risks and his exceptional display somehow helped revitalize Joe's flagging spirit.

SKY HUNTERS

Safely behind the dike, Dennis Carbary handed Joe his radio microphone and said, "Gaffney wants you to call, RIGHT NOW! He says if you don't have a dime then please call collect!" Back on the "freak," Joe was ready and able to help Gaffney unleash onto the bad guys. Just about every available weapon system the battalion had at its disposal was now ordered up. The Navy, helicopter gunships, and more importantly the A-1 Skyraiders from Betty all stormed into action. Armed with four 20mm cannons and an assortment of small bombs and rockets, the A-1s skillfully flown by the South Vietnamese were an effective platform. From the cemetery, First Platoon was forced to pop smoke as attacking aircraft lit up the VC bunkers. Rapid bursts of cannon fire spat hundreds of hot casings onto the beleaguered paratroopers below.

When the fast-jet boys arrived, they were low enough for everyone to feel their engine heat. Liebler listened in on the net as one Phantom pilot reported seeing tracer arcing up at him. Flying even lower, the F-4s returned and blew their attackers into dust. For the next two hours, Joe coordinated and looked on as bombs fell, napalm burnt, and artillery exploded. Lieutenant Alexander derived great pleasure in watching the destruction as a succession of ground-shaking 500, 750, and 1,000lb bombs exploded onto target. Between them, Alpha and Bravo had used the entire monthly ammunition allocation for II Corps in one afternoon!

"Frenchy" Coulon regained consciousness when concussion from an exploding bomb physically lifted him into the air! Although blind, Coulon could hear his colleagues calling from behind the berm to stay down. But when another massive blast showered him with debris, Coulon decided to make a frantic dash toward the voices. As "Frenchy" hit the low dirt bank, he fell forward into the hands of omnipresent Doc Jones, who immediately shot him full of morphine.

It had taken Sergeant Mike Mullican from Joe's Second Squad nearly 20 minutes to crawl out of the kill zone. Behind a burial mound, Mike – known to all as "El Can" – was reloading when a 750lb bomb exploded and sent him flying headlong back into the carnage. His shoulder dislocated and under covering fire from Gary Alberhasky, Mike – along with Sergeant Louis Oswald – managed to reach Colone and drag him back to safety. As Carl Yoshida leapt to assist Mullican and Oswald, a bullet struck his arm and spun him backward behind the berm.

Several times Alexander overheard the fire support officer asking for aircraft to hold and allow a medivac to fly in. As more wounded were being evacuated, Alexander crawled and walked with some assistance toward Second Platoon's perimeter and PZ. Seeing Gaffney by the CP, Joe felt compelled to report before leaving. Bleeding and on the verge of tears, Joe tried to salute as he mumbled, "Sir, my platoon fought courageously and are proud and brave warriors." Unable to stem the flow of overwhelming emotion and embarrassed by this unexpected outburst, Joe turned and dropped his gaze. Gaffney grabbed hold of the young lieutenant's chin and in restoration of dignity lifted his head back to eye level. The look of sorrow on Tom's face was undeniable as he patted Joe supportively on the shoulder. "Yes, Joe, they are proud warriors, each and every single one of them ... and you, my lad, have nothing whatsoever to feel ashamed of ... do you understand me? Now go get yourself on that damned helicopter."

"Flint" Purcell from Yoshida's squad had been trying to stabilize Colone's head and airway. At the CP, face covered in blood, "Frenchy" Coulon clung to a photograph of his wife. As Colone suddenly grew lucid, he shared a couple of self-effacing words with Ray Mayfield. John's light-hearted comments masked the fact that his life now literally hung by a thread due to massive hemorrhaging.

During his five-minute chopper ride, Sergeant Colone slipped away and was declared dead on arrival at Betty. One hour later, Curt Washington came running into the overwhelmed clearing station from the death tent to advise Andy Lovy that he had seen John's toe twitch. Although the doc thought it was rigor mortis, Curt would not let go. Annoyed, Lovy stopped what he was doing and begrudgingly made his way through to the tent. Placing his spectacles against John's lips, Andy was rendered utterly speechless when a tiny spot of exhaled moisture appeared on the lens! Immediately, John was rushed into surgery and brought back to life. Afterward, the sergeant recounted hearing voices and a feeling that he was falling … it was truly a miracle. But it would take many more miracles of hard, painful rehabilitation before Colone was able to return to some sort of "normality."

TALES FROM THE RIVERBANK

Over the last few hours, Second Platoon had created a modified perimeter facing the river. From here, Sergeant Fellmann directed his men carrying ammunition and water from LZ to the graveyard. When medic John Melgaard reached the front line, he immediately went to work with Mark Jones, prioritizing casualties for extraction.

Plagued by mosquitoes, Harrison's men dug in as day gave way to night. Over at the CP, Gaffney's radio burst into life, "Alpha 6, this is your friendly dragon, can you identify your positions please?" Spooky could see the Ca Ty as Tom explained his platoon locations and confirmed, "Each will light up a number of flares and everything north of that line is yours." After Spooky had done its work, John Melgaard joined with Ramos and CSF medic John Wendelschaefer as Gaffney and Liebler handpicked around 20 volunteers and moved forward. Ramos was hungry, tired, and suffering, but found comfort in having the two Johns by his side. Fires from burning farms gave off an eerie, deep-red luminescence. As "Flint" Purcell approached one motionless body, he was relieved to find the individual still very much alive! Private first class "Magoo" Howell from Third Squad had lain motionless for over five hours and was equally relieved to see "Flint." Ed Clark and Stephen Howe from Coulon's squad had also survived unharmed. With the addition of Bob Griffis, the final toll for Third Platoon was eight dead and 13 wounded. Captain Gaffney put Joe in for the Silver Star and Mark Jones the Army Commendation Medal with "V" for Valor. Unbelievably, one day after the Rattees were officially notified, Carl's sister Carol lost her life in a car wreck.

TIME FOR THE LIVING

Free world Armageddon continued throughout the night as bullets whipped overhead from Bravo's raging battle in Phan Thiet. There was no time to mourn or feel the luxury of sympathy. Completely spent, Mark Jones – clothes stained with blood – sat in his foxhole and quietly shared a cold coffee. The dead were dead, the wounded were gone, and the battlefield now passed back to the living.

Looking across to Ca Ty's southern bank, Alpha breathed a sigh of relief at the new sunrise. The 20th was Ed Bassista's 22nd birthday and despite everything that had happened, Ricky Ellison made him a cake out of C-Rations. Ed put on a brave face as he thought about "Pete" Knight, Tom Vaughan, and others now lying silently in the morgue. As Joe Alexander was on his way to the 36th Evac with Doc Lovy, Jose Ramos doctored himself up and returned to duty. Subsequently, many openly despised his actions, but he would have to live with this, too. For Ramos, life would never be the same; time, however, is a great healer and eventually he found forgiveness.

Lieutenant Colonel Elton arrived with Major Mairs, who set about apologizing to Gaffney, although the "incident" was never officially admitted or recognized. When Alpha went back to recover lost weapons, Ed Bassista noticed a distant figure traversing the smouldering moonscape. How anyone other than a cockroach could have survived was a total mystery. First Platoon fired at least 100 rounds before the guy fell slowly to the ground in a bizarre lazy run.

Early on the 21st, C Co and Mike Force air assaulted into Alpha's location. One of the Green Beret NCOs had worked with Gaffney a few years before. After a quick catch-up, Gaffney asked Mike Force to screen his flank down by the river, where it was felt they would be more effective.

Over the next 24 hours, the multi-force swept west along Highway 1, supported by two Dusters, Quad-50s, and jeep-mounted recoilless rifles. Along the railway, with ARVN on their extreme right flank, Gaffney, Alitz, and the Australian-led CIDG headed toward Ap Xuan Phong. The troops had not gone far before they started receiving enemy fire. A crusty SAS warrant officer walked over to John Harrison and in full view raised his SLR to indicate the enemy position.

By this time, John had thrown himself into the dirt as bullets cracked around the Australian's head. Harrison took the handset from Hal Dobie and put in a call to Gaffney for artillery. With the advance once again under way, John noted a small plantation of banana trees and radioed headquarters to advise his concern. Not impressed with John's message or that the advance had stalled, Gaffney responded, "This is 6, banana trees … why do you wanna pick one? Go ahead, be my guest, but for Christ's sake keep that line moving!"

As Harrison feared, the plantation burst into life with automatic weapons and rockets. By then, Mike Force were caught in the open and decided to engage. John's platoon took cover behind a nearby farmhouse as the "Yards" disappeared into the smoke. It did not take long for Gaffney to show up, and as John outlined his situation, a flight of Tiger Sharks went after a nearby battery of mortars. Glowering, Tom ordered John to regroup with the CIDG and get everyone back on line. The lieutenant blew his whistle and motioned for the "Yards" to hold so he could catch up.

As Alpha broke out into a huge paddy, they came under fire from an anti-tank gun and took seven casualties. The skin and muscle on Vaughan Dewaay's arm were peeled back as if butchered by a boning knife. The stretcher party seemed unnaturally quiet as they carried him toward the medivac. When Ronnie Ford looked down, Dewaay immediately fixed him with an intense, wide-eyed stare. Weirdly, although no words were said, Vaughan seemed to derive a pitiful form of comfort from this deep exchange that remained unbroken until he was placed on the helicopter.

Each platoon now had a Quad-50 and M40 106mm recoilless rifle attached. Harrison's jeep-mounted 106 was operated by Company Clerk Scott Johnson, who actually had the correct qualifications to use it. By 1000hrs, the Americans were once again receiving heavy mortar fire and moved quickly to get inside the arc. A succession of air strikes and artillery finally drove scores of enemy troops into the open. Leaving behind over 50 dead, the VC began retreating out of Disneyland.

By this point, Ronnie Ford was on the edge of no return after being ordered to exhume one of the 40 graves that were found nearby. This was done to confirm the circumstances in which an individual or individuals had died. Afterward, Sergeant Raynor ordered his squad to dig out a nearby bomb shelter. The roof had partially collapsed and as the guys stripped down under a hot sun, Ron came across a dead baby, its mouth and eyes filled with dirt. Further digging revealed two women whose lives had been spared by the roof.

A bullet grazed Mike Krawczyk's wrist while he reluctantly followed Captain Alitz on point. Their sweep inflicted more VC deaths, destroyed dozens of bunkers, and saw three suspects detained for questioning. Unbelievably, the intelligence gained indicated a third attempt against Phan Thiet was now being planned.

Constant mortar fire had left a small fragment of shrapnel embedded in Ron Ford's left shoulder. Back at Betty, the clearing station was still struggling with priority patients. Amidst the pitiful cries for absent mothers, Ronnie sat and patiently waited in the corner. The removal procedure was surprisingly quick and after being sutured, Lovy sent him back to Alpha.

Rejuvenated by his trip to Hong Kong, Mike Trant was desperate to tell everybody about his "holiday romance." But Mike's mood was quickly dampened by Joe Alexander's recent heavy losses. "Skip" Rattee's death in particular brought about a grim realization as Trant went to see Doc Lovy. Knowing Mike only had a few weeks left in country, Andy made an appointment for him in Vung Tau. The specialists there were able to confirm a problem with Mike's left ear. Back at Betty, the doc wrote Trant up for light duties and arranged a quiet job over at Alpha HQ with new First Sergeant Gilbert Verbist.

Chapter 17

"After the Storm"

The Bowl – February/March 1968

The weeks and months following Tet would run into a blur for the old sweats as they continued to chase their enemy across three provinces. Although largely contained by the ARVN, the third significant assault from the Viet Cong against Phan Thiet erupted on February 25. Two companies from the 482nd Main Force rose from their tunnels and hit northeasterly targets while the remainder, along with 480th Local Force Company, attacked government troops from within. That night, as the downtown beach fight raged toward a catastrophic VC defeat, the boys from Alpha were rewarded with a rare day off.

Following Gaffney's instruction, upon their return to base, Bill Norris was waiting for A Company with a trailer filled with ice-cold beer. Although it was a fabulous gesture, many just wanted to curl up with their upset stomachs and sleep. Chris Adams was feeling OK and headed down to the Beach Club for a joint and a game of cards. Later, while on his way to the MARS Shack, he waved at Ronnie Ford and Stacy Raynor sunbathing drunk on the roof of their bunker. MARS allowed each soldier a free five-minute "call" to their families, all facilitated by a network of home radio enthusiasts. The MARS guy made contact with a HAM operator in California, who patched Chris through to his parents. After a brief but welcome catch-up, Adams was surprised to learn that despite constant news coverage, his battalion's struggle in Phan Thiet had been largely overlooked. However, along with home-front hearts and minds, the long-term impact of Tet would actually signify a beginning of the end in terms of US involvement.

Later that evening, as Headquarters Company sat outside watching John Wayne in *The Green Berets*, a deep rumbling sensation began to ripple underfoot. Two miles away, over by the main entrance, a huge mushroom cloud suddenly erupted high into the night sky. Six heavy mortar rounds, probably fired from an offshore sampan, had just landed in the middle of the ARVN ammunition dump. The attack set off a chain reaction of massive explosions, launching chunks of metal hundreds of feet in all directions. The earth-shattering blast was like nothing anyone had ever heard or felt. Debris covered the runway, damaged a dozen aircraft, and reached as far as Battalion HQ, completely knocking out power to the Tactical Operations Center.

Clutching a half-full bottle of Jim Beam, Captain Gaffney sprang into action with John Harrison. Out of the flame-filled horizon, a seven-inch chunk of shrapnel ripped into Ricky Ellison's lower back. Grabbing a portable stretcher, revolver in hand, Ed Bassista rushed his screaming friend toward the medics only to be delayed by B Co who were on base security detail. When Bassista arrived at the clearing station, most if not all of the medical staff had disappeared underground into the emergency TOC.

DARK SKIES

Nick Nahas had just relocated to the secondary operations center when a call arrived from an isolated outpost half a mile away along the beach. Amidst the chaotic earthquake of exploding ammunition, a young truck driver on bunker duty had spotted a sampan through his night vision scope. The boat, purposefully heading toward Betty's two enormous circular fuel storage tanks, was of immense concern. Nick immediately called up the nearest available Spooky and requested a couple of "warning" bursts be fired across the bow. However, when the sampan failed to change course or reduce speed, Nahas had little choice but to order its destruction. A couple of hours later, the captain's decision seemed justified when two Vietnamese bodies washed up carrying ammunition and explosives.

Over the last four weeks, the task force as a whole had lost a total of 91 dead and 569 wounded. However, the VC and NVA casualties had been far greater, with around 1,000 killed and conservatively double that number wounded. During the penultimate attack on Phan Thiet, despite the North Vietnamese employing ever-more daring tactics, the lack of experience shown by their reinforcements directly contributed to final failure. Civilian casualties amounted to an estimated 100 killed, 650 wounded, and 16,000 left homeless. Until proper refugee centers could be established, most sat out the nightly curfews on Phan's beaches in French-supplied tents. Captain Robert Bates from the battalion's Civil Affairs Department and Doc Lovy did their best to provide humanitarian assistance while countering the growing cases of typhoid and cholera.

Depleted, the enemy withdrew and press-ganged every available male aged between 13 and 45. By no means beaten, the 482nd VC disappeared into the vast Hong Phong Forest. Leaving behind a series of diversionary rear-guard actions, the plan now was not active engagement but to quietly filter northwest and rearm. Meanwhile, 3/506 began to develop new concepts for detecting the enemy. One of these was the introduction of a bespoke helicopter force specifically designed to reduce night movement. Crucial to its success was a group of trooper volunteers who stepped forward to become aerial spotters. The utility choppers were fitted with starlight scopes designed to intensify ambient light. Assisted by flare and gunships from the 162nd Assault Helicopter Company, the "night hunter" pilots flew hundreds of missions, keeping Betty's perimeter and wider area secure. Simple and effective, by use of tracer, the troopers indicated targets for waiting Tiger Sharks, whose pilots followed up with their mini-guns and rockets.

At least a temporary return to base meant decent hot food. Ray Mayfield and Ed Bassista were waiting in the chow line when a military policeman suddenly collapsed in front of them. The man's helmet liner rolled away to reveal blood and brain matter as two medics stepped out to help the stricken soldier. Bizarrely, a .50-caliber ricochet from Phan Thiet had flown over two miles to inflict the mortal wound! As the cooks declared "service open," everyone shuffled forward and nonchalantly stepped around the unfortunate victim ... such was life and death in the Republic of Vietnam.

The following morning, Alpha launched an operational sweep to the northeast of Bartlett, destroying bunkers, weapons caches, and equipment. Company B remained behind to assist with the ammo dump clean-up and base security mission. In the aftermath, using shipping containers, it was decided to create a special subterranean hospital. Completed during March, the new facility was christened "Spider's Treatment Parlor."

Sixteen kilometers northeast of Phan Thiet, a new radio relay station codenamed "Whiskey" was installed on the summit of an imposing hill known as Nui Ta Dom. At 386m, "Whiskey Mountain" was conveniently situated next to Highway 1 and sat adjacent to the northwest tip of the Hong Phong Forest. The forward base would go on to become a vital communications link for Betty, as well as a dust-off and "arrow" re-supply point for all future localized operations.

By chance, Joe Alexander was en route from hospital in Vung Tau to Phan Rang for convalescence when his twin-engine Caribou made an unscheduled landing at Betty. Intent on reporting for duty, within minutes Joe was "AWOL" and heading toward Battalion Headquarters. Not only was the lieutenant surprised to see all the recent building damage, but he now also had a new company commander.

Previously battalion adjutant, Ed Dowdy took over Alpha on March 3. While trying to figure out what to do with his unexpected guest, Dowdy put Joe down for transfer to HHC, where a slot for battalion liaison officer was soon coming available. After hearing Joe was on base, Tom Gaffney, now Task Force Air Planning Officer, came over to see how his favorite son was doing. Before returning to the Tactical Operations Center, Tom offered Joe the opportunity to run his nightshift. The job entailed logistical planning and tasking of all Infantry, Artillery, Aviation, and Naval Gunfire Support. Although it would take a few weeks to arrange, Joe was excited and thrilled by the idea of working as Gaffney's assistant.

The latest commander of First Field Force, Lieutenant General William R. Peers arrived at Betty to introduce himself. At the time, Bill Landgraf had just handed over command of Bravo to Mike Pearson. Bill was taking over Logistics from "Dee" Dallas, who was preparing to leave for a new role with First Brigade as CO of Headquarters Company. The brigade had not long relocated back to Phu Bai and a number of other troopers across the battalion were also in the process of being reassigned north.

CHASING THE WIND — LRRPS

The Shock Force was now being reorganized into a full-blown reconnaissance role under the new leadership of Roy Somers from C Company. With all the right credentials, Roy, a former enlisted man and Ranger, had occasionally been known to "paint himself up" for missions with the CSF.

The old Quick Reaction role was gone, leaving the new "Currahee Raiders" to field several independent six-man "Romeo Teams" designed to be inserted covertly. With direct Rifle company support, Battalion LRRPs, as they became known, quickly established a solid reputation. With specific information now coming in from Somers, it was becoming evident that small elements of VC were operating out of a valley to the northeast between Bartlett and Whiskey known as "the bowl."

Romeo Team 2, led by Jerry Ochse, was out near Bartlett when point man Tim Keller froze as 20 VC crossed the railway line directly in front of him. Artillery was called and as the team advanced, Corporal Jim Atwood clocked a trio of stragglers scrambling across the embankment. Within a second, the patrol opened fire, killing all three Vietnamese. Sergeant Sam Jacobs cautiously called his colleagues to a trail hidden in a strip of trees. As Jacobs emerged from the undergrowth, he shot dead a Viet Cong soldier nonchalantly drawing water from a spring.

The patrol pushed on through a graveyard and into a field, where they decided to go firm. As night fell, the men noticed dozens of shadowy figures slowly moving toward them. Again, artillery was called in from Bartlett. Scanning the rear through binoculars, Texan Jacobs was horrified to see another group of around 150 strong forming to skirmish. The Americans could clearly hear screams as their next barrage exploded among the larger force. Despite being bombarded, the enemy managed to regroup into a ramshackle line.

Regardless of the overwhelming threat and dangerously low on ammunition, Ochse threw out flares and called for Tiger Sharks. Luckily, the gamble paid off and after a brief exchange of small-arms fire, the helicopters arrived and went to work. The boys laid down one last burst and withdrew for extraction. Totally out of ammunition, they sprinted the last 200m and threw themselves onto a hovering chopper!

Earlier that same day, March 12, Captain Dowdy was planning a memorial service during Alpha's stay at Bartlett for those killed during the Second Battle of Phan Thiet. At the time, "Jay" Eckhart was awaiting transfer north to 2/327 along with "Magoo" Howell and dozens of others. The process, officially called "infusion," was a program that enabled experienced personnel to be shuffled between commands. Simplified, this was to avoid a clash of "overseas return" dates, thus reducing the number of high-value troops leaving Vietnam. Many felt that things would have gone smoother if the battalion had been rotated with another similarly cohesive outfit, but this was not part of the military strategem. Sadly, over the coming months more than a dozen boat boys would lose their lives fighting with their new surrogate outfits along the DMZ.

A loss of airborne role also signified the inevitable arrival of drafted "leg" replacements. Ed Bassista made it clear to his FNGs or "Fucking New Guys" that he would not be bothering to learn or remember their names for at least two months. One of the frequently asked questions was how deep should a foxhole be. The standard flippant answer was always, "You'll know when the time comes."

It was to be a tough time for the boat troopers, who felt that their tight-knit bond was being torn apart and tossed away without any thought toward operational cohesion. Many people of color or from poorer minority backgrounds saw the draft as another way of discriminating and this reflected in attitude and motivation. Back home, black or white, many of the conscripts had been rooting for liberal Democrat Senator Eugene McCarthy, who was not only standing for president but also part of the growing anti-war movement.

WE SHALL OVERCOME

Since the end of February, one more name had been added to the list of KIAs … A few days earlier, despite being top-heavy with new people, it had been First Platoon's turn for ambush duty. That night, Ed Bassista's squad were in position when a heavily laden enemy soldier strolled right through their claymore defenses. The moment he realized something was wrong, the man raised his AK to shoot. Bassista was livid and returned fire as the ambush unraveled into a chaotic exchange.

Despite Ed's orders to rally, the replacements lost their nerve and ran back toward Len Liebler, abandoning a .45 automatic pistol and radio. By the time the missing items were reported, it was close to morning. Stepping out into the first light of dawn, Liebler, Bassista, Keith Rowell, and Marshall Nelson had no choice but to go back. Corporal Nelson had served with Bassista since his early days on Brigade LRRPs. The three regulars covered Ed from nearby foxholes as he moved forward to retrieve. A few feet ahead, Ed noticed what looked like a spider hole and as he dropped in a grenade, the tree line crackled into life. Bassista hit the deck and burned off several magazines while attempting to withdraw. Ignoring direct orders, Nelson broke cover and was bearing down on his friend when a bullet ripped through his chest and it was all over.

Not expecting to leave Alpha until the 24th, Joe Alexander was also attending the ceremony at Bartlett. The company had undergone several recent changes. Len Liebler handed command of First Platoon to John Harrison, while Arthur Quesada and Roland Belanger were reassigned from HHC to run Second and Third. However, Joe was overjoyed when Dowdy bestowed on him the very special honor of leading his old crew in formation. Afterward, a commotion broke out among the ARVN, who had just brought in an enormous dead python. Like some sort of surreal metaphor, the Vietnamese laughed and repeated the words "chop chop" as they carried their lifeless prize past the grieving Americans.

Chris Adams had just got back from Bangkok and while awaiting transport to Bartlett happened to be walking by the clearing station. As a soldier standing outside smoking waved hello, Adams noticed a Rolex on his wrist almost identical to Andy Daniel's. Thinking there was no way, Chris carried on before curiosity kicked in. The guy was gone by the time Adams returned and as he stood looking, Jim Gains wandered up from the beach. The two headed for Betty's refrigeration unit but the trooper was nowhere to be found. Thirty minutes later, just as Chris was about to give up, the individual hove into view. After a brief altercation, Chris forcibly removed and checked the watch that as he suspected had Andy's initials etched into its rear plate. Leaving the despicable lizard bleeding and broken on the ground, Chris and Jim made sure he knew exactly who they were and the reason for their violent response. Soon to be infused north, Chris did not care about repercussions, although nothing further happened. After DEROS, Chris went to visit "AJ's" mother Suzie near Demopolis, Alabama. Before saying goodbye, Chris presented Suzie with her son's watch as a forever keepsake.

COLLATERAL CARNAGE

James Mezzetta had not long taken over from John Melgaard as medic for Second Platoon. Although replacement airborne, Jim like so many others appeared to be nowhere near as fit as expected. Unable to keep up on his first patrol, Jim had to face Ron Ford, who regrettably berated, "You're here for me, mother fucker – not the other way around!" Moments later, two more FNGs fell out with blisters, causing the entire squad to be recalled back to Bartlett.

Mike Pearson spent his first week with Bravo patrolling and screening around LZ Judy. Moving eastward, the company carried out several highly successful ambushes. Herb Hohl was now executive officer, while "Joe" Noah jumped across to Second Platoon with two new lieutenants, Josef Choc and Ronald Butler, heading up First and Third.

Split into smaller groups, a couple of days later, "Paladin" deployed his three platoons onto several local creeks and trails. Within 30 minutes, "Joe" Noah came under heavy contact and was only able to extract owing to skillful Spooky support, Tiger Sharks, and artillery. The next morning, it was Choc's turn. At first contact, his point man, Dave Markievich, was lucky not to have been injured. A quick aerial check from the C&C revealed a number of bunkers directly ahead. After calling in the Red Legs, "Paladin" asked Choc if he needed additional help, but the answer came back negative and he continued to flank.

By midday, Joe Jerviss was maneuvering along an old watercourse when Corporal Butler McKinnon impaled his shin on a concealed Punji stick. As they waited for medic Stephen Oliphant, "Pineapple" happened to notice a note written in Vietnamese pinned to a wooden stake. Radio operator Joe Garrett called Choc to request their "Kit Carson" translator. As "Pineapple" turned toward Garrett, everyone heard the unmistakeable metallic ping of a grenade. The blast left Jerviss temporarily blind, peppered by shrapnel, and with an index finger dangling by a single thread of tendon. To make matters worse, a smoke canister attached to his webbing ignited and enveloped everyone in a cloak of acrid, bright yellow smoke. The VC booby trap also took out Staff Sergeant Garrett, Doc Oliphant, Dave Markievich, and Canadian Mike Shepherd – who along with Jerviss were all safely picked up and flown out to Vung Tau.

The platoon carried on and in an exchange a couple of hours later, Corporal Bennett Herrick was shot in the mouth. The Huey that came to lift the mortally wounded RTO had its own radio destroyed by ground fire. A highly coordinated artillery effort and

Tiger Shark attack allowed the dust-off to escape, but it was touch and go. Before returning to Betty, Pearson's men were successful in neutralizing the bunkers and recovered several boxes' worth of useful paperwork. Before extracting, the head of an exhumed insurgent was stuck on a pole along with a stern warning note addressed to the 482nd VC.

When Bob Mairs handed over to Major Richard Johnson, Betty was in the middle of a minor dysentery epidemic. Mairs was now replacing Houston Hauser as battalion executive officer. Leaving Bob to hold the fort, Lieutenant Colonel Elton, Major Johnson, Bob Robinson, and Captain Morely – the commander of the Fire Support and Coordination System (known as FISCORD) – flew out to gauge the current situation around Whiskey Mountain. A few days after, "Fat Cat" contracted the intestinal affliction along with dengue fever. Despite this, Mairs flatly refused Doc Lovy's advice for treatment in Japan and instead opted to remain in isolation on light duties at Betty. Over the next three horribly debilitating weeks, Bob's weight plummeted. Desperately trying to make light of his hideous situation, now little more than a bag of bones, much to everyone's amusement, Mairs decided to change his call sign to "Twiggy."

Toward the end of March, on a sweep around Whiskey, Arthur Quesada and Second Platoon came across the bodies of three adults and two kids in a burned-out bunker. Four others were still alive and they were flown back to Betty for treatment. Chris Adams watched in moral horror as one of the ARVN officers working alongside Alpha began to interrogate a group of prisoners. Frustrated by silence, the lieutenant struck one VC several times across the forehead with his pistol before angrily pulling the trigger. With that, the others burst into a cacophony of terrified chatter as Quesada took out his notebook and quietly added the dead man to his body count list.

That night, as President Johnson announced he would not be standing for re-election, Quesada's men were digging in alongside a small lake. By now, everybody knew Harold Rodney was terrified of most reptiles. Looking for a little entertainment to lighten the mood, Ronnie Ford threw a snake into his buddy's lap. Ron thought it was hilarious when Harold jumped like a jack-in-a-box from his foxhole and threatened to have Ford buried alive!

An order began to circulate that under no circumstances was anybody to use the lake for drinking or even washing. Speculation over its condition grew after a re-supply of potable water was flown in. At dusk on the third day, there was a brief exchange of fire when a lone insurgent ran into one of the troopers. Shortly before 0200hrs, John Hass woke Ed Blanco for his turn on watch. Earlier, John had heard a noise and for a short while the two listened intently before Hass returned to his position. Five minutes later, the enemy opened up with a machine gun and Ron Ford almost lost the top of his head as he strained to ascertain direction. Keeping low, Ronnie blew his claymores and with rifle above parapet, emptied ten magazines toward the enemy tracer. Blanco fired his thumper and suddenly everything went quiet. Ed was elated and lobbed over another round. Jubilation quickly turned to terror as a thump of nearby enemy mortars filled the air. Piercing their bodies with scorching hot shrapnel, the first shells slammed in close to Blanco and Danny Lopez. More attacks followed and by morning – when Ed and Danny were evacuated by the medics – almost every tree surrounding the American positions had been scythed to stumps.

Chapter 18

"Watch and Shoot"

April 1968

April Fool's Day marked one year since reactivation at Fort Campbell. Contacts were still sporadic as the Viet Cong continued with their ongoing northern migration plans. Intelligence now concluded that the 482nd was moving toward the Central Highlands. While Billie Kirk, "Paladin," and Gaffney sat in the TOC reminiscing about Chassion, outside, the first of two lifts carrying C Co and elements of 4.2-inch heavy mortars were flying to the next province. Doug Alitz was now operating with three brand-new platoon leaders – Gordon "Gordy" Gant, David Bentley, and Donald Whiteman. After clearing the LZ, Sergeant O'Neil Newkirk set off toward nearby foothills. Newkirk suddenly spotted VC gathering further along the trail in preparation to ambush Lieutenant Gant. Fearing compromise, O'Neil dropped to one knee, raised his rifle into careful aim, and gently squeezed the trigger. One man fell as the others took off under a cloud of mortar shells. Newkirk's perfect long-distance headshot turned out to be an NVA officer who ironically became the 506th enemy soldier to be killed by the Currahees.

RAGE OVER HOPE

The day after Martin Luther King Jr. was murdered, 3/506 began returning to Betty for a special three-day stand-down. Dr. King's death triggered a turning point in attitude across many of the battalion's new African American Leg replacements. When the Hook carrying TOC Headquarters took off from Hill 305, its under-slung load broke away and disappeared into the dense canopy of the Hong Phong Forest. At that moment, "Paladin" agreed with Gaffney that if a helicopter were ever to go down, then B Co would head out to assist with security and recovery. Unbelievably, 30 minutes later, while Charlie was being extracted from its recent area of operations, it happened.

Inside a flood of external rotor wash, pilot Dave Timm's slick began to violently yaw back and forth. Struggling for clearance, the main rotor struck a tree and after a brief distress call, Timm's radio fell silent. Another slick returned and hovered above the crash site. Thick with bamboo forest, it took well over an hour for anyone from C Co to reach the downed helicopter. Minus its tail section, the Huey was lying on its side, turbine humming, as the rescuers began hauling out casualties. Trapped beneath a landing strut, Lieutenant Whiteman was found unconscious. By sheer brute force, the main compartment was lifted enough to release Don, who had suffered catastrophic injuries to his head.

A dust-off arrived and began winching up survivors. Timm was dead, as were C Company's Sergeant Alan Guymon and replacement Private John Havlick. Timm's body was the last to be extracted, leaving Alan and John to be carried back to the PZ on stretchers, along with weapons and personal equipment. True to his word, "Paladin" flew out and removed anything that could be recycled before the bird was destroyed. Replaced by Alfredo "Louis" Suarez, Whiteman remained in a coma for several weeks before being returned to the States.

Unaware of the accident, everyone was looking forward to the upcoming United Service Organization Show. Drawn by trailers of free beer and soda, the apron was already packed several hours before the event was scheduled to begin. From a hangar opposite Battalion HQ, Bob Elton took to the stage and informed his men about those who had just died, along with the recent passing of Dr. King.

After a respectful one-minute silence, the show brought in from Oz finally got under way. The main attraction was an all-girl singing act backed by The Digger Revelle Band. The gig was a great success and its four provocatively dressed ladies lifted everyone's spirits immeasurably. Despite the bad news, Mike Trant's spirit was already stratospheric owing to the fact that in a few short hours he would be heading home to the real world.

OUT OF ACTION

After two days' rest, Bravo and Alpha were waiting out by the Can Do for a night combat assault as LRRPs secured their LZ east of Whiskey. Second Lieutenant David Glenn had taken over First Platoon from John Harrison, who was back in his old familiar role as exec. Both companies landed safely and by 2200hrs were en route to their pre-designated ambush sites. Early the next morning, Sergeant John Howland and replacement Private Bobby Green from Glenn's platoon were wounded and 4.2-inch Mortar Forward Observer Wayne Jester critically injured.

For several hours back at Betty, Doc Lovy and his team worked hard to save Wayne before finally airlifting him out. Andy and Curt took turns on the chopper with cardiac compressions and mouth-to-mouth. Halfway to Vung Tau, Andy pulled the plug and ordered the helicopter's return to base. As the exhausted team sat over Jester's body, their pilot reported a loss of cyclic pitch and told everyone to brace for emergency landing. Incredibly, the pilot pulled off an 80-knot, fixed wing-style approach before safely sliding the Huey to a stop!

By early evening, three miles northwest of Whiskey, Bravo was heading toward Nui Xa To or Hill 251. Searching thickets along the way, "Paladin's" men discovered various crude traps and punji stakes. Pearson reached his objective early the next morning and patiently waited for "Joe" Noah. At the same time, Lieutenant Colonel Elton and Richard Johnson set off for a rendezvous to discuss Roy Somers' latest intelligence. With migration and focus almost certainly now shifting toward the

Highlands, "Paladin" was re-tasked northwest of Phan Thiet to block potential movement.

Waiting at the PZ for his slicks to arrive, Pearson took a call from Romeo 4. His friend and colleague Sam Jacobs was working a few miles away and embroiled in a fight with around 35 insurgents. As Joe Choc was having radio problems, "Paladin" mobilized Noah and Butler, and flew direct to Sam's assistance. After saving Jacobs' ass, "Paladin" elected to settle in with Ron Butler's platoon for the evening.

Just after 0230hrs on April 13, eight heavily armed men walked into Butler's kill zone. Private Jerry Eisman triggered his claymores as both M60s choked into life. Thirty seconds later, the platoon came under direct RPG and automatic weapons fire. Two further attacks were repulsed before everyone fixed bayonets and prepared for a third. Sergeant Steve Cook's squad bore the brunt of initial casualties. The Fire Direction Center at Betty had every salient feature plotted and using these pre-recorded coordinates, Pearson systematically placed his 4.2-inch mortars onto the enemy. The VC retaliated with their own concentration as they attempted to flank Butler's platoon. One shell fell close to Pearson and radio operator John Brasher. Splinters spattered Platoon Sergeant Arthur Terronez in the face and also struck Sergeant Mark Needham and privates Bob Blackson and Joe Kelley. Eisman caught a fragment in his back while Staff Sergeant Eddie Steward was hit in the chest by a bullet.

Terronez, Steward, and Eisman were all lifted out through the dense canopy during a daring early morning basket hoist. The incredible skill shown by the dust-off undoubtedly saved their lives. Although hit in the leg and shoulder, still able to walk, Sergeant Steve Cook refused "Paladin's" order to join his wounded colleagues. By 0515hrs, the enemy had withdrawn deeper into Hong Phong, where Spooky and Naval Artillery pounded them for the next hour. Nine enemy soldiers were captured, including two NVA squad leaders and an officer who blew himself up before Pearson had a chance to fully interrogate him.

Entangled in three different contacts, by 1130hrs "Paladin" managed to identify a line of bunkers. One VC was shot out of a tree as Bravo took a step back to avoid enemy mortar fire. The withdrawal was by no means easy, carrying five wounded and their heavy personal equipment. From here, Pearson stopped and called in fast air, artillery, and Tiger Sharks. Regaining control, Mike was able to bring in a helicopter to take away sergeants Cook and Needham, along with Private Sylvestre Primous, who had just received multiple shrapnel wounds to his right leg.

With his platoon now down to 18 men, Lieutenant Butler replaced Terronez with Roger Shannon. As Pearson's re-supply bird took off, around 30 insurgents decided to attack from behind. Although wounded, Sergeant Terry Thomas remained with three other troopers to provide covering fire as Bravo turned and faced the threat. Following a successful repulsion, "Paladin" went back to his search and soon found discarded weapons, several rucksacks, and two Honda motor scooters.

Shortly after Private Ernest Ironhawk lost a foot to an anti-personnel mine, Ron Butler's platoon returned to Betty while the company settled into a new support base dedicated to Paul Cline. While at LZ Cline, low on ammunition and supplies, "Paladin" took delivery of 28 sweet-smelling Leg replacements. At the same time, Herb Hohl, "Spider," and the planning officer from First Field Force arrived to discuss Bravo's imminent return. Once back at Betty, despite having to prepare paperwork for an upcoming court martial, "Paladin" made time to visit the wounded at Vung Tau with "Spider," "Bucky" Cox (who was now the executive officer for C Company), and "Snake" McCorkle. All the patients seemed to be doing well except perhaps for Joe Garrett, whose face was completely unrecognizable.

LOVE AND WAR

Finally, Ron Ford's eight-day pass for Australia arrived. The Whisky a Go Go in Sydney was heaving when a group of girls inquired if they could share his table. While they made themselves comfortable, Ron smiled, pinched himself, and ordered the most expensive bottle of champagne on offer. Good fortune continued and before long the young sergeant was on the dance floor shaking his booty alongside Maureen Little. With her dark hair and piercing blue eyes, Maureen was sophisticated, refined, and full of fun, and for the next week they became inseparable.

While Ron was enjoying RnR with Maureen, Captain Gaffney told Joe Alexander that he had been selected to host a representative from the American Red Cross. Joe tried to wriggle out but raising a hushed finger, Tom turned away, masking an unusually playful smile. Before breakfast, Alexander put on the set of jungle fatigues he had been saving especially for DEROS. After inspecting his jeep and driver, Joe headed for Betty's Military Terminal to greet the aircraft scheduled for 1000hrs. Joe nearly choked on his coffee as a perfect vision of apple pie beauty stepped from the C-123 Provider's loading ramp, her short blonde hair neatly tucked beneath a headscarf. The name badge above her ample right breast did not immediately register as Joe escorted the young woman toward his waiting vehicle. But when the lieutenant stepped back and made full eye contact, he realized Gaffney had set him up.

An old friend from school, Rachel smelled fabulous as she threw her arms around Joe. First stop was Colonel Elton and a tour of the TOC, followed by staff offices, new underground hospital, and Battalion Headquarters before lunch. Rachel was scheduled to depart at 1500hrs, but her plane was delayed for an hour and as the driver had other duties, Joe took over and headed for a remote stretch of beach. After parking up, they sat watching Vietnamese fishing boats and a couple of LARC-V amphibious transporters moving supplies off in the distance. As Joe apologized for being such an idiot back in college, Rachel punched him lightly on the bicep. Instinctively, Joe put his arm around and gently stroked her shoulders and back. Without saying a word, she turned and right there and then kissed him. Time stood still as the couple found somewhere more comfortable nearby to "catch up" before saying goodbye.

Chapter 19

"Let the Light Shine"

Operation *MR-6*, April 26–May 16, 1968

Through special agents and aerial photography, "Spider" was now developing a flexible plan to accommodate movement across three key provinces at the heart of Military Region 6. Most of the data pointed to a specific area of foothills along the border with Lam Dong. Working alongside Lieutenant Colonel Elton's men would be two LRRP platoons from First Field Force, Third Battalion 44th ARVN, First CIDG, and Montagnard tribesmen from 208th Mike Force.

Prior to the main helicopter assault on Friday, April 26, the 482nd Main Force had been mainly using low ground to get about. Two LZs were selected around the target area, designated "Jester" and "Seebee," the latter being used by Mike Pearson and Doug Alitz. Inserted directly inside Lam Dong, Mike Force was tasked with a very specific series of night ambush patrols.

A few kilometers southeast of the suspected enemy headquarters, LZ Jester was the destination for A Co, Forward Tactical Operations Center and D Battery, 27th Artillery, for whom Captain Dowdy and his men were also providing security. For additional support, Red Legs had been instructed to anchor in with the guns from B/27 stationed 15km due north of Whiskey Mountain.

Several Romeo Teams were inserted onto the lower highland slopes, each with individual missions to patrol north. Team 3, led by Sergeant Elmer "Lee" Bradford, was jinxed from the start. Bradford's pilot was replaced at the last minute and this resulted in them being inserted at the wrong location. Communicating his concerns to Intelligence Officer Captain Bob Robinson, "Lee" was asked to hold while Battalion tried to sort things out. Shortly before dusk, a pair of American jets flew in and attacked. The unprovoked bombing left Bradford's radio operator Ed Zewert mortally injured. "Lee" and Corporal Henry Salas desperately worked to resuscitate Zewart but like the light, he slowly faded and died 20 minutes later.

First positive contact came from Mike Force when they engaged five armed men among high peaks bordering the adjoining province of Binh Thuy. At the same time, B and C companies flew out to LZ Seebee two miles west of the border with Lam Dong. Despite being set down in the wrong place, Bravo went to work screening two nearby valleys. As darkness fell, thankfully so did the level of insect activity. The next day, after removing several enormous blood-gorged leeches, Lieutenant Butler came upon a freshly built bamboo base camp. Among paperwork belonging to a local commander named Chien To, Butler discovered 300lb of rice and several hundred rounds of ammunition.

By May, after transferring to Battalion LRRPs, Tony "Alphabet" Martisauskas found himself on beach outpost duty back at Betty alongside Californian Richard Landers. Although generally quiet, with most people out on operations, several targeted attacks had recently taken place around the perimeter. At the time, Richard and his wife Dianna were expecting their third child and naturally bunker chat focused heavily on their new baby. That night, through the image intensifier, while Richard slept, "Alphabet" noticed a sampan sailing toward him. Several warning bursts were fired before enemy mortar shells began landing around the American post. Using his thumper, Landers tried to defend but was soon overwhelmed. Richard bled out as his friend lost the top of his skull to a bullet. The VC raiders, thinking "Alphabet" was also dead, searched his body before being forced back into their boats. Incredibly, Tony survived and after spending two weeks in a coma returned home, albeit permanently paralyzed from the waist downward.

THUNDER IN THE MOUNTAINS

Alpha handed over control of LZ Jester to Bravo and moved on to patrol the vast slopes overlooking Whiskey Mountain. Jester was a welcome break for "Paladin," with cold beer and clean cots. Mike was surprised when a re-supply bird brought in six new parachute-trained replacements, including 21-year-old Private John Viktoryn from Cleveland. Pearson sat the guys down for a relaxed 60-minute "welcome" talk, before sending them across to Joe Choc, who was just about to fly out in support of Romeo 1.

Meanwhile, Pearson gathered up the rest of his men and headed southwest to tie in with Romeo 2, who had been shadowing a VC platoon. Dressed in camouflage fatigues and bush hats, the Cong were moving along a shallow valley heading toward an abandoned hamlet called Dang Gia. Bravo had not been on the ground long when Romeo 2 was forced into action. As Corporal Carl Locklear moved forward to check a body with his radio operator Tim Keller, the enemy came charging around the track bend. Two days later, Keller was mortally wounded while searching for two American nurses thought to be held captive across the Provincial Border. "Paladin" flew northwest into a forested valley to assist Romeo 5, where Staff Sergeant Jerry Ford had spotted six black-suited VC in a half-built base camp. When Pearson and Third Platoon dropped in, the VC had already gone, but a later search revealed an indigenous woman and a boy who both tried to escape.

Named in honor of Jim Bunn, Captain Dowdy was now working from Firebase Bunn situated on a high plateau close to the settlement of Bao Houi. C Company was making good progress further west on Nui Song Len Mountain, where Alitz uncovered a small base camp.

Even further west, Sergeant Sam Jacobs and his Romeo Team had been inserted into the Suoi Kabet River Valley. By now, Jerry Gomes had left S&T and was a member of Sam's crew. The first couple of five-day patrols were a steep learning curve but Gomes was more than ready for his new challenge. A "Kit Carson Scout" had been leading them to a hidden cache of weapons when Jacobs decided to stop for the night at an old abandoned complex. Jerry was enjoying his specialist LRRP rations when a VC suddenly appeared in front of him. The guy was talking to someone behind as Jerry and the others stood to. Turning on his heels, the man disappeared back down the trail with the Americans in hot pursuit. After a few minutes, the boys came across six rucksacks containing women's clothing and other girly supplies, plus a number of bags filled with what appeared to be cannabis. Next to each "ruck" was a pair of flip-flops all neatly facing toward the "lay-up point," as if the occupants had simply stepped out and flown away!

Over the next few days, 3/506 and its associates fought dozens of skirmishes across the Southern highland slopes, killing and capturing several more insurgents, plus seizing a harvest of camps, bunkers, weapons, rice, and equipment. Battalion LRRPs were constantly in the shadows watching and waiting. Staff Sergeant Mifflin Tichenor's point man Homer Sutton emerged from a bamboo thicket and suddenly opened fire. Twenty-five meters away, a camouflaged lookout fell dead from a tree. As Mifflin and scout "Chia" went forward to check the body, they came under aggressive but relatively innacurate fire. The Tiger Sharks were overhead in less than three minutes and several large secondary explosions followed their attacks. A quick ground sweep afterward revealed that the VC had not been infantry but a group of demolition engineers out training for an upcoming mission.

Again, Sergeant Homer Sutton was on point during a night patrol in the hills when another deserted base camp revealed its treasures. After reporting their location, Sutton located a second complex of around 14 bunkers containing boxes of mortar shells and sacks of rice. After waiting all night, the men monitored a VC squad as it moved toward the cache. A fierce gun battle ensued, resulting in seven Vietnamese dead and one prisoner. When questioned, the 14-year-old detainee explained that he was a runner for what they were calling an "arrow team" created specifically to train new recruits.

When acting as medic for one of the Romeos, Tom Lundgren's host team ran out of water in thick triple-canopy jungle. A Hook soon appeared overhead, with a bright-orange tube dangling from its underbelly. Everyone knew this was not going to end well and sure enough, Tom was soon seeking cover in a nearby rock formation. Suddenly, "Spider" excitedly announced over the radio that he was going to direct them toward the enemy gunfire. At that point, the dehydrated troopers did not have the energy to go chasing ghosts. Instead, they began taking rough potshots at the C&C helicopter. Unable to determine from where these bullets were coming, everyone cheered as Elton announced it was no longer safe for him to remain on station. Late on May 5, from separate locations, Bravo departed the foothills in pouring rain and flew south to a large walled settlement along Highway 8 known as Ap Binh-Lam.

Surprisingly, activity from the 482nd VC had again been on the increase and fearful of another attack, "Spider" wanted "Paladin" to take care of business. First Sergeant Roberts arrived on the re-supply early the next morning with more replacements, including new Platoon Sergeant Fred Pickrell. Fred had been pulled across from C Company to join Ron Butler, whom he remembered from time spent as an instructor at OCS.

By lunchtime, supported by Dusters from Betty, Mike was herding his force alongside a canal in the general direction of Whiskey Mountain. Just after sunrise the next morning, as one of "Joe" Noah's men was gathering in his claymores, he was shot in the shoulder at long range. But when the Dusters were inexplicably recalled to base, morale took a significant drop. Adding to the problem, Noah and his troops were picked up and flown north for "Palace Guard" or TOC security duty at Firebase Bunn.

The sun had been up for several hours as Bravo shadowed the railway line toward Muong Man. By midday, Joe Choc was on task and moving to reconnoiter, while "Paladin" and Butler hooked up with Romeo 3 for a series of ambushes. Suddenly, the shit hit the fan when Sergeant Terry Thomas detonated his claymores. The enemy responded with mortars and rockets as "Paladin" ordered Ron Butler to send a squad up to support Terry. A few minutes later, the FAC spotted 20 VC moving toward a line of bunkers. While the gunships were driving home their attack, Pearson ordered Joe Choc into position with First Platoon.

Almost immediately, Choc ran into trouble. Butler tried to help but continual harassment delayed him for almost 45 minutes. Three of Choc's men were wounded while trying to reach Sergeant Rich Gonzalez. The dust-off held for almost an hour as Tiger Sharks blasted the VC with everything they had. When the first Skyraiders arrived, Gonzalez, who had been Joe Jerviss' original radioman, and new trooper John Viktoryn were both recovered dead. By 1800hrs, Alpha hurriedly flew in to reinforce, but by then the enemy had melted away and was nowhere to be seen.

After evacuating 11 wounded, Bravo picked itself up and continued west. "Paladin" thought he was being followed and sent Lieutenant Butler up a nearby hill as top cover. "Joe" Noah stopped off and by mid-afternoon engaged ten insurgents. In the firefight, Squad Leader Preston Howell was killed.

During the early hours, Pearson was awoken by Lee McCray after the sergeant heard voices less than 100m away. By first light, "Paladin" sent McCray and his squad out to investigate. The voices belonged to a company from the 482nd Main Force Battalion who had arrived and dug in during the night. Lee called in the Tiger Sharks and Skyraiders, who successfully neutralized the positions. By mid-afternoon, Bravo was on the move again and rotating back to LZ Bunn for Palace Guard. The last two weeks had been some of the most physically tiring that Pearson had experienced in a long while. Returning to Betty with "Joe" Noah and his men, Mike soon found himself briefing a handful of "experienced" new arrivals from the 187th Airborne and 2/506, who included Staff Sergeant Bob Hardin and Sergeant Tom Cox. "Paladin" was not sure about Cox, who a few days later suspiciously fired into his own foot during an attack.

SONG MAO

Captain Doug Alitz left C Co and moved on to Phu Bai. By coincidence, when Captain David Hillard took over on May 11, the enemy chose to rise up across Vietnam in another mini-offensive. At that time, the VC were besieging several ARVN outposts along Highway 1. Most of these localized attacks came from the sun-bleached sand dunes and paddies south of Song Mao. Captain Hillard had not even properly introduced himself before his company was ordered into action.

Sandwiched between Mao and Luy rivers, the area was inter-cut by dozens of smaller waterways and irrigation canals. Sergeants Tommy Williams III and Manuel Huitron had only just cleared the LZ when they became targets for an enemy machine-gun crew. Manny and replacement Frank Zustiak were hit. Blasted by a concussion grenade, although deaf and bleeding, new Third Platoon leader Lieutenant "Louis" Suarez was luckier than Gordon Gant, who had been shot in the arm. As battle commenced, the entire company became pinned down by heavier fire coming from a nearby canal.

Several new guys risked all to retrieve their two colleagues. While the wounded were being treated, "TW3's" radio operator Tim Barnes calmly called up Carl Decker to ask for help. From a distance, David Bentley and Second Platoon looked on as Tommy took his remaining men and stormed an enemy observation post. In a manic exchange of fire, Barnes killed one NVA at close range with a thumper. Decker's radio crackled with activity as Bentley set about trying to move all three elements on line. Then a message from First Platoon revealed that a small team had been sent to support "TW3" and was now in desperate need of a replacement radio. Captain Hillard momentarily suspended Bentley's advance and granted permission for Decker to go forward with his "25" and join the rescue team. Carl made Bentley's medic, Doc Bolt, promise not to come after him if he went down. Attaching some surgical tubing around Decker's upper arms, Bolt reluctantly agreed and wished him luck. At that moment, word came down from the

FAC that Captain Hillard's request for an air strike was awaiting authorization.

Impatiently, Carl sprinted out through scraggy brush toward the three troopers, who were anxiously beckoning from a streambed. Decker had not gone far when he caught sight of an anti-aircraft gun on a dike over to his right. Its North Vietnamese crew were hand-cranking the weapon down and around toward him. Thankfully, fast air arrived and the crew immediately retrained their heavy-caliber gun skyward. While Decker was requesting a strafing run, the spotter plane took a direct hit through one wing and was forced back to Betty for repairs.

The aerial interruption probably saved Carl's life, but there was no time to reflect. Pumped full of adrenaline, Decker sprinted like a lunatic and jumped in on top of the rescuers. With the sun now setting, trapped in no-man's land, it looked like "TW3" and his boys would soon be surrounded. As a consequence, Hillard decided to send out another squad led by Lieutenant Bentley to reconnoiter a secondary extraction route. A full moon reflected brightly off white sand, but as Bentley was preparing to move, Spooky arrived and the enemy began to withdraw.

Bravo had already been mobilized in support of Hillard and was inbound by road from Betty. Captain Pearson had not traveled far along Highway 1 when things began to unravel. A few minutes into his advance, the captain was forced to stop. Blocking the road, a mine strike had disabled a large fruit truck, which then had to be cleared by demolition engineers. Further along the highway, Mike came under fire from a group of twitchy ARVN. As his trucks accelerated to keep pace, one hit a large bump and launched two men over the tailgate. Finally, upon arrival at Song Mao, "Joe" Noah and First Platoon were put on immediate standby for an early morning sweep. After flying in to take over Suarez's platoon, "Bucky" Cox joined forces with Noah to clear the napalm-drenched dunes. Although 12 bodies were recovered, incredibly there was nothing left to indicate any previous mass occupation apart from a few scattered, blood-soaked bandages.

Chapter 20

"Return to the Graveyard"

Operation *Rockne Gold*, May 19–27, 1968

After Song Mao, attention again turned westward toward the Ca Na Peninsula. The situation here on Cape Padaran had not really changed since Operation *Rose*, except now the 610th NVA Battalion had made it their new operational home. Reconnaissance teams from 20th Infantry had already been on the ground for two days. However, after scrambling up rugged sea cliffs south of Son Hai, Team 33 had been compromised and extracted back to Tan Son Airbase at Phan Rang.

As Doc Lovy and his medics boarded their Chinook, Bravo and Charlie were being airlifted from Song Mao by the 192nd Army Helicopter Company to the Dragon's Graveyard. Using its original base for Operation *Rose*, the TOC would be coordinating alongside Red Legs artillery and Mike Force security. A number of other Mike and Ranger units were also being employed alongside a small force of Koreans and the Fletcher-class destroyer USS *Uhlmann*.

202nd Mike Force drove south along Highway 1 from Tan Son toward the sea to rendezvous with A Co down in the valley. The meeting point between coastal massifs was below a newly established radio relay station. David Hillard and Charlie were inserted onto the high plateau in readiness to protect "Spider's" incoming Forward Command Post. Meanwhile, a protective shield of Romeo and LRRP teams was deployed across Nui Geo and Nui Da Bac. While all of this was happening, Bravo flew into their old stomping ground among the salt fields near Son Hai.

The next afternoon, on May 20, Captain Robinson arrived at "Paladin's" location to drop off a VC prisoner. The man, nicknamed "Con," had agreed to lead Bravo toward his previous base situated a few miles further north. "El Torro," the Naval Gunfire Observer from *Uhlmann*, inquired what "Paladin's" final plans might be for "Con." When Pearson asked why, the Marine audaciously explained that he was seeking revenge after the recent death of his brother. "Paladin" was not about to sanction murder and shut "El Torro" down immediately with a few choice words and threats.

Two days later, as Bravo traversed beneath "Con's" old camp at Nui Cha Bang, they came under heavy mortar fire from the ridge above. During a brief exchange, Sergeant Ken Keithley was seriously wounded while a follow-up air strike badly injured Lieutenant Butler, his platoon sergeant Fred Pickrell, Sergeant Bill Harvin, and Private Larry Walker. After Butler and the others were airlifted out, frustrated by the futility of events, "Paladin" placed Staff Sergeant Bob Hardin in temporary command of Ron's platoon.

Before midday on the 23rd, A Co flew in, allowing Lieutenant Choc and his boys to move west in support of "Paladin." Almost immediately, Alpha began picking up sniper fire and while ascending a small river valley, shot and killed two insurgents. Thirty-five minutes later, Dowdy and his men were elated to discover dozens of concealed bunkers and another 25 fighting positions on high ground across to their right. Dowdy's ecstatic reconnaissance-in-force had just uncovered a major training camp. Further investigation revealed caches of clothing, rice, medical supplies, weapons, and ammunition. Training aids and US aircraft recognition documents were also recovered. Piles of mimeographed leaflets caused a ripple of amusement, stating, "You are now a prisoner of war. You are in safe hands, except for attacks from your own artillery, mortars, and air strikes. If you need anything, ask our interpreters. Thank you for your assistance."

The next day, Bravo walked into "Con's" abandoned camp. The triple feature overlooked Route 407, with commanding views back to the coast and Son Hai. While "Con" was showing "Paladin" around, he spotted a booby trap and saved Joe Choc's life. Not wishing to go any further, "Paladin" decided to call for an "arrow" and dug in for the night along a nearby ridge.

As the last day of Operation *Rockne Gold* loomed, 3/506 withdrew by helicopter back to Highway 1 in preparation for an upcoming motor march. A couple of hours after Third Platoon Bravo flew out to Phan Thiet, everyone else boarded trucks and headed for Song Mao. One hour into his journey, "Paladin" received a call from the C&C helicopter reporting a VC unit moving southeast of the airstrip. Tiger Sharks were sent but found nothing to engage. That night in the club, Pearson was drinking with Dave Johnson from Maintenance, when informed that his company and Red Legs were to remain as rear guard for the next few days.

On May 28, "Paladin" took his remaining two platoons and headed northeast in torrential rain. Overnight, thick storm-laden clouds had arrived to usher in monsoon season, and with it a rapid rise of trenchfoot. After crossing the swollen River Mao, Choc and Noah split to carry out their own individual patrols. Some four hours later, "Paladin" and Choc came under fire and called in artillery before making camp. The next morning, a burst of enemy machine-gun fire rang out from across the clearing, mortally wounding Corporal Harold Mason. As "Paladin" mobilized the Red Legs in response, Lieutenant Colonel Elton swept down and evacuated the 21-year-old New Yorker in his C&C chopper.

IN HONOR OF A FRIEND

Mason's body was dropped off outside Battalion Headquarters as Lieutenant David Rivers prepared to take over Gordon Gant's old platoon. When Rivers graduated West Point in mid-'67, his class went on to have the highest KIA ratio in Vietnam. Dave and fellow cadet John Brown followed identical paths through Airborne and Ranger School. On December 16, Rivers married his high school sweetheart Emily before heading off with John and another friend Mike Deane to join the 82nd Airborne.

When North Korea captured the intelligence ship USS *Pueblo*, Rivers was an executive officer and expected to be in the States for at least another year. However, as the *Pueblo* crisis developed, his unit was issued winter clothing and put on ready reaction mode. As Tet unraveled, Dave and around 100 other "all-American" juniors were ordered to Vietnam. Rivers and his two friends arrived at the 90th Replacement Company on May 11, before being sent to Bien Hoa for P Training. Ten days later, Dave said goodbye to his chums, who were being posted north to 2/502. Tragically, shortly after arriving at Camp Eagle, John Brown was killed and Mike Deane mortally wounded in one of the worst sapper assaults of the war.

As news filtered through about the attack on Camp Eagle, Nick Nahas became 3/506 Task Force adjutant and appointed Jim Kessinger as his assistant. Once or twice a week, a transport plane would fly in from Phan Rang delivering supplies and replacement personnel. Nick and Jim decided to station an NCO at the base to facilitate movement and fill any extra space with PX goods, such as beer and sodas, specifically for the troopers when they were stood down.

WHAT MAKES THE GRASS GROW?

Commanded by Captain Kenneth Waylonis and with "Louis" Suarez as executive officer, a fourth rifle company coded "Delta" formed from the battalion. Likewise, another was created to encompass HHC's previous combat support functions such as 4.2-inch heavy mortars, LRRPs Platoon, ground surveillance radar, and air defense sections. Known as E Company, Joe Alexander took on a dual role as its executive officer and 4.2-inch Mortar Platoon leader. Recently arrived, First Lieutenant George Blakay agreed to take temporary command of the 81mm mortars. Like most new officers, George was now parked in a slot awaiting an opening within one of the line platoons.

Joe Alexander's new posting under Captain Bill Knowlton was a gift to his increasing skill set. E Company's main mission was to provide muscle for LZ Betty. The fire support officer (FSO) assigned

E Company its targets based on range and firepower. Fire missions would also come in from the perimeter towers and local ARVN. But before launching, Alexander always had to get clearance from FISCORD Captain Morely, who processed and managed all Task Force Artillery, Aviation, and Naval assets.

On occasion, when Joe's heavy mortars were tasked to operate "outside the wire," it was necessary to split down into smaller sections. During one of these excursions, Major General Melvin Zais, the new 101st commander, flew in to personally award Alexander his Silver Star for February 19. During another forward mission, new Battalion Executive Major Osborne accompanied Joe in support of the Phoenix Program. For several days, Joe took his orders directly from the CIA, who never fully explained the true nature of his specific targets.

On June 1, "Paladin" and "Spider" spoke a few solemn words at a joint memorial service in front of Battalion Headquarters at Betty. "Paladin" and Bravo then led an E Co Task Force into the Western foothills to support LRRPs, who were monitoring a surge in VC movement. Devoid of any roads or tracks, the remote area was covered in hideously thick vegetation and rocks. By nightfall, after finding no sign of any enemy presence, "Paladin" called a halt and set up his night perimeter. With monsoon season now well and truly under way, and after a night of pouring rain, B Company made their way to the top of a ridge and settled into ambush. Ten suspects were soon caught and choppered away. The slick also brought in four new "Kit Carson Scouts," who had previously belonged to the 482nd and 186th Main Force VC.

A day or so later, Pearson's men were picked up and flown 10km south to assist LRRPs who were in trouble. One of their guys, Sergeant Dennis Sutton from Romeo 3, had been mortally wounded and with no available Tiger Shark support, the dust-off could not get in. The 22-year-old was eventually extracted by "Spider" in the C&C and flown back to Phan Thiet, where Doc Lovy was unable to save him. Ironically, Dennis had just returned from compassionate home leave following the death of his sister and was now only one month short of going home.

Chapter 21

"The Bitterest Pill"

Operation *Banjo Royce* and Beyond – June/July 1968

Previously in late May, the 186th Main and 810th Local Force VC Co had attacked Da Lat with around 500 fighters, throwing the town into crisis. Once again, its tarmac mountain airstrip at Cam Ly and US-built Atomic Center were both under threat. While America reeled from Bobby Kennedy's recent assassination, B Co plus Romeo and 20th Infantry LRRPs flew into Cam Ly. Kennedy was staunchly against the war and as prime successor to Johnson, his murder in Los Angeles meant nothing would change anytime soon.

The next morning, C Co arrived by C-130 from Phan Rang alongside Alpha. Although beaten back into the mountains by government troops, at least two companies of VC were still active. Much had changed in the capital of Tuyen Duc since 3/506 last drove through its colonial streets. Since then, the former Imperial fiefdom had been badly damaged during Tet. Da Lat's ten-day battle cost several hundred lives as ARVN, aided by cadets from the nearby Military Academy and American MPs, slogged it out to defend the city.

Second Vietnamese Ranger Group plus three companies from Mike Force and elements of the 44th ARVN would all be joining 3/506 for this mini-expedition. Earlier on June 1, the Vietnamese 11th Rangers had engaged with 186th Main Force in a high, rugged valley overlooking Cam Ly. Despite being well trained, enemy losses were high, with over 50 killed and wounded. More skirmishes took place 10km further south, close to a minor mountain road that linked into the airfield. Covered by dense forests, the majestic high ground concealed hundreds of camps and bunkers. Many had already been destroyed by South Vietnamese troops, who forced the insurgents to dilute into much smaller groups.

Joe Edwards Jr. was Lieutenant David Glenn's new African American platoon sergeant. Edwards always joked that he had received his "OJT" during the riots in Detroit. At the time of Joe's arrival, one of the new legs in Ed Bassista's squad was actively trying to stir up anti-racial feeling. Before the soldier arrived, everyone, no matter what their ethnicity, felt they were in this war together. When several black troopers complained about the young "Panthers'" constant negative rhetoric, Joe Edwards was compelled to take action. After making an incision in his own arm, Joe called Ed Bassista over. Without hesitation, Ed presented as Joe gently sliced into him before locking forearms. Turning toward the agitator, Edwards spat, "See, you asshole, our blood is all the fucking same ... so either you drop this now or face retribution ... the choice is yours; do you understand me?"

TO DARE AND DIE

A three-day-old insurgent camp consisting of over 40 bunkers was uncovered on a 1,600m-high mountain peak 3km due west of the airfield. This particular base had commanding views far beyond Da Lat. At the same time, David Bentley prepared to take over both 4.2-inch and 81mm platoons while George Blakay moved across to B Co. During the reshuffle, "Joe" Noah became exec and handed over his Second Platoon to new leg officer Wallace Brown.

By June 10, A Company was shadowing a westerly track, away from the road leading to Cam Ly. Scouting beneath Nui Dro Mountain, Captain Dowdy and his men thwarted a supply party of five teenage girls and their VC security guard hauling over 300lb of rice. One of the girls agreed to lead Dowdy to a nearby settlement where a further three tons had been stored in a tin shack. From here, the 16-year-old agreed to take Alpha northwest up valley to her base camp. Again, due to the monsoon, all waterways in the vicinity were at overflow, making covert local movement painfully slow and challenging.

En route, Arthur Quesada's guys from Second Platoon engaged two VC trail watchers who were trying to kill the girl. Biven Patterson was on point and managed to take one down, but the other fled into dense undergrowth. When Quesada ordered his M60 team into action, their gun jammed. Shrapnel from a thumper round, launched by Danny Lopez, struck Quesada's radio operator, Arthur Gaudreau, in the neck. Medics Max Sclair and Jim Mezzetta started an IV as the platoon set about clearing a makeshift PZ for medivac. Sclair was a conscientious objector and usually worked in the clearing station at Betty alongside another pacifist, James Shaughnessy. Everyone thought Gaudreau, who had joined Alpha in mid-January, was going to be OK, but sadly the gifted young artist died a few days later in hospital.

Nearby, "Paladin" was extracted and returned to Betty for a special disciplinary hearing against three Bravo absentees with Civil Affairs Officer Captain Robert Bates. Heavily tattooed, Bates—from Beacon Falls, Connecticut—was ex-Special Forces and still deeply involved with the Phoenix Program. Bob also spoke fluent Vietnamese and was a long-time friend of Tom Gaffney's. Initially, Lieutenant Colonel Elton intended for Bates to take over from Pearson, who was now preparing to leave for First Brigade. However, on June 17, as Doc Lovy headed for Tokyo, Captain Dowdy was evacuated to hospital and Bates switched across to Alpha. Nicknamed "The Man in Black," due to his penchant for wearing traditional Vietnamese "pajama-style" clothing, Bob was also known to have taken part in several undercover assassinations and had achieved a fearsome reputation.

Colonel John Collins from First Brigade was trying to get Elton to extend his tour. Torn, "Spider" asked Captain Nahas for advice. Nick basically told him, "You have done your time, now jump on the helicopter and get out of here." Shortly afterward, it was announced that Lieutenant Colonel Walter Price from Stillwater,

Oklahoma was to be the new CO. Price, call sign "Brown Badger," took over on June 18, in a special ceremony and medal presentation at Bao Loc. Leading the handover along with Collins were Major General William Peers from First Field Force, Deputy 101st Divisional Commander Lieutenant General Frank Clay, and 4/503 boss Lieutenant Colonel John Cleland from the 173rd Airborne Brigade. At the time, Cleland was running a small local task force soon to be redesignated "South" and amalgamated with 3/506, 44th ARVN, and 2nd Ranger Group. Leaving "Joe" Noah in temporary command, "Paladin" took the opportunity to say goodbye to Nahas and Kessinger before heading off to Bien Hoa with "Spider."

By early afternoon, Lieutenant Colonel Price began moving westward to assist the 503rd, who were heavily engaged in a valley south of Highway 20. Near the confluence of the Da Rgna and Da Riam rivers, the 503rd had suffered seven dead and 33 wounded after stumbling across a multi-bunkered enemy base camp. Belonging to C-740 Local Force, the facility was heavily protected by a network of World War I-style trenches and barbed wire entanglements.

Hampered throughout by bad weather, codenamed "Harmon Green," the new assignment began on June 17, with several independent Search and Destroy missions. During the first day, 3/506 found ten camouflaged caches on covered platforms. Among these initial hauls were a huge variety of weapons, explosives, flour, rice, dried milk, and communications equipment. Early the next morning, Lieutenant Quesada was leading his troopers through bone-soaking rain toward a highland settlement called B Kuac. Coming under attack, Quesada took a squad and skirmished uphill. Shrouded by mist, an entrenched enemy platoon lay in wait and within seconds the lieutenant was dead. Three hours later, Alpha found 12 rucksacks belonging to 145th Main Force full of penicillin and morphine. As Captain Bates uncovered his own enormous weapons, ammunition, and cannabis find, word arrived that two helicopters had gone down somewhere in the local area. Joe Choc and First Platoon B Co were airlifted to the second crash site, where they recovered a dead pilot and crewman from the 192nd Army Helicopter Company. Afterward, Choc was collected and flown a short distance south to where Bravo had established a new Fire Support Base named after Ed Zewert, who had been killed in April.

While things were fairly uneventful for David Hillard and C Co, Bob Bates continued to find more enemy caches in the vicinity of B Kuac village. Likewise, operating over to Alpha's west, government troops from 408th Scout Company also had great success. Although 3/506 played a relatively small part in Harmon Green, it had been vital in helping locate and recover a huge amount of arms and equipment essential to the 145th Main Force war effort.

While the battalion extracted back to Phan Thiet, Charlie were sent to secure LZ Bartlett before it reopened. Dave Rivers, Max Cadena, and their platoon were on the first lift. Cadena had only just returned from hospital and everyone was overjoyed to see him back on the line. However, Max's alcoholism had grown worse and only "Bucky" Cox and Ron Newton were able to "control" him when intoxicated. Only the day before, when they found a VC supply point, Max disappeared with a few bottles of wine and left Rivers to set up their night perimeter defenses. On the plus side, Cadena still retained his uncanny sixth sense of what tactics would work in this strange war of micro-combat.

After Hillard and his men screened the area surrounding Bartlett, a squad of engineers armed with metal detectors arrived to check the LZ. Upon completion, the choppers began arriving with artillery, ammunition, equipment, and people. Later in the afternoon, Rivers and Cadena were patrolling Bartlett's lower slopes when they heard a terrific explosion from the helipad. Before they realized it was an IED, one of Dave's men questioned why nobody had called "Fire in the hole!"

Everything stopped as all personnel were gathered for roll call. Lieutenant Dennis Kinnard, the new forward observer for Alpha, was still unaccounted for when his radio operator staggered in badly concussed. After a frantic search, David Bentley found Kinnard's mangled remains about 30yds away from the pad in a clump of bushes. When called back, the engineers found a second charge. The battery-operated device utilized a 105mm howitzer shell fitted with a cleverly designed bamboo pressure pad. Kinnard had just waved off his Huey when the accident happened. As Tom Gentry was gathering Kinnard's possessions, he found a letter from Den's wife Carol announcing she was pregnant with their first child.

SEE YOU IN THE REAL WORLD – JULY 1968

Working from LZ Betty, Lieutenant Colonel Price was now part of Task Force South and supporting ARVN Forces across the region. Further to this, Roy Somers established a LRRP training school and his first in-house course was so successful that it became a regular fixture for the 44th ARVN's junior officers.

Underneath a stormy night sky, Sergeant Ed Taylor and his squad from First Platoon Alpha waited patiently in ambush. Silhouetted by a bolt of lightning, a shadowy figure walked past and unwittingly kicked over a claymore. As Taylor triggered his remaining mines, a sound of wailing encouraged John Harrison to launch a flare. The cupola of light showed a VC mortarman kneeling next to his wounded assistant. Speaking in Vietnamese, Bob Bates convinced them both to surrender and sent two teams forward to help. Later, when more wounded began to appear, Bates instructed each to crawl toward him on all fours. Throughout the night, others seeking medical attention also came in voluntarily, including a company executive officer and platoon leader.

On cloverleaf patrols, if Lieutenant Harrison wanted his guys to come back, he would blow a whistle. Months before, Tom Gaffney had given one to each Alpha Platoon leader to use as a last resort during the heat of battle. Although a whistle did not need batteries, when used it could and often did attract enemy fire.

Several times over the last few months, Ed Bassista's RnR requests for Australia had been brushed aside. After being told by Captain Bates to get ready for eight days in Oz, Ed was ecstatic. Naively, Bassista assumed that upon his return he would be in line for a cushy rear echelon desk job and began saying his goodbyes. One guy he was really going to miss was Sergeant Keith Rowell. Over the last few months, both men had grown closer than brothers.

Keith confided in Ed on many things, including his complex and turbulent personal life. Before going overseas, Keith and his wife Ann had been experiencing marital issues, but all that had changed. During his recent leave to Hawaii, Keith managed to patch things up with Ann and they were now back stronger than ever.

Ed was still saying goodbye to his friend when the chopper arrived and burst his euphoric bubble. Bassista's leave allocation was no longer available and, freaking out, he started screaming and swearing at Bates. About half an hour later, the captain called Bassista back to his CP and offered a last-minute cancelation for Kuala Lumpur. The city had only just opened as a destination for American troops and was still largely unknown. Ed thought for a moment before deciding to accept. What followed was beyond Ed's wildest comprehension and his only regret was to take a short break from the English-speaking debauchery and go hunting wild boar.

Unlike Bassista, Ron Ford did get a job at Betty about a month before release. As NCO in charge of bunker guard, he figured it was safe duty, until one night when a VC rocket skimmed his head by inches. It seemed like a lifetime since Phan Rang when Ford struck up a conversation with a homeward-bound grunt. The guy had given Ron his "lucky" wallet and Ford had carried it religiously for 259 days before dutifully handing it on to another "virgin" as he left Vietnam on July 15.

It was pretty much the same for Cleo Delong and Mike Krawczyk, who had also now been removed from the field. Mike loved this last assignment and quickly adapted to lazy French bunker life. Occasionally, his peace would be shattered by a mortar or rocket attack that nearly always threw the new guys into panic. Like so many end-of-tour veterans, Krawczyk now had that unmistakeable hollow-eyed look and referred to all his draftee bunker buddies as "kids" even though they were mostly older.

Joe Alexander finally got leave to Sydney, where he hoped to meet a lush, blue-eyed blonde and somehow managed two! Both were English and working on a cruise ship docked out in the harbor. Athletic and affectionate, the girls took him to see the Everly Brothers, who were in residency at Chequers Nightclub. Joe had always been a big fan of Don and Phil Everly, who came from Knoxville, Tennessee, just a few miles down the road from where he grew up.

SONS OF THE NEW STORM – WHISKEY MOUNTAIN – JULY 17, 1968

The last major "boat trooper" engagement took place on July 17 when government troops encountered a large entrenched enemy force 4km due south of Whiskey. All of "Brown Badger's" Rifle companies were recalled to prearranged PZs from their respective missions. At the time, Alpha and Delta were ten miles west of Whiskey. Further north, Dave Rivers' First Platoon was working with Bravo while the remainder of C Company were at Phan Thiet. Shortly after 1300hrs, C Company abandoned their security mission and took off from Betty. Captain Hillard was followed by Bravo, while Alpha and Delta landed further southeast. Although C Co and 3/44 ARVN successfully connected, Bravo was unable to do the same with 2/44 due to unduly heavy resistance.

By late afternoon, Alpha and Delta made first contact when 482nd VC unleashed a barrage of mortars and rockets from a nearby tree line. As Alpha tried to consolidate and deal with its many wounded, Captain Bill Knowlton and B Co arrived on their left flank. Alpha were now slightly behind Bravo on the other side of a small clearing. Medic Tom "Swede" Lundgren was working with B Co when Knowlton decided to try to complete the encirclement before nightfall. Everybody dropped their rucks and rushed forward, leaving Tom behind struggling to remove his aid bag. Once out in the paddy, Lundgren could feel bullets cracking overhead. Raising a finger, each exposure was met by a burst of machine-gun fire. Knowlton's First Platoon bore the initial brunt and saw Lieutenant Steven Simpson and several senior and junior NCOs badly wounded as they tried and failed to reach the ARVN.

Staff Sergeant Willie Washington led a team through heavy fire in an attempt to extract the wounded. One casualty, a thumper guy, handed Tom Lundgren his M79. The medic immediately put it to good use and obliterated the enemy machine gun with a volley of 40mm. Another trooper brought in was suffering with a serious entry wound just below the collarbone and an exit above his scapula. Then a tall blond guy casually strolled over. Flat on his belly, Tom could see a shallow groove from a bullet just above the man's larynx. As Lundgren went to stand … it happened again. By some miracle, this second round also skimmed across the guy's throat. The trooper began hollering like a maniac and only calmed down when issued with a field medical tag and sent off toward A Co and helicopter extraction point.

Lundgren tried several times to start an IV on another casualty. The black soldier appeared to be fading as Tom asked, "If you die, everyone back at base will think I'm an asshole, so for my own self-respect please hang on … at least until we can get you to the medivac!" Tom grinned with satisfaction as his now-revitalized patient shouted abuse and gave him the finger while being loaded and flown away. A call came through to attend another soldier lying in full view of the enemy. By this time, Lundgren was exhausted with dehydration and disregarding any thought of safety, walked out into the open. Luckily for him, the enemy were low on ammunition and withholding fire.

Wally Brown's medic, Corporal Donald Smith, had been lightly wounded earlier while scuttling back and forth with his casualties. Captain Knowlton had already flagged up the risks but Don laughed and shrugged it off. Later, when word went round that Smitty had been killed, Tom Lundgren joined four volunteers and moved northwest toward Alpha to help. In the course of retrieving Smith's body, three members of the rescue group were shot and wounded. Suddenly, Tom found himself alone with a black sergeant who suggested they use smoke. The screen worked and they managed to drag Smith back into cover. When Tom examined Don's chest, he counted five entry wounds in the rough shape of a pentagram.

After dark, Captain Knowlton took over Steve Simpson's platoon as they were trying to reorganize and recover Private Doug Henning. Ex-CSF, Henning had only just been posted in from Battalion LRRPs when he volunteered to go out and look for a couple of missing men. Accidentally exposed by an Alpha flare, Henning immediately drew sniper fire. Captain Knowlton managed to get Doug back to safety but the young boat trooper from New York died shortly afterward. As a gap still existed between B Co and 2/44 ARVN, the nearby Ranger Force Company was called forward but frustratingly failed to respond.

Sporadic small-arms fire continued throughout the night, as did "danger close" artillery directed by Bravo's Forward Observer Charlie Moseley. Between each barrage, lines of green tracer struck out at the arriving medivacs; however, this soon stopped as gunships, air strikes, and Spooky saturated the enemy positions. Last contact was around 0200hrs, when D Co came under heavy 60mm mortar bombardment. Despite this, by sunrise 482nd VC had recovered most of their 60 dead and melted through the southeastern gap toward the Hong Phong Forest.

While peering from his foxhole, Tom Lundgren noticed the tail fin from a Chinese B40 rocket. As he picked it up, a captain arrived with Wally Brown. The officer, who was probably Bill Knowlton, had his back to Tom as he angrily spluttered, "That one rocket could have killed us all!" Lundgren casually waved the fins above Knowlton's head and grinned mischievously at Wally, who tried his best not to laugh. Despite Tom's gallows humor, 2/44 ARVN had suffered five dead and 45 wounded, plus an alarming number of their M16s were also missing. Among 3/506's 30 casualties were many recent replacements from March and April. Private James Shaugnessy from newbie Lieutenant Barry Myerson's Second Platoon Alpha became the third KIA when he died later at Long Binh. Shaugnessy had only recently been assigned to Jim Mezzetta as a medical assistant. Previously taken off the line by John Harrison, Shaugnessy, then a rifleman, was revulsed by killing. Despite the danger it placed on his squad, everyone could not help but like the young kid from California who did not want to lacerate his soul with human blood.

After the battle, A and B companies flew back to LZ Betty while C and D went to support 17th Cavalry at LZ Zewert west of Bartlett. One platoon from Bravo dug in 3km further southeast at an abandoned settlement codenamed "LZ Red." That first night, radio operator Carl Decker was tasked to direct Spooky fire.

The crew had Decker "walk" their Gatling guns to the very edge of Zewert's perimeter. This was simply achieved by throwing out flattened C-Ration boxes tied to para-cord like frisbees. When each full firing circle was complete, the cardboard was pulled in to see if it had been struck. No holes meant Spooky could tighten its arc and repeat the process until the "frisbees" were hit ... and danger close confirmed. During his stay at Zewert, Dave Hillard handed over command to Captain Wayne Wheeler. Two days later, Ranger Force clashed again with the 482nd VC 10km northeast along Highway 1 between two villages – Ap Hoa Tan and Ap Phu-Trung. 44th ARVN, APCs, and 3/506 were requested as reinforcements. By late afternoon, the battalion rendezvoused nearby and headed toward the enemy, where Alpha came under rocket and small-arms fire.

With less than two weeks left until DEROS, Doc Lovy's war ended on the wrong LZ. His medivac shuddered as it came in to recover one of Bates' badly wounded troopers. Raked by bullets and mortars, Andy was almost blown out of the door as the helicopter aborted. An onboard medic asked to be examined and as Andy went to stand, he found that his legs were completely numb. Thankfully, he was OK, but an examination back at Betty revealed a piece of shrapnel had passed through the medic's flak vest and lodged in Andy's belt!

Back at Ap Phu-Trung, Artillery and Tiger Sharks eliminated further threat as Lieutenant Colonel Price tried to establish another cordon with the South Vietnamese. But as before, the northern encirclement could not be fully completed. Subsequently, during the early hours an attempted breakout was beaten back by Alpha. Two hours later, when government troops arrived to close the breach, they lost two men killed and 15 wounded through friendly artillery. This tragic accident was entirely due to a lack of communication between American and South Vietnamese assets. However, positive lessons were learned and better future liaison agreed between all element commanders and the Fire Support and Coordination System. The following morning, Doctor Lovy woke up deaf in one ear. After being diagnosed with a perforated eardrum, Andy was sent to Vung Tau for treatment, where he happily convalesced before DEROS.

Chapter 22

"The Protected Will Never Know"

August–October 1968

Task Force South's overstretched procedures across three provinces did not particularly suit 3/506, who preferred the old, smaller platoon-level tactics. Of course, having responsibility for one of the largest patches of real estate was never going to be an easy fix. As a direct consequence, more emphasis was being placed on the long-range patrol teams, and a number of key Romeo players were sent for additional training at the LRRP School in Nha Trang. After incurring such heavy losses, the 482nd VC were understandably quiet. Despite communication problems, the recent American/Vietnamese operations had greatly reduced insurgent numbers throughout Binh Thuan. Things were peaceful enough for a second USO stand-down at Betty, where upcoming chart-toppers Peaches & Herb headlined the show. Two days later, a memorial service held on the bluffs at Betty paid respects to those killed on July 17. Although it was quiet, the enemy was still active elsewhere. As a convoy from D Co returned from Long Binh on August 5, one of their sergeants was shot and killed by a sniper along Highway 1.

Alpha had been patrolling the undulating low coastal area south of LZ Judy with little success. Sergeant Ed Bassista stopped briefly for a bite to eat when three insurgents were spotted nearby. Immediately, as per SOPs, Ed secured his perimeter and deployed claymores. At the time, Mexican-born replacement Lieutenant James Delardo had just taken charge of First Platoon. Delardo was Ed's sixth leader and expected to be treated with the respect commensurate of his rank. But as a butterbar, fresh out of OCS, he got none of that from Bassista or any of the other senior NCOs. Delardo started to panic and ordered Bassista and his assistant John Matkin to prepare the platoon for attack.

Ed and John told Delardo to remain calm and let the guys rest and finish their food. Delardo did not take kindly to this insubordination and repeated his instructions as a "direct order." Again, Bassista and Matkin explained what they were going to do and, dumbfounded, Delardo backed down. When the platoon was ready, John and Ed moved forward and found the three Viet Cong obliviously eating lunch. The two sergeants charged forward screaming and did what had to be done. This behavior was a common tactic that served not only to confuse but also nullify a person's ability to move and react.

THE BATTLE OF DAI HOA-XUAN PHON

Early on Sunday, August 25, Lieutenant Colonel Price received a report from MACV that the enemy were believed to be digging in a few hundred meters west of the old Van Ta house at Dai Hoa. At the time, Price's Forward TOC and Supply Base (codenamed "Sherry"), along with a battery of 155mm guns from 27th Artillery, was located a few miles further north. After combined support from Artillery, Navy, and Spooky, Ranger Force went in and found a handful of VC bodies. One hour later, the South Vietnamese came under sudden attack from what appeared to be a platoon of VC. Working together with 44 ARVN and Binh Thuan's Provincial elite, A and B companies were placed on alert. By midday, Bravo were ready to extract from Bartlett but heavy thunderstorms slowed down the move. Government anti-tank and Armored Cavalry assets had also been assigned to Bill Knowlton, who was designated as Team B. Within two hours of landing, Team B had swept west into heavy enemy resistance north of the railway at Ap

Dai Hoa. During the fight, a sergeant from Second Platoon, Teo Rios-Rosario, was mortally wounded. Teo was medivaced with colleague Jimmy Huggins, who held his sergeant's intravenous drip all the way back to Betty. Knowlton was eventually able to temporarily supress all incoming heavy mortar and rocket fire with more artillery and air support.

Less than 1km further west, the blocking force provided by 4/44 ARVN also came under attack. South of Judy, A Company prepared for extraction. James Delardo's platoon would be leaving first to secure an LZ east of Ap Dai Hoa. Meanwhile, under way from Bartlett, D Co was flying across to reinforce Team Bravo's right flank. While First Platoon was waiting to board, Ed Bassista's squad were on overwatch nearby. Bassista had noticed some unexpected movement and ran over to the CP to ask Captain Bates if he knew of any localized enemy activity. "No, sergeant, we got patrols all over, so you don't need to worry about a thing!" It was a different mindset by that time and Bassista accepted what Bates had said and went back to his guys. The first chopper came in and as the troops began to climb aboard, it came under fire. The pilot went to full throttle, violently pulled up, and flew away at top speed. It was then Ed heard over the radio that someone had been killed. Bassista and his men quickly converged onto the LZ, where they found Keith Rowell surrounded by his men. It looked like a 7.62mm round had entered below Keith's left armpit and penetrated into his chest. Everything pointed toward an accidental discharge by one of the door gunners, but it could just as easily have been an AK round. Incensed, Ed stormed across to Captain Bates. The futility of Keith's death had pushed Bassista completely over the edge as he threatened to kill his company commander. While Ed was going at him, Bob never uttered a word. Bates could easily have had Bassista busted and jailed, but he simply sat and accepted the verbal beating.

Shortly before midnight, Alpha relocated and connected in with Ranger Force and D Co to completely seal off the 482nd VC's northeastern escape routes. Now totally surrounded, the enemy were pounded mercilessly into oblivion throughout the night with artillery. At dawn, a battlefield sweep gave up 24 identifiable enemy bodies and two prisoners, both of whom were officers. Twelve bunkers were bulldozed, burying a plethora of human body parts. In total, apart from Keith and Teo, the one-day action resulted in five South Vietnamese troops dead and 14 American and 41 ARVN wounded.

Enemy activity decreased significantly during September as VC/NVA forces took time out to rebuild and restructure. Continual reconnaissance threw up the usual base camps and caches. Ray Mayfield was acting as Tom Gaffney's firebase representative and working at FSB Sherry when it was heavily mortared on September 2. The base north of Phan Thiet was supposed to be Ray's "retirement post" when the unexpected attack killed a member of Battalion LRRPs. Bill Flint's death was followed a few days later by Paul Clement's radio operator Jerry Miller, who walked into a booby trap. Clement was also badly injured in the blast, along with one of his riflemen, John Bittner.

A small task force was established on September 10, for a combined operation from Bravo, 4/44 ARVN, and a 105 battery from 320th Artillery along the coast east of Song Mao. Nearby, as a salvo landed on a suspected base camp, Carl Locklear and his LRRP team moved forward for a closer look. Within a few seconds, they were engaged in a bizarre firefight with five heavily armed women. One woman was killed and the others scattered on hearing more incoming artillery. Moving into the camp, Locklear recovered 17 rucksacks, two B40 rockets, 30 grenades, and 900lb of rice.

When Ed Bassista finally left the fight on September 25, there were only 17 originals remaining from A Company. Not wishing to leave, Jerry Gomes loved the camaraderie so much that he went on to do two further tours with LRRPs, but as October arrived, most of the remaining boat troopers were heading for home.

OPERATION *PHUONG HOANG* AND LE HONG PHONG

By October 1, a combined operation with South Vietnamese District Headquarters, National Police, and elements of 44th ARVN prepared for the latest mission. Lieutenant Colonel Price was expected to provide a joint cordon allowing five local villages to be thoroughly searched. During the ten-day operation, there were several close encounters, the last being the early evening of October 4, when Wayne Johnson from D Co was killed and three others wounded. Private Johnson had only been in country for a month when hit by a Chinese-made rocket while closing in on Phu Sum. Overall, *Phuong Hoang* served its purpose by the detaining of over 100 suspects for questioning.

Another joint effort was thrown into Le Hong Phong Forest a few days later. The vast area encompassed around 400 square miles of dense vegetation and the only significant water source were two lakes in the southeastern corner. A stronghold since the 1950s, the insurgents had been long-established here, with hundreds of bunkers, bases, and covert trails. Slowly but surely, the enemy began to react before things came to a head on October 22. Third Platoon from Delta married in with the ARVN infantry and armor near a small village called Long Hoa close to Highway 1. The government troops had already been there for a couple of days and came under night attack shortly after Delta arrived. Had it not been for the South Vietnamese tanks and APCs, the entire force would have been overrun. During the furious battle, the enemy used everything they had at their disposal and by morning 35 of them lay dead alongside Sergeant Fred Jackson.

For the next three months, five more joint missions all codenamed "Double Eagle" would be conducted with the 44th ARVN Regiment. For Third Battalion's extraordinary efforts shown during Tet, nobody really gave a damn when the offer of a prestigious Presidential Unit Citation was downgraded to "Valorous." By the end of January 1969, total enemy losses levied by 3/506 amounted to over 800 killed, hundreds of weapons captured, and over 42,000 rounds of ammunition and 1,800 base camps destroyed. Additionally, hundreds of tons of rice, flour, and wheat were successfully located, removed, and redistributed. The division as a whole accounted for over 8,000 enemy dead and captured more than 2,500 weapons of various calibers. It could be argued that America was militarily victorious in Vietnam, although from Hanoi's perspective the focus was always going to be long-term political strategy and in terms of that America was clearly losing. All politics aside, 3/506 would continue to fight and suffer. Another 80 died and hundreds were wounded under stewardship of five consecutive commanders before the battalion was disbanded in May 1971. From 1965 to 1972, the division suffered 20,390 battle casualties which, bearing in mind the extended time frame and different table of organization, was almost double that of its World War II ancestor.

By August 1968, as overall American casualty figures continued to rise, anti-war protest leader David Dellinger was planning to march in Chicago during Eugene McCarthy's Democratic Party Convention. Although the vice president realized growing militancy was a destabilizing force for his own goals, he was still happy to co-exist with older activists like Dellinger. However, Chicago's autocratic Mayor Richard Daley refused Dellinger a permit and deployed 26,000 police and National Guard. Shortly after the first demonstration commenced, Daley's police charged and ferociously attacked Dellinger's 5,000-strong crowd. It was total state-sanctioned anarchy and over the next two days, unbelievable scenes of unrestrained violence played out on domestic TV screens. Any chances of McCarthy ever becoming president were crushed along with Dellinger's protest as Richard Nixon quietly resurfaced on a naive promise of "peace and honor." By now, the media was portraying a new front line as America descended into a protracted pseudo "civil war." However, this overreaction in Chicago seemed to mirror a general lack of humanity by the US government. Arguably the "revolution" on Mayor Daley's streets went on to spawn a new rationale against the war. Ironically, "the anti-war movement" would never freely admit any responsibility toward the carnage that followed when America did finally pull out of Vietnam in April 1975. After capitulation, thousands of innocent people were murdered, imprisoned, or sent to work camps. The scale of human suffering visited upon the South by Ho Chi Minh would and could never be fully understood by those who had not sweated and bled into the dust and dirt that was Vietnam.

Epilogue

A Handful of Wounds That Never Healed

John Harrison sat patiently on the 7-0-Quick freedom bird waiting for takeoff … he was going home. After a 16-hour flight to swinging San Francisco, John checked into the Mark Hopkins Hotel from where his uncle had agreed to pick him up the next morning. Of course, there was no glorious flag-waving, patriotic offers of free beer, or the warm embrace from a grateful nation. San Francisco was the first stop on a long but carefully planned trip to DC. When he eventually reached his mother's house in Washington, every external door was locked and bolted in fearful paranoia of America's new riot culture. It was only then she told him that two of his school friends had been killed in Nam and his beloved dog Penny had passed over the rainbow bridge. Before leaving the Army in '69, John took up the post of specialist weapons and tactics instructor at Fort Benning. After graduating from George Washington University, Harrison became a lawyer and realtor. Over the next 30 years, John worked on many high-profile cases before retraining in 2004 to teach high school History and Law. Since "retirement" in 2012, John has authored several wonderful books, short stories, and articles from his home in Maryland, all based on his life experience both during and after Vietnam.

Promoted to full-bird colonel, **"Mal Hombre"** agreed to extend his tour when assigned south to command First Brigade, 9th

Infantry Division in the Mekong Delta. By June '68, leaving her oldest daughter Vicki back home in college, Rita Geraci relocated to Clark Air Force Base in the Philippines with her remaining children. Tragically, the following February, Rita passed away in her sleep. Devastated, John was reassigned to the School of Infantry at Fort Benning as director of company operations before becoming director of the Ranger Department. "Mal Hombre" eventually succumbed to cancer in 1996 aged 70, leaving behind a legacy of military service that to this day still engenders enormous family pride.

Totally burned out, **Ronnie Ford** had saved $3,500 and the first thing he did was purchase a brand new Volkswagen Beetle. As he was still only 20 years old, Ford's mother had to sign the paperwork before he could drive the "Bug" away. By August, Ron packed up and headed for Lake Tahoe, where an old school friend was working on a new extension for the Sahara Casino. Ron got a job laboring with Dell Webb before moving on to less strenuous kitchen work at Zephyr Cove. Tahoe never slept and was a great place to meet chicks, but after two months' endless partying, Ford returned to his hometown of Newhall, where he bumped into Lois, who had just turned 18. Set to join the Air Force, Lois remembered Ronnie from school. Romance followed and shortly after Ron turned 21 in the January of '69, they were married and eventually settled into a one-bedroom house. Rene was born in 1971, shortly before the violent earthquake at nearby Sylmar. Picking up the pieces, Ron started a two-year apprenticeship as a retail meat cutter. But when Ronnie Jr. came along, Lois and Ron decided to buy a plot of land in Billings, Montana and build their very own "Little House on the Prairie." Here, under the endless sky, Ron was able to pursue his passion for hunting and fishing while expanding his career in the meat business with Lois. Retirement at 55 brought with it the opportunity to travel and enjoy what they had built as a family from the ground up. Despite having to overcome the loss of Ronnie's son Jacob, life for the Fords is still an adventure to be embraced and savored unconditionally ... God bless you, Ron.

Immediately upon returning home, **Wayne Warren** visited Bob Baldwin's parents in Texas, who took him to their son's monolithic-style grave. Bob had been sent home in a closed coffin but when his father Hoyt mentioned that the wristwatch they had given him was missing from the personal effects, Wayne could not bring himself to explain the reasons why. Before Wayne left, Hoyt whispered that Bob's ex-girlfriend had dropped in shortly after his obituary appeared in the local *Cleburne Times*. Brazenly, she argued that none of this was her fault even though she had actively encouraged their son to get involved in the war.

After being transferred to the States, **"Bucky" Cox** was serving with the 7th Special Forces at Fort Bragg when he bumped into **Max Cadena**. Since leaving Vietnam, Max had been downgraded several times and assigned to the 82nd Airborne. "Bucky" had a nice pad on base and invited him over for dinner. Afterward, he tried without success to get Cadena back into the field with a Special Forces training unit. Eventually, Cadena dropped off the grid and it was only years later that "Bucky" learned that his old pain-in-the-ass buddy had passed away in '85 from chronic liver disease. When the Army tried to post "Bucky" back to Vietnam, he decided to leave, and after college enrolled in university, where he also worked as a campus security officer. Three years later, Cox began a new career with the FBI that eventually took him all over the world. Ongoing investigations often led him to London, while investigating cases of international money fraud. "Bucky" has now long since retired and is living the good life with second wife Chris in North Carolina.

Then a captain, **Ron Newton** eventually returned to the States and remained in the Army until entering the Los Angeles Police Academy in early 1970. Later that same year, Ron married Marilyn, whom he had met at Fort Lewis. Over the next six years, they had two girls, Suzanne and Michelle. While working the mean streets of LA, Ron put his old Army skills to good use with the Reserves after becoming a company commander in the California National Guard. Newton retired from the LAPD with the rank of lieutenant in 1997 and became a Police Monitor and Human Rights Investigator with the United Nations International Police Task Force in Bosnia and Eastern Europe. The following year,

Newton returned to regular law enforcement and joined the Los Angeles County Police as assistant chief until 2004. Over the next few years, while working as a high-level training, planning, and anti-terrorism contractor, Ron took on important assignments in Africa and Afghanistan before finally hanging up his boots in 2014. Grandparents seven times over, Ron and Marilyn currently live in Williamsburg, Virginia.

On October 2, 1968, **"Jay" Eckhart** opted for early release and was processed through Oakland. Back home in Rapid City, Illinois, awash with cash, "Jay" splashed out on a brand-new Camaro and went to work across the Mississippi at the Alcoa Plant in Bettendorf, Iowa. A couple of girls who knew "Jay's" sister had been pen pals during his time in Nam. One, a trainee nurse, became "Jay's" wife in May 1970 and two years later their son Ben was born, followed by a daughter in '74. Factory work was where young men go to grow old and before long "Jay" was bored and looking for a new challenge other than booze or weed. By chance, a Marine recruiter who lived in the same apartment block kick-started a new career and on April 24, 1974, "Jay" left for boot camp at Parris Island. Although it was one of the smartest things he ever did, the move also signified the start of a long, difficult break-up that ended with a divorce in 1985 and sobriety. "Jay" met his future wife Bobbie at an AA meeting while stationed in 29 Palms and the couple tied the knot in March 1990. Everyone said it would never last but of course it did. Upon retiring from the Marines, "Jay" studied at college for three years before taking a job at the Betty Ford Center. Four years later, he gave notice and did a succession of other jobs before retiring aged 62. Bobbie and "Jay" currently reside in the Yucca Valley, California, where they enjoy a quiet, loving, comfortable relationship, keeping everything simple and their life in clear perspective.

Volunteering for a second tour, **Mike Krawczyk** took on an assignment to 5th Special Forces Group followed by MACV-SOG. Mike ran RECON and Hatchet Force missions and was wounded again on December 28, 1969. Discharged five months later, Mike went into law enforcement and was working for Porter County

Indiana Sheriff's Office when he and Donna married on February 13, 1972. The Krawczyks raised two great kids and have four lovely grandchildren, and after retiring in 2007, now live in Purcellville, Virginia. Despite serious health issues, Mike served on the 101st Airborne Division Association Board of Directors and is currently president of Task Force 3/506 Airborne Infantry Association.

If it had not been for his mother's disagreement, **Ed Bassista** would have gone OCS and then SF "Special Ops." After 30 days' paid leave and separation, Ed took his 26-week entitlement to unemployment benefit and with $6,000 in the bank accepted a job trout farming before taking a month off to go deer hunting across several states. Ed used to get a buzz out of hunting but after tracking humans in Vietnam, it was never the same. In January '69, he met Wilma through a cousin and married four months later, raising two fabulous kids, Kristen and Matthew. Bassista eventually joined an engineering company producing laminating machines and after 13 years of night school graduated with a master's degree in Heating, Ventilation, and Air Conditioning. A number of management engineering jobs followed with several large companies until Ed finished up in Computer and IT Support with Maintech Incorporated New Jersey before retiring in 2011.

After a short spell at Parachute School, **Nick Nahas** moved his family to Fort Benning for the Officers' Advanced Course or OAC. At Benning, Rosalie received a call from the Infantry Assignment officer, who was inquiring as to whether her husband would like to go back to Vietnam or Graduate School. That evening, when Nick arrived home, Rosalie explained he was going to the University of Arizona to study Nuclear Engineering. So, off they went to Tucson, where two years later, Nick graduated with a master's degree. Not long afterward, Nahas was sent to Korea for a short tour, where he became aide-de-camp to the Chief of Staff Eighth Army General John H. Michaelis. "Iron Mike" had famously led the 502nd Parachute Infantry Regiment during Normandy and Holland. Returning from Korea, Nahas attended the Command and General Staff College at Leavenworth. Again, he received a phone call from Infantry Assignments, who asked if he wanted to

SIGN HERE FOR SACRIFICE

be a professor at the Naval Academy in Annapolis, Maryland. Nick was not even aware that they had Army officers stationed there, but decided to give it a go and spent the next three years teaching midshipmen submariners Mechanical and Nuclear Engineering.

After Annapolis, Nick went back to Germany on a three-year assignment initially as executive officer with the 1/30 Infantry Battalion at Schweinfurt. After becoming secretary of the general staff for 3rd Infantry Division in Würzburg, Nick accepted command of a battalion at Fort Jackson in South Carolina. Again, the Infantry branch came calling and asked if he wanted to go to Naples as a nuclear staff officer. Having a teenage daughter, Nick and Rosalie decided that Italy would not be such a good idea and instead won the default prize to Pacific Command Headquarters in Honolulu. The couple could not believe their luck and spent three very happy years in Hawaii. Promotion to full-bird colonel gave way to a final assignment at the Pentagon as assistant to the secretary of defense for atomic energy. Retiring in 1986, Nick went on to work for the Science Applications International Corporation. In all, Nahas spent a further 22 years working for the defense company developing and managing their business interests in Japan.

After recovering from his physical wounds, **Jim Schlax** was assigned as a Basic and AIT testing officer in California. Upon leaving the Army, he enrolled at the University of Illinois and earned a bachelor's degree in Accounting. After his marriage to Barbara in 1970, Jim continued and graduated with an MBA from the University of Chicago. Eventually, Schlax joined the oil industry, where he worked for Amoco and then BP as an accounting manager and financial analyst. Jim and Barbara raised three kids, retired to La Crosse, Wisconsin, and dote on their six grandchildren.

Assigned to Fort Bragg and before marriage to Rikki, **Joe Alexander** joined the Special Forces Warfare School on full jump pay. By March '69, post-ETS, Joe re-enrolled back into East Tennessee State University and joined the National Guard in Lenoir City. During his time in the Guard, Alexander's skills were not always accepted or used to improve things. But he and others such as Charlie Arce and Ron Newton slowly helped to change things from a beer-drinking social club to a semi-professional force capable of mobilizing alongside the Regular Army. Skills learned from 3/506 transferred down to the generation that went to war in Iraq nearly 40 years later. Joe retired as a colonel to his long-established family farm and small herd of Angus Beef.

For a long time, the veterans of Vietnam were seen as pariahs, but eventually, after three decades, public attitudes began to change to a deeper respect and understanding. One autumnal afternoon in 2012, Joe Alexander learned that cancer had finally taken his friend **"Pete" Dozier**. When it came to the funeral, Weapons Platoon felt a compulsion to attend. "Pete's" wider family had grown up hearing about his beloved airborne brothers but they were not expecting ten middle-aged white guys. Although the intervening decades had left America divided and broken, forged from battle, Dozier's blood ties with guys like Alexander, Colone, Coulon, Mullican, and Ed Bassista still ran deep and forever true. These survivors valued their Ameritocracy and esprit de corps earned from a time and a place where the only thing that really mattered was complete trust and respect. Perhaps now, those who signed on for sacrifice have found their legitimate place in history, as the war in Vietnam begins its inevitable drift toward the end of living memory.

The final epitaph should go to medic **"Joe" Ramos**, who spent the rest of his life struggling with demons from that fateful afternoon in February 1968. Shortly after returning to Los Angeles, "Joe" married Sylvia and raised a beautiful family. In 2002, he began a campaign to fix his past and recognize the service, honor, courage, and loyalty of those who had served the United States in that faraway war. Eventually, his persistence paid off when in 2009, Governor Arnold Schwarzenegger designated March 30 as "Welcome Home Vietnam Veterans Day" and signed it into Californian State Law. Contrition comes in many ways and Jose Guadalupe Ramos finally accepted those things he could never change. "Uncle Joe" passed away peacefully on September 3, 2017.

Bibliography

PRIMARY SOURCES

Personal interviews with the following:
Chris Adams, Joe Alexander, Ed Bassista, Ed Blanco, Ralph Burdett, Steve Cook, Wylie "Bucky" Cox, Freeman "Dee" Dallas, Carl Decker, "Jay" Eckhart, Ron Ford, Jerry Gomes, Gary Gressett, John Harrison, Joe Jerviss, Mark Jones, Mike Krawczyk, Andy Lovy, Tom Lundgren, Bob Mairs (RIP), Ray Mayfield, Nick Nahas, Ron Newton, Dave Rivers, Jim Schlax, Mike Stuart, Al Thompson, Mike Trant (RIP), Frank Vinales, and Wayne Warren.

SECONDARY SOURCES

Combat Surgeon in Vietnam, self-published by Andrew Lovy, 2004
Imperial Heights by Eric T. Jennings, published by University of California Press, 2011
Echoes from Vietnam: Whispers from the Disposable Soldiers, Christopher Adams, published by DP Diversified, 2020
My Gift to You, self-published by Jerald "Jerry" Berry, 2006
Post-Knoll Battle transcription notes dated July 16, 1968 from the US Army Center of Military History, featuring interviews with: Ron Barnes, Braxton Baston, Max Cadena, "Bucky" Cox, Jerry Hill, Mike Hill, Jim Moore, Graham Morris, Mike Munson, Ron Newton, Everette Parham, and Gary Wisnier via Mike Stuart
Recorded interviews with Tom Gaffney via John Geraci Jr.
Research notes on Captain Gaffney and multiple first-hand interviews regarding the Battle of Ca Ty River with Joe Alexander, Ed Bassista,

Marcel "Frenchy" Coulon, John Colone, Mark Jones, Mike Mullican, Gary "Flint" Purcell, Jose Ramos, and Gale Shire via David Rattee

Steel Rain, the Tet Offensive 1968, self-published by John Harrison, 2016

The Stand-Alone Battalion, self-published by Jerald "Jerry" Berry and Joe Alexander, 2002

The Viet Cong Tet Offensive: Phan Thiet 1968 by RVNAF via Mike Krawczyk, published by Printing & Publications Center (A.G./Joint General Staff)

Third Battalion (Airborne), 506th Infantry Regiment, 101st Airborne Division After Action Reports 1967–68, US Army via "Dee" Dallas

Third Battalion (Airborne), 506th Infantry Regiment, 101st Airborne Division Morning Reports 1967–68, US Army via Mike Krawczyk

Unlucky Moon, self-published by Edward Blanco, 2022

Various articles from *The Screaming Eagle* Magazine 1967/68 via David Rattee

Vietnam: The Ten Thousand Day War by Michael MacLear, published by Thames Methuen, London, 1981

War Diary of Tom Gaffney via David Rattee

War Diary of David "Mike" Pearson via Mike Krawczyk

War in Peace by Sir Robert Thompson, published by Orbis Publishing, 1981

Index

References to maps are in **bold**.